Tourism in Iran

Iran has long been regarded as an international pariah state in some parts of the international community. However, its negative image in many countries disguises its history of tourism and rich cultural and natural heritage. Following the July 2015 nuclear deal and the reduction in sanctions, Iran is focusing on international tourism as a means to generate economic growth in addition to its substantial domestic tourism market. Given the significance of tourism in the Middle East and in international politics, as well as restrictions on international mobility, this volume brings together the first contemporary collection of research on tourism in Iran.

Written by experts based both within and outside of Iran, the chapters engage with a number of crucial issues including the importance of religion, the role of women in society, sustaining Iran's cultural heritage, Iran's image and the resistive economy to provide a benchmark assessment of tourism and its potential future in a troubled political environment. The book will undoubtedly be of interest not only to those readers who focus specifically on Iran but also those who seek a wider understanding of Iran's role in the region and how tourism is utilised as part of national and regional economic development policies.

Siamak Seyfi is a Ph.D. candidate in the Department of Geography at the University of Pantheon-Sorbonne, France. Using primarily qualitative and mixed methods his research interests are sustainable tourism, community development, political ecology and tourism, power and the environment.

C. Michael Hall is a Professor at the University of Canterbury, New Zealand; Docent, Department of Geography, University of Oulu, Finland; and Visiting Professor, Linnaeus University, Kalmar, Sweden. He has published widely on tourism, regional development and global environmental change.

Contemporary Geographies of Leisure, Tourism and Mobility

Series editor: C. Michael Hall, *Professor at the Department of Management, College of Business and Economics, University of Canterbury, Christchurch, New Zealand*

The aim of this series is to explore and communicate the intersections and relationships between leisure, tourism, and human mobility within the social sciences.

It will incorporate both traditional and new perspectives on leisure and tourism from contemporary geography, for example notions of identity, representation, and culture, while also providing for perspectives from cognate areas such as anthropology, cultural studies, gastronomy and food studies, marketing, policy studies and political economy, regional and urban planning, and sociology, within the development of an integrated field of leisure and tourism studies.

Also, increasingly, tourism and leisure are regarded as steps in a continuum of human mobility. Inclusion of mobility in the series offers the prospect of examining the relationship between tourism and migration, the sojourner, educational travel, and the second-home and retirement travel phenomena.

The series comprises two strands:

Contemporary Geographies of Leisure, Tourism, and Mobility aims to address the needs of students and academics, and the titles will be published in hardback and paperback. Titles include:

An Introduction to Visual Research Methods in Tourism
Edited by Tijana Rakić and Donna Chambers

Tourism and Climate Change
Impacts, Adaptation and Mitigation
Daniel Scott, C. Michael Hall and Stefan Gössling

Tourism and Citizenship
Rights, Freedoms and Responsibilities in the Global Order
Raoul V. Bianchi and Marcus L. Stephenson

Co-Creating Tourism Research
Towards Collaborative Ways of Knowing
Edited by Carina Ren, Gunnar Thór Jóhannesson and René van der Duim

Tourism in Iran

Challenges, Development and Issues

**Edited by Siamak Seyfi and
C. Michael Hall**

First published 2019 by Routledge

2 Park Square, Milton Park, Abingdon, Oxon OX14 4RN
605 Third Avenue, New York, NY 10017

Routledge is an imprint of the Taylor & Francis Group, an informa business

First issued in paperback 2022

British Library Cataloguing-in-Publication Data
A catalogue record for this book is available from the British Library

Library of Congress Cataloging-in-Publication Data
A catalog record has been requested for this book

ISBN: 978-1-138-50512-4 (hbk)
ISBN: 978-1-03-233890-3 (pbk)
DOI: 10.4324/9781315146409

Typeset in Times New Roman
by Sunrise Setting Ltd, Brixham, UK

Contents

Figures

Tables

Boxes

Contributors

Niloofar Abbaspour, Ph.D. Student in Tourism Management, Allameh Tabataba'i University, Tehran, Iran; orcid.org/0000-0003-1238-4112

Marjan Abdi, Ph.D. Student in Tourism Management, Allameh Tabataba'i University, Tehran, Iran; orcid.org/0000-0002-2593-442X

Habib Alipour, Faculty of Tourism, Eastern Mediterranean University, Famagusta, TRNC, Via Mersin 10, 99628, Turkey; orcid.org/0000-0001-5517-3118

Somayeh Amiri, Graduate Student in Tourism Management, Allameh Tabataba'i University, Tehran, Iran; orcid.org/0000-0002-6061-6785

Hamid Ataeishad, Department of Urban and Regional Planning, Tarbiat Modares University, Tehran, Iran; orcid.org/0000-0003-4339-4188

Fabio Carbone, School of Marketing and Management, Faculty of Business and Law, Coventry University, Coventry, West Midlands, UK; orcid.org/0000-0002-6711-4892

Hamideh Dabbaghi, Allameh Tabataba'i University, Tehran, Iran; orcid.org/0000-0001-7801-112X

Banafsheh M. Farahani, Department of Hospitality and Tourism, Maziar University, Iran; orcid.org/0000-0002-8789-0928

Fereshteh Fazel Bakhsheshi, Independent researcher, 11 Bidhendy, Mansoori St., Resalat Ave. Post code 1671783393, Tehran, Iran; orcid.org/0000-0002-8421-3892

Zahed Ghaderi, International Tourism Management, Deggendorf University of Applied Science, Pfarrkirchen, Germany; orcid.org/0000-0001-6666-1635

C. Michael Hall, Department of Management, Marketing and Entrepreneurship, University of Canterbury, Christchurch, New Zealand; orcid.org/0000-0002-7734-4587

Shiva Hashemi, Department of Urban and Regional Planning, School of Housing, Building and Planning, Universiti Sains Malaysia, George Town, Malaysia; orcid.org/0000-0002-2728-781x

Najmeh Hassanli, University of Technology Sydney, Business School, NSW, Australia; orcid.org/0000-0002-3392-0829

Bahareh Hassanzadeh, Faculty of Tourism, Eastern Mediterranean University, Famagusta, TRNC, Via Mersin 10, 99628, Turkey; orcid.org/0000-0001-9686-7810

Saman Hassibi, Department of Management, Marketing and Entrepreneurship, University of Canterbury, Christchurch, New Zealand; orcid.org/0000-0001-9521-1350

Joan Henderson, Nanyang Business School, Nanyang Technological University, Singapore; orcid.org/0000-0002-8417-1135

Nina Khamsy, MPhil candidate in Social Anthropology, Green Templeton College, Oxford University, UK; Research Associate, Amir Kabir Research Center, Mashhad; orcid.org/0000-0002-2362-8808

Anahita Lohrasbi, Department of Economics and Management, University of Ferrara, Ferrara, Italy; orcid.org/0000-0003-1303-4667

Anahita Malek, School of Marketing and Management, Faculty of Business and Law, Coventry University, Coventry, West Midlands, UK; orcid.org/0000-0003-3423-6567

Azizan Marzuki, Department of Urban and Regional Planning, School of Housing, Building and Planning, Universiti Sains Malaysia, George Town, Malaysia; orcid.org/0000-0002-1035-4908

Adel Nikjoo, Department of Tourism Management, Shandiz Institute of Higher Education, Iran; orcid.org/0000-0003-1468-9948

Hossein G. T. Olya, The Oxford School of Hospitality Management, Oxford Brookes Business School, Oxford Brookes University, Oxford, UK; orcid.org/0000-0002-0360-0744

S. Mostafa Rasoolimanesh, School of Hospitality, Tourism and Events, Faculty of Hospitality, Food and Leisure Management, Taylor's University, Subang Jaya, Malaysia; orcid.org/0000-0001-7138-0280

Hamed Rezapouraghdam, Faculty of Tourism, Eastern Mediterranean University, Famagusta, TRNC, Via Mersin 10, 99628, Turkey; orcid.org/0000-0001-8190-6565

Amir Sayadabdi, University of Canterbury, Christchurch, New Zealand; orcid.org/0000-0002-8071-1966

Siamak Seyfi, University of Pantheon-Sorbonne, EIREST Research Lab (Interdisciplinary Research Group for Tourism Studies), Paris, France; orcid.org/0000-0002-2427-7958

Bardia Shabani, ACECR Institute of Tourism Research, Iran; Ph.D. Candidate, Université Paul Valéry, Montpellier, France; orcid.org/0000-0002-1267-7858

Moji Shahvali, College of Health and Human Development, Department of Recreation, Park and Tourism Management, Pennsylvania State University, PA, USA; orcid.org/0000-0001-9330-0739

Mohammad Sharifi-Tehrani, University of Isfahan, Iran; orcid. org/0000-0002-9979-5477

Sahar Soltani, Academic Center for Education, Culture and Research (ACECR), Khorasan Razavi branch, Iran; orcid.org/0000-0001-8253-0985

Masoumeh Tavangar, Institute for Tourism Research (ACECR), Department of Geography and Urban Planning, Shahid Chamran University of Ahvaz, Iran; orcid.org/0000-0002-6608-9154

Hazel Tucker, Associate Professor, Department of Tourism, School of Business, University of Otago, New Zealand; orcid.org/0000-0001-8110-137X

Fatemeh Vossughi, Professor, Department of Urbanism, Azade University of Mashhad, Mashhad, Iran; Deputy, Amir Kabir Research Center, Mashhad; orcid.org/0000-0003-3753-2249

Afsaneh Zareei, Department of Tourism Economics, Academic Center for Education, Culture and Research (ACECR), Khorasan Razavi branch, Iran; orcid.org/0000-0003-0686-6078

Mahmood Ziaee, Department of Tourism Management, Allameh Tabataba'i University, Tehran, Iran; orcid.org/0000-0001-8518-3640

Preface and acknowledgements

My thanks are extended to various friends and colleagues for their advice and warm encouragement at times of despair. Most noteworthy among them have been Adel Nikjoo and his generous and lovely family, Bardia Shabani, Babak Hassan-zadeh, Masood Samimi, Reza Rezvani, Mohammad Sharifi-Tehrani, Masoumeh Tavangar, Farangis Khoshbin, Hani Bayat, Hessam Emami, Hamed Mehrabi, Arman Dehghan, Abolfazl Siyamian, Ebrahim Bazrafshan Salar Kuhzadi, Kourosh Esfandiar, Vahid Ghasmi, Jafar Bapiri and Arman Hosseini. Nobody has been more important to me in the pursuit of this project than the members of my family. I would like to thank my parents, and especially my late father whose love and guidance are with me in whatever I pursue. And, last but not least, I wish to thank my loving and supportive wife, Mina, for her enduring love and patience – *Siamak.*

Michael would like to thank a number of colleagues with whom he has under-taken related research over the years. In particular, thanks go to Dorothee Bohn, Tim Coles, Hervé Corvellec, David Duval, Alexandra Gillespie, Martin Gren, Stefan Gössling, Johan Hultman, Dieter Müller, Girish Prayag, Yael Ram, Jarkko Saarinen, Dan Scott, Anna Dóra Sæþórsdóttir, Allan Williams and Maria José Zapata-Campos for their thoughts on tourism, as well as for the stimulation of Agnes Obel, Ann Brun, Beirut, Paul Buchanan, Nick Cave, Bruce Cockburn, Elvis Costello, Stephen Cummings, Chris Difford and Glenn Tilbrook, David Bowie, Ebba Fosberg, Aldous Harding, Father John Misty, Mark Hollis, Margaret Glaspy, Aimee Mann, Larkin Poe, Vinnie Reilly, Henry Rollins, Matthew Sweet, David Sylvian, and *The Guardian*, BBC6, JJ and KCRW – for making the world much less confining. Special mention must also be given to Koppi in Helsingborg, Balck and Postgarten in Kalmar, and Nicole Aignier and the Hotel Grüner Baum in Merzhausen. Finally, and most importantly, Michael would like to thank the Js and the Cs who stay at home and mind the farm.

We would both like to extend special thanks to Jody Cowper-James for her invaluable help in checking references and editing, Mehdi Kazemi Biniaz for helping with the design of Figure 1.2, and we would also like to acknowledge the support of all at Routledge and especially Emma and Carlotta.

Abbreviations

ACECR	Academic Center for Education, Culture and Research
APPA	Appreciative Participatory Planning and Action
CAO	Civil Aviation Organization
CBT	community-based tourism
CCAs	Community Conserved Areas
GEC	Global Environment Facility
IAIA	International Association for Impact Assessment
ICCIMA	Iran Chamber of Commerce, Industries, Mines and Agriculture
ICCROM	International Centre for the Study of the Preservation and Restoration of Cultural Property
ICHTO	Iran Cultural Heritage, Handcraft and Tourism Organization
ICOMOS	International Council on Monuments and Sites
IMF	International Monetary Fund
ITTO	Iran Touring and Tourism Organization
JCPOA	Joint Comprehensive Plan of Action
NGOs	non-governmental organizations
OPEC	Organization of Petroleum Exporting Countries
REST	Responsible Ecological Social Tours
RICHT	Research Institute for Cultural Heritage and Tourism
RTSC	Rural Tourism Steering Committee
SCI	Statistical Center of Iran
SCO	Shanghai Cooperation Organisation
TPB	Theory of Planned Behavior
UNDP	United Nations Development Programme
UNWTO	United Nations World Tourism Organization
VFR	Visiting friends and relatives
WEF	World Economic Forum
WTO	World Trade Organization
WTTC	World Travel and Tourism Council

Part I
Context

1   Tourism in Iran: an introduction

Siamak Seyfi and C. Michael Hall

Introduction

Tourism generated US$1.220 billion in revenue worldwide in 2016, and tourism arrivals had continued their long upward trend to reach 1.235 billion. This number is projected to reach 1.8 billion arrivals by 2030 (UNWTO, 2017). Thus, tourism is considered as one of the main engines of development for all countries at very different stages of development and is receiving vital focus in all geographical regions of the world (Hall & Page, 2017). Despite this global trend, however, the Middle East region has failed to capitalize on its resources to reap the benefits of international tourism and this region's share of the pie remained one of the lowest in the world estimated at about only 4% (UNWTO, 2017). Consequently, the region as a whole remains one of the world's least developed tourism regions (Hazbun, 2004, 2008; Morakabati, 2011, 2013; Cohen & Cohen, 2015; Isaac, Hall, & Higgins-Desbiolles, 2015). The image of the Middle East is one that has been portrayed as a theatre of war and conflict, from the Arab–Israeli conflicts to the more recent war against Islamic extremists in Syria and Iraq, Syria's civil war, Turkish aggression against the Kurds, Saudi Arabian-led intervention in Yemen, and the nuclear issues in Iran. This long history of political instability along with ongoing security events and crises has negatively affected the development of tourism in the Middle East despite its vast natural, historical, and cultural resources as well as its abundant collection of unique tourist sites, diverse climate, exotic food, and hospitable hosts (Mansfeld, 1999; Bassil, 2014; Isaac, 2013; Morakabati, 2011, 2013). Hence, all these issues have presented significant challenges to the inbound flows of international tourism to the region.

The recent 'Arab Spring' with its new round of regional leadership competition and the advent of Islamic radical groups has also had significant negative impacts on the tourism industry in the Middle East (Avraham, 2015; Tomazos, 2017). Although Iran is classified as being in the South Asia region by the World Tourism Organization (UNWTO, 2017; Hall & Page, 2017), it is primarily covered as a Middle Eastern country in the international media (Ebadi, 2017). Iran has a strong geopolitical presence in the Middle East with longstanding tensions and rivalry and mistrust between Sunni countries under the leadership of Saudi Arabia and

Shia countries such as Iran (Zamani-Farahani, 2010). This centuries-old sectarian rivalry between Sunni and Shia Islam is embedded in the regional politics of both Iran and Saudi Arabia as they compete for leadership in the Islamic world. This competition has been extended into the internal politics of other Arab states (Hinnebusch, 2010) and is one of the key factors defining the Middle East security complex today with significant implications for tourism.

With respect to Iran, given its vastness of tourism, its complicated institutional set up along with its highly centralized and bureaucratic development model, and paucity of reliable data as well as lack of awareness of tourism per se, researching tourism development in this country has been a difficult task (Alipour & Heydari, 2005). Therefore, Iran's tourism has remained one of the least studied sectors so far and has a very limited coverage in the international tourism literature (Seyfi, Hall, & Kuhzadi, 2018). Furthermore, with regard to domestic policy, encouraging tourism in Iran has become a hotly debated issue between two main political factions in the ruling elite (Alipour & Heydari, 2005). The Reformists view tourism as a driver for job creation, economic growth, and development as well as a means to modernize and promote international links, whereas the Fundamentalists and conservative clerical establishments considers tourism as a means of globalization and a threat which undermines the 'soul' of Islamic values and norms (Alipour & Heydari, 2005; Morakabati, 2011; Zamani-Farahani, 2010). While the Reformists and moderate groups believe in establishing friendly relations with the West, creating a conductive political and social atmosphere for foreign investment and promoting inbound tourism mainly from main tourism-generating countries, the hard-liners and conservatives tend toward an isolationist strategy in foreign policy and reject foreign investment, and are suspicious toward foreign tourists. The latter group fears the erosion of religious devoutness and conventions, and shows little demonstration of interest in hosting foreign tourists, especially non-Muslims (O'Gorman, McLellan, & Baum, 2007; Baum & O'Gorman, 2010; Butler, O'Gorman, & Prentice, 2012; Morakabati, 2011). Thus, despite the country's untapped potentials (e.g. ancient and historical sites, coastal areas, mountains, deserts), the tourism industry has been either ignored or given little attention, and experienced a tremendous setback due to the upheavals of the 1970s, the Iran–Iraq war of the 1980s, and a range of political instabilities and changes in different administrations' ideologies (Alipour & Heydari, 2005; Seyfi et al., 2018). Moreover, lack of a formidable and stable tourism organization with a long-term strategy, along with an ad hoc approach to the sector, and heavy dependence on the lucrative oil and gas sector (which accounts for around 80% of the government's total export earnings and 60–75% of its total budget) have curtailed such a promising sector. Iran has therefore failed to capitalize on its resources to reap the benefits of international tourism, and its share of the world's tourist receipts remained as one of the lowest in the world, as low as 0.003% for the year 2016 (UNWTO, 2017).

After a decade of a tension and antagonism with the West and a crippled economy as a result of sanctions during Ahmadinejad's presidency (2005–2013), known as the 'new conservative era' in the political discourse of the country

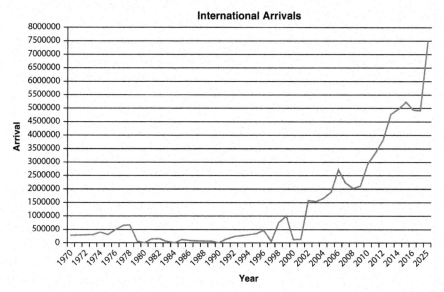

Figure 1.1 Inbound tourism to Iran.

Source: ICHTO, 2018; UNWTO, 2017.

(Ehteshami & Zweiri, 2007), a moderate president took office in 2013. In the wake of the nuclear agreement of 2015 and the subsequent easing of sanctions and reconnection to the world, a new chapter opened in the contemporary history of the country and Iran is viewed as the world's biggest emerging economy to rejoin the global trading system since the collapse of the Soviet Union over two decades ago (McSmith, 2016). As a result, Iran, which had long been avoided by international tourists, became a booming destination (Khodadadi, 2016a, 2016b). More than 5 million inbound tourists visited Iran in 2017, nearly three times the number in 2009, according to official data (Figure 1.1) (ICHTO, 2018; UNWTO, 2017). A similar such surge in tourism to the Islamic Republic is also thought to have occurred after the victory of reformist president Mohammad Khatami in the late 1990s. Tourism is the core of attention of Rouhani's administration which has called for its revival, which could create jobs for millions of young Iranians at a time when youth unemployment remains stubbornly high at 26% (Mozaffari, Karimian, & Mousavi, 2017; Pratt & Alizadeh, 2017).

In light of this easing of sanctions, European airlines such as Air France, British Airways, and Lufthansa, and regional airlines, such as Air Asia, resumed direct flights to the country. The Iranian authorities also relaxed visa requirements and updated a part of its aging air fleet by ordering nearly 200 planes from Airbus, Boeing, and ATR, worth $36 billion (Khodadadi, 2018; Seyfi et al., 2018). Following the easing of sanctions, Iran has managed to attract considerable investment in tourism-related infrastructure (Khodadadi, 2018). For instance, in light of skyrocketing demand for accommodation, foreign investors such as French group

Accor Hotels, UAE-based Rotana, Spanish Meliá, and other Turkish and German companies have invested in the country's hotel sector (Khodadadi, 2016c). Iran has also made significant investment in rail transport by working with the Italian state rail company to build a high-speed train between major cities inside the country which will have significant implications for domestic mobility (see also Chapter 2, this volume).

This introductory chapter provides a comprehensive introduction to tourism in Iran and the challenges it faced before, and faces post, the lifting of sanctions and given relations with the United States as well as countries in the surrounding region. It also outlines the growth and history of tourism in Iran, and identifies key tourism related issues and challenges in the country with links to the chapters in the book. These issues and their respective implications for the tourism industry in Iran will set the context for the book. The chapter ends with a brief overview of the organization of the book.

An overview of tourism in Iran

Tourism resources of Iran

In Persian literature, Iran (meaning 'land of the Aryans') has been the title of the country since the Sassanid era (also known as the Neo-Persian Empire) (224–651 BC) and became the official international title for the country in 1935 (Yarshater, 1989). In Western countries, Iran had been traditionally known as Persia until 1935 or as a 'combination of Persia and Islam' (Baum & O'Gorman, 2010, p. 175). While Iran is classified as being in the South Asia region by the World Tourism Organization (UNWTO, 2017; Hall & Page, 2017), it is being mostly covered as a Middle Eastern country in the international media (Ebadi, 2017). It occupies an area of 1,648,195 km^2 (636,372 miles^2) and is regarded as the second largest country in the Middle East and the seventeenth largest in the world (World Bank, 2018). It is inhabited by over 81 million people and is the world's eighteenth most populous country (Statistical Center of Iran (SCI), 2018).

Iran, which was a Zoroastrian country before the conquest by the Arab armies of the early Islamic state in the seventh century (Katouzian, 2010) is home to one of the world's oldest civilizations and incredible antiquities, and is a treasure trove of medieval and pre-Islamic architecture with ancient ruins, glittering mosques, and spectacular landscapes (Alavi & Yasin, 2000; O'Gorman et al., 2007; Baum & O'Gorman, 2010). Historically, Iran has had a strategic location along the Silk Route between the Ottoman and Mughal empires. This ancient route "is one of the best known of the world's historical trading routes, traditionally running from Xian in Northern China through Iran and on to Istanbul" (O'Gorman, 2009, p. 785). Throughout history Iran has been of geostrategic importance owing to its central location in Eurasia (Ghirshman, 1951), and its abundant natural resources, especially petroleum, are a factor in colonial and superpower rivalries. Following the occupation of Iran by the Islamic armies coming out of Arabia in the seventh century (known as the Muslim conquest of Persia or the Arab conquest of Iran), Zoroastrian, a monotheistic religion with its long history and association with Persian history, heritage, and culture was substantially replaced by Islam. Another major change with respect to the religion in Iran came during the Safavid period (1502–1736), when Shia Islam was recognized and established as the official religion of the country (Pierret, 2017).

Iran is not an Arab country (Almuhrzi, Alriyami, & Scott, 2017) yet it is often perceived as such given its situation in the Middle East. This misperception, however, may be a reflection of the Islamic regime's failure to generate a strong positive country image (Jalilvand & Samiei, 2012) and potentially renders the country remaining relatively less explored by the outside world. Whereas Islam is the main religion in many Arab and non-Arab societies (i.e. Persian, Turkish, Kurdish society), these societies are neither identical (Hourani, 1992) nor have many cultural similarities with respect to the lifestyle, and social norms and customs (Hourani, 1992; Almuhrzi et al., 2017). Despite the invasion by the Arabs and some initial efforts to impose the Arabic language, the Iranians did not lose their language or their identity. In fact, the failure of the clerical elite of Iran in keeping Iranian youth under Islam has led to many Iranians referring to themselves as being Persian rather than Muslim-Iranian and tending to trace their heritage back to the time of Cyrus the Great (the founder of the Achaemenid Empire, the first Persian Empire between 559–530 BC) despite Iran's clerical establishment's continued efforts to emphasize the religious-Islamic component of Iranian identity and downplaying the nation's pre-Islamic history (Baum & O'Gorman, 2010).

The landscape of Iran is dominated by the Alborz and Zagros mountain ranges and two vast deserts: Dasht-e Kavir and Dasht-e Lut (Ghaderi, 2017). The country's environmental assets (Hall, 2019), a rich array of intangible cultural heritage, diverse ethnic and linguistic groups combined with a versatile climate, and major heritage assets, and most importantly a young population (with a median age of 30.1 years) provide it with a sound platform from which to build a diverse, unique, and dynamic tourism industry (O'Gorman et al., 2007; Butler et al., 2012; Alavi & Yasin, 2000; Morakabati, 2011). As of early 2018, 21 historical sites and one natural site are listed under the UNESCO World Heritage List (Figure 1.2), while 56 more sites are tentatively listed (UNESCO, 2018). Iran has also 13 elements listed as part of the World Intangible Cultural Heritage (UNESCO, 2018). Therefore, according to UNESCO, Iran is one of the top countries in the world in terms of the richness of its ancient and historical sites. However, having attractions alone is not enough for tourism development (Zamani-Farahani, 2010).

In addition to its rich cultural heritage, Iran possesses a rich and diverse set of natural tourism assets. With four seasons throughout the year, climate in the area is pleasant and attracts increasing numbers of tourists. Iran has set aside a large number of protected areas including 48 nature reserves, 285 forest parks, and reserves of which 25 have been prioritized, 43 wildlife refuges (5.586 million ha.), 33 wetlands (1,483,824 ha.), 35 natural national monuments (37,576 ha.), and 28 national parks (almost 1.986 million ha.), many of which, such as Mian Kaleh Wildlife Refuge, the salt lake of Namak, and Golestan National Park contain unique habitats of international importance (Alipour & Heydari, 2005;

Figure 1.2 Iran's properties inscribed on the World Heritage List (2018).

Mirzaei, 2013). "Other natural tourism resources include Iran's hot and cold mineral springs, its therapeutic mud, and lake areas with health spa potential, especially the hot volcanic springs in the Sabalan Mountain range and therapeutic mud of Lake Orumiye" (Alipour & Heydari, 2005, p. 45).

Iran is attractive for international tourists, especially those who are interested in history and archaeology (Baum & O'Gorman, 2010). Iran is often associated with a destination for pilgrimage, religious, and cultural tourism, and has a vast historic, religious, and cultural heritage which has great appeal to tourists, not only Western visitors but those from other Islamic states with similar beliefs to those of Iran (Butler & Suntikul, 2017). Apart from cultural and religious tourism, there are some other various forms of tourism. The development of medical and health tourism has gained attention from successive Iranian administrations, together with its mineral water springs and resorts (Moghimehfar & Nasr-Esfahani, 2011).

Geographical proximity along with high-quality medical services especially in organ transplant surgeries and aesthetic surgeries at low cost (mainly due to the exchange rate fluctuations) in comparison with developed and regional countries, have also contributed to reasons behind the government's decision to promote medical and health tourism. Since 2010, Iran's medical tourism sector has shown a growth rate of 20–25% (ICHTO, 2018). Based on Iran's fifth economic development plan (2017–2022), the number of health tourists is aimed to increase to up to 600,000 every year. Also, by 2025, Iran plans to increase revenue from health tourism to $2.5 billion. However, despite all the advancements in recent years, the set targets appear difficult to reach, given the challenges that need to be addressed, including: lack of integrated management, insufficient advertising, and an insufficient number of approved travel agencies, and hospital and medical centers to accept foreign patients (Bizaer, 2016).

With regard to the different types of tourism in Iran, Table 1.1 shows the different categories of tourism in Iran in 2017 identified by the Iran Cultural Heritage, Handcraft and Tourism Organization (ICHTO), along with the number of arrivals as well as the main provinces in which each type of tourism occurs.

With respect to the main tourism market, since the Iranian revolution in 1979, the majority of foreign visitors to Iran have been religious pilgrims. In Iran there are many Shi'ite Shrines, the three main ones being Imam Reza Shrine in Mashhad, Fatimah al-Ma'sūmah Shrine in Qom, and Shah e Cheragh in Shiraz, and each year they attract millions of pilgrims from Iran and other Shi'ite countries like Iraq, Azerbaijan, Palestine, Bahrain, Saudi Arabia (Shi'ites are concentrated in the country's Eastern province, chiefly Qatif and Al-Ahsa), Pakistan, and Afghanistan who come to Iran to make pilgrimage to these holy places. These Shi'ite tourists have been among the most important markets for the Iranian state administration since the

Table 1.1 Main types of tourism in Iran as identified by ICHTO (2017)

Type of tourism	Number of arrivals	Main provinces in which this type of tourism occurs
Pilgrimage	2,223,648	Mashhad-Qom
VFR	1,177,284	
Business	562,118	Tehran
Historical and cultural tourism	429,676	Tehran, Isfahan, Shiraz, Kerman, Yazd
Health and medical tourism	273,375	Tehran, Shiraz, Tabriz, Yazd, Mashhad
Eco-tourism and nature-based tourism	149,534	Guilan, Mazandaran, Kerman, Tehran, Yazd, Shiraz
MICE, educational and sport tourism	95,924	Tehran
Total	4,911,920	

Source: ICHTO, 2017.

Islamic revolution. There are around 200 million Shia Muslims in the world today (Shia accounting for almost 20% of the 1.6 billion Muslims around the world) and between 70 million and 75 million Shias live in Iran (89%), representing nearly half of the world's Shia population. This has made Iran the spiritual center of the Shi'ite world. Since the overthrow of Iraq's Saddam Hussein in 2003, and the establishment of a Shi'ite administration and the rapprochement with Iran, the number of Iraqi Shia pilgrims to Iran has risen fast (Table 1.2). Moreover, the escalation of Iraqi violence in 2011 and the appearance of ISIS have also encouraged more Iraqi Shia pilgrims to come to Iran (Majidyar, 2018). However, the majority of the above-mentioned countries have low average incomes, and this limits tourism spending (Zamani-Farahani & Henderson, 2010).

However, in the wake of the Arab Spring (2011) and the Syrian conflict, inbound tourism to Iran has been affected. In January 2016, Saudi Arabia along with its allies cut diplomatic relations with Iran following the attack on the Saudi Arabian embassy in Tehran and its consulate in Mashhad, and this has led to a decline in the number of religious pilgrims (Shi'ite Muslims) to major religious destinations such as Mashhad, Qom, and Shiraz (Zamani-Farahani, 2010). The situation led to an 80% decline of foreign pilgrims along with a 20% decrease in domestic

Table 1.2 Inbound tourism to Iran in 2017

Inbound tourists (by nationality)	Number of arrivals	Market share
Iraq	1,392,243	28.34%
Azerbaijan	979,319	19.94%
Afghanistan	683,172	13.91%
Turkey	415,011	8.45%
Pakistan	242,002	4.93%
Iranian diaspora	152,873	3.11%
Turkmenistan	104,769	2.13%
Bahrain	93,885	1.91%
India	77,307	1.57%
Kuwait	74,560	1.52%
China	73,135	1.49%
Germany	61,541	1.25%
Lebanon	55,997	1.14%
Oman	41,899	0.85%
France	41,431	0.84%
Italy	38,131	0.78%
Russia	27,066	0.55%
Georgia	25,666	0.52%
South Korea	21,035	0.43%
Netherlands	17,849	0.36%
Other countries	293,029	5.97%
Total	4,911,920	100.00%

Source: ICHTO, 2018.

Table 1.3 Primary and secondary target markets for Iran tourism

Asia-Pacific region		Arab and African regions		Europe and North America region	
Primary	Secondary	Primary	Secondary	Primary	Secondary
Turkey	Taiwan	Saudi Arabia	Algeria	Italy	Netherlands
Azerbaijan	India	Kuwait	Syria	Germany	Spain
Turkmenistan	Bangladesh	Bahrain	Egypt	UK	Greece
Kazakhstan	Tajikistan	Qatar	South Africa	USA (Iranian	Poland
Armenia	Afghanistan	Oman	Tunisia	diaspora)	Ukraine
Georgia	Uzbekistan	UAE		France	Denmark
Pakistan	Singapore	Iraq		Russia	Balkan
Malaysia	Indonesia	Lebanon		Canada	countries
Japan				Sweden	(Croatia,
China				Switzerland	Bosnia,
Australia					Albania)
South Korea					Belarus

Source: Zargam & Shalbafian, 2014.

tourists to Mashhad, which most Shia tourists visit for the Shrine of Imam Reza, the eighth Shia Imam, and has had a tremendous negative effect on the city economy and the employment in Mashhad has dropped by 50% (Khodaei, 2017). With respect to cultural tourists, the main generating markets are Germany, France, and Italy. ICHTO has defined some target countries for inbound tourism (Table 1.3) and tourism overseas representatives have been established in 25 countries for promotional purposes and to attract investors in the tourism and hospitality sector in Iran (Zargam & Shalbafian, 2014).

Despite the significant growth of tourism in the country since 2013 and the country's potentiality, the effects on the economic health of Iran's tourism industry are still glaring. According to a recent World Travel and Tourism Council report (WTTC, 2017), Iran was ranked thirty-fourth in the world in terms of travel and tourism's direct contribution to its Gross Domestic Product (GDP) in the year 2016. Its position is therefore now considerably lower than other countries in the region, such as the United Arab Emirates (ranked 21) and Turkey (ranked 14), which it had previously outperformed in this respect. According to WTTC (2017), the direct contribution of travel and tourism to Iran's GDP was $11.9 billion in 2016—2.9% of the total GDP which is substantially lower than Turkey ($29.1 billion), the United Arab Emirates ($18.7 billion), or Egypt (EGP87.4 billion) (Table 1.4).

According to the travel and tourism competitiveness report of 2017, Iran is on the first rank in terms of price competitiveness (Table 1.5). This is mainly due to the exchange rate fluctuations since 2012 which have meant that the currency has lost more than 80% of its exchange as a result of rising tension with the West and the tightening of US-banking sanctions and the EU ban on Iran's oil imports (Pratt & Alizadeh, 2017).

Table 1.4 Travel and tourism's share of total national investment in Iran in comparison with the UAE, Turkey, and Egypt

% of whole economy GDP	2005	2006	2007	2008	2009	2010	2011	2012	2013	2014	2015	2016	2017	2027 estimate
Iran	3.5	3.3	3.4	3.2	3.3	2.9	2.7	2.8	3.0	3.1	3.2	3.3	3.4	3.9
Turkey	9.3	8	6	7.8	10.8	8	10.4	8.5	9.2	11.4	11.7	12.3	12.2	12.5
Egypt	12.8	13.7	14.0	13.4	13.0	12.4	12.5	12.3	12.8	12.8	12.0	11.9	11.8	12.4
UAE	2.6	3.4	5.1	5.5	4.5	5.8	6.5	6.4	6.5	6.6	7.2	7	6.7	11.2

Source: WTTC, 2015, 2017.

Table 1.5 Comparisons between Iran and regional competitors in the Travel & Tourism Competitiveness Report 2017

Indicators	Iran	Turkey	Egypt	UAE
International openness	109	50	102	75
Prioritization of travel and tourism	117	87	37	31
ICT readiness	94	72	89	15
Human resources and labor market	105	94	102	23
Health and hygiene	93	64	68	63
Safety and security	87	116	130	2
Business environment	79	63	78	5
Price competitiveness	1	70	2	56
Environmental sustainability	119	112	67	40
Tourist service infrastructure	116	42	93	27
Natural resources	100	70	97	91
Cultural resources and business travel	38	16	22	50
Overall rank	93	44	74	29

Source: WTTC, 2017.

Background to tourism development in Iran

The contemporary history of tourism development in Iran dates back to the 1930s where the first tourism facilities, including some guesthouses and hotels, were built and steps were carried out to promote and encourage tourism. Since the establishment of the first official tourism organization in Iran in the 1930s, tourism development has confronted many challenges. In fact, historically tourism has not featured as a major economic priority, although it has shown some occasional development. The organizations responsible for tourism development, its planning and marketing have confronted a wide range of changes from names and structures to objectives and policy (Alipour & Heydari, 2005). Strengthening inbound tourism and its role as an economic and cultural pursuit has been a common goal and favored by various state systems and administrations in modern Iran (Mozaffari et al., 2017). This is true of both the Pahlavi Monarchy (1925–1979) as well as its successor state system, the theocratic Islamic Republic (1979–present). Before the arrival of Reza Shah Pahlavi and the establishment of the Pahlavi Dynasty (1925–1941), there was no formal international tourism industry in Iran as it was formed in the aftermath of the Industrial Revolution and after the First World War (Ghaderi, 2017). In part as a result of linkages to Western powers during Reza Shah's reign, many significant political, socio-cultural, and economic reforms were introduced, ultimately laying the foundation of the modern Iranian state and the extensive policy of Persianization with the aim of creating a single, united, and largely homogeneous nation (Matthee, 1993; Chehabi, 1993). It has been asserted that the international prominence of Iran had sharply declined during his predecessor dynasty, Qajar rule (1789–1925), and was significantly rejuvenated in his reign (Ghods, 1991). The first attempt to organize and administer Iran's tourism occurred in 1934 (Zamani Zenouzi, 1980). It was then, an official bureau inaugurated under the auspices of the Ministry of Interior and called the bureau of tourism. A significant number of tourism facilities including guesthouses (called Jalbe-Saiahan), hotels, a national railway, and public transport network were built and major attractions were developed. Unfortunately, no official tourism statistics for this period are available to compare the number of visitors.

In 1941, the last shah of Iran, Mohammad Reza Pahlavi took power and succeeded his father. During his reign (1941–1979), extensive relationships with the West, especially the United States were established and, in turn, tourism was considered as an important strategy to introduce Iranian history and culture (Morakabati, 2011), most notably the celebration of 2,500 years of Iran and the Persian Empire held in Shiraz. As one of the principal events in this period, this gathering consisted of an elaborate set of festivities that took place on October 12–16, 1971. The intent of the celebration was to demonstrate Iran's old civilization and history to showcase its contemporary advancements under Mohammad Reza Pahlavi. In this period, the tourism budget increased considerably (from 3.9 billion rials to 8.9 billion rials) (Mozaffari et al., 2017) and the Ministry of Information and Tourism established a substantial marketing and promotion program. The tourism plan focused on promoting tourism in summer as well as winter activities, religion, and cultural tourism. The number of tourist arrivals increased steadily from 200,000 in 1969 to more than 700,000 in 1977 (Bureau of Statistics and Marketing, 1978) and the main tourism markets in this period were Western Europe and the United States (Mirzaei, 2013).

With the increasing numbers of inbound tourists, tourism facilities and services along with the first tourism master plan were established. However, the development of tourism was interrupted by the Islamic revolution in 1979 and the industry faced dramatic socio-economic impacts as a result of the change of political system. The most considerable effort in promoting tourism in Iran before the Islamic revolution was in the 1970s, when the government appointed a Swiss consultant (Tourist Consult) to develop a comprehensive plan for the expansion of tourism. It was an extensive study of Iran's existing and future tourism markets, policies, resources, priorities, and potentials, along with detailed analysis and suggestions. However, the study could not be implemented as the country faced several events, including political developments, pre- and post-1979.

The government took various steps to develop tourism facilities and services and the arrival of international and multi-national companies and investment in luxury hotels, and the training of human resources with the establishment of hospitality schools to accelerate the development of tourism in the country. The first Hospitality Higher School was established in 1963 followed by the Hotel Management School in 1966 (Ziaee, Saeedi, & Torab Ahmadi, 2012). In this period, hotel investment was supported by management contracts with major international chains such as Hilton, Hyatt, Intercontinental, and Sheraton and the national airline, Iran Air, was established and by the late 1970s was the fastest growing airline in the world and one of the most profitable (Baum & O'Gorman, 2010). By 1976, Iran Air was ranked second only to Qantas as the world's safest airline (Morakabati, 2011). Currently, with respect to its safety record, Iran Air cannot secure a place in the top 30 airlines in the world, which can, to a large extent, be attributed to the lack of availability of authentic spare parts and maintenance issues as a result of sanctions (Jalilvand & Samiei, 2012).

With the collapse of the Pahlavi monarchy and the establishment of a type of political Islam in the form of a theocratic Islamic revolution governed by a strict Islamic state (Zamani-Farahani & Henderson, 2010), tourism activities were hampered by the revolution together with political turbulence, conflicts, war with Iraq (between 1980 and 1988), and socio-cultural barriers. This transition from monarchy into a theocracy with its legacy, with a complex political framework and the Islamic religion has had profound consequences for destination conditions and inbound and outbound tourists, and has been influential in determining the content, direction, and implementation of tourism policy (Zamani-Farahani, 2010). Religious ideology continues to affect the governance of Iran, and changes in political leaders are not always matched by agreement with religious leaders because of clashes over religious ideology and interpretation. Iran is a good example of how tourism can be stopped and at least slightly restarted as a result of changes in the ruling elite and the specific ideologies which are espoused (Butler & Suntikul, 2017). This has meant that Iran, despite a wealth of unique tourist attractions, has drawn relatively small numbers of inbound tourists from the developed countries that are the major generators of international flows.

In the early years after the 1979 Islamic revolution, hardline elements in the clerical establishment advocated destroying some of the country's most important pre-Islamic sites, including the ruins of Persepolis, a 2,500-year-old palace complex. This was aligned with the revolutionary states' desire to play a prominent cultural and political role in the Middle East region, based on its proclaimed ambition of leading the Islamic world by "exporting the revolution" to neighboring countries (Esposito, 1990). Tense political relations with Western countries, and particularly the United States, which were the main tourism markets for Iran, and the Iran–Iraq war (1980–1988) interrupted the growing trend of tourism in Iran and the number of tourists started to decrease considerably from 700,000 in 1977 to less than 100,000 in 1988 (Mirzaei, 2013). Following the above-mentioned changes, which were intensified by the occupation of the American Embassy in Tehran and the Iran hostage crises (from November 4, 1979 to January 20, 1981) and imposing a round of sanctions on Iran, the tourism market experienced major changes and shifted to neighboring countries including Pakistan, Afghanistan, and India, which was favored by the clerical ruling elite of Iran. While North America and Western Europe had a market share of more than 40% in 1978, by 1988 Pakistan, Afghanistan, and India with more than 44% market share were the main tourism market in Iran. Many leisure and entertainment centers and resorts were closed and social constraints on travel and leisure were imposed, especially in coastal resorts, as they were believed to be contrary to the Islamic values of the ruling elite. Moreover, hotels and residential facilities which were run by international chains under the control of the Pahlavi foundation (e.g. Hilton, Vanak, Evin, and Darband) were confiscated by religious and revolutionary organizations. This was also the case for many amusement and entertainment centers that were considered against the Islamic norms and values and, more importantly, were one of the rationales behind the revolution. The challenges facing the country's tourism were aggravated just one year after the revolution by the eight-year war with Iraq (1980–1988). Since the closure of most international chains, the hotel sector in Iran has been dominated by the local players (Khodadadi, 2016c). In addition, hospitality and tourism training centers were shut down and foreign tourists were faced with serious limitations. All these issues presented significant challenges to the image of Iran as a tourism destination.

The second presidential election in the aftermath of the Islamic revolution led to the Hashemi Rafsanjani administration (two terms, 1989–1997), also known as the 'construction period' or 'post-war reconstruction period' in the economic and political discourse of the country following the ending of the Iran–Iraq war in 1988. Iran's diplomatic relations with most European states began to improve at the end of the war when the newly formed Supreme National Security Council adopted a pro-Europe foreign policy (Molavi, 1999). However, following the issue of a fatwa against Indian-British writer Salman Rushdie and calls for his death by Iran's supreme leader, Ayatollah Khomeini on charges of blasphemy for his novel *The Satanic Verses* in 1989, Iran broke its diplomatic relations with the United Kingdom and most European countries (Rule, 1989). Ayatollah Khomeini, the Supreme Leader of the Revolution died at the end of the 1980s, ushering in a new chapter of revolution.

By supporting a free market policy and favoring privatization of state-owned industries and avoiding conflict with the United States and the West, new stages of development were launched in the country with the aim of reconstructing a country which had suffered considerably in the eight-year Iran–Iraq war. With respect to the tourism industry, the first comprehensive tourism master plan in the aftermath of the Islamic revolution of 1979 was launched and a new chapter opened in Iran's relations with its neighboring countries, which became the main Iranian tourism markets. The state of the hotel industry which was nearly bankrupted as a result of Islamic revolution began to improve. Tourism training centers were reopened and the first tourism program at higher education level along with the first hospitality undergraduate program were launched at Allameh Tabataba'i University (ATU) in 1995 in Tehran. Since then, there has been a substantial increase in the number of universities and colleges offering tourism programs. In the immediate aftermath of the war, there was a specific focus on post-war protection and preservation of heritage in general and that of war-related heritage in particular. As a form of 'dark tourism' focusing on conflict sites (Stone, 2006), war tourism was officially but implicitly promoted (Heidari & Najafipour, 2014). This sub-sector of tourism continues to be promoted to the present and is funded by powerful organizations, including the Foundation of Preservation of Works and Dissemination of Values of Holy Defense, rather than tourism bodies (Mozaffari et al., 2017). These organizations have established several war museums in Tehran and other cities. Organized tours led by Rahian-e Noor, an organization affiliated to the Basij, the volunteer paramilitary wing of the Revolutionary Guards to battlefields from Iran's 1980–1988 war with neighboring Iraq have been largely established with the aims of visiting graves and commemorating the fighting primarily for domestic tourism purposes. Moreover, during Hashemi Rafsanjani's presidential period, the collapse of the Soviet Union opened potential opportunities for the Iranian inbound tourism market. However, the Iranian state could not take significant advantage of this situation by expanding its market's share from newly independent states due to the lack of an effective marketing strategy (Ghaderi, 2017). Although, following the economic policies of the state, a new social class was created in the community that increased the demand for outbound travel.

During Mohammad Khatami's two presidential terms (1997–2005), known as the 'reform period' in the political discourse of the country, liberalization, foreign investment, and reform policy were supported and a new chapter between Iran and the West was opened in the wake of his political discourse of "Dialogue among Civilizations" as a response to Samuel Huntington's *Clash of Civilizations* theory. The United Nations proclaimed the year 2001 as the United Nations' Year of Dialogue among Civilizations, on Khatami's suggestion and the theory gained a lot of international support. As a result, the image of Iran as an emerging tourism destination was substantially improved. As a result, inbound tourism was increased from fewer than a million people in 1997 to over 2.5 million in 2005 and the number of international arrivals experienced an average growth rate of 27.2% between 1990 and 2000 (Mozaffari et al., 2017). A large part of the growth is attributed to Iranian expatriates returning to visit, which was an outcome of reformists' policies in easing up travel to Iran without fear of being penalized. Tourism was placed in the government priorities for national and regional development and hence a new tourism master plan was prepared in 2002. The success of the reformists had also brought fresh air into the foreign policy arena which has resulted in a far better relationship with some regional powers (Saeidi, 2002; Kazemi, 2003), although domestic tensions with clerical establishments and pressure groups continued to affect inbound tourism.

In this period, the tourism organization started inscribing Iranian heritage sites on the UNESCO list which had been stopped between 1979 and 2002. A new plan was launched to attract the Iranian diaspora to visit their home country and a comprehensive tourism plan was developed in cooperation with the UNWTO and the United Nations Development Programme (UNDP). Following the invasion of Iraq in 2003, the fall of Saddam Hussein's Sunni regime, and its eventual replacement by a Shia-led Iranian-supported government, Iran could attract more Iraqi Shia pilgrims (Majidyar, 2018).

During Ahmadinejad's presidency (two terms, 2005–2013) which is known as the 'new conservative era' in the political discourse of the country (Ehteshami & Zweiri, 2007), notable for increasing tensions with the West as a result of nuclear dispute and uranium enrichment as well as his anti-Zionist ideology, a new round of tensions with the West were intensified and the tourism industry again experienced a dramatic stagnation and a new round of sanctions imposed on the country with significant consequences for the country's economy. The rial suffered significantly and the inflation-racked currency made Iran a cheap tourism destination which enabled the entry of Chinese tourists to Iran (Ghaderi, 2017).

The stringent economic sanctions and the extremist policies of the unpleasant security state under Ahmadinejad have affected negatively the destination image of Iran. A political movement (the Iranian Green Movement, also known as the Persian Awakening or Persian Spring by the Western media) arose after the 2008 Iranian presidential election, in which protesters demanded the removal of Mahmoud Ahmadinejad from office following widespread electoral fraud. The Green Movement protests were a major event in Iran's modern political history and claimed as the largest protest since the Iranian revolution of 1979 (Dabashi, 2011). In this period, the formation of a Shi'ite ruling elite in Iraq and the development of stronger relations with Lebanon led to an increasing flow of Shi'ite tourism from Iraq and Lebanon to Iran. In the second presidential term of Ahmadinejad (2008–2012) there was a gradual rise in domestic tourism and continuing sharp decline in outbound tourism because of the runaway inflation in the country and currency exchange fluctuations. The gradual rise in domestic tourism may be attributed to the political restrictions forced by Ahmadinejad's administration, controlling travel to destinations such as Turkey and Thailand and cancelling direct flights to a number of destinations (Mozaffari et al., 2017), affected outbound tourism and substantially increasing domestic tourism.

In 2013 a more pragmatist candidate was elected in the presidential election with moderate views toward domestic policies and reconciliation along with a desire to foster ties with the international community and end the crippling economic sanctions along with the country's isolation. During the Rouhani administration (from 2013 onward), the necessary measures were taken to restore the economy and improve the rocky relations with Western nations and terminate the nuclear dispute. However, his foreign policy has been contained by the Iranian hard-liners and other conservatives who fear change with their xenophobic beliefs (Alipour & Heydari, 2005). With the election of Rouhani to the presidency, a new spirit of vitality emerged and the image of the country was substantially improved and the volume of travel to Iran was significantly increased (Table 1.6). Following the nuclear deal of 2015 signed between Iran and world powers along with the easing of visa requirements and creating on-arrival visas for a majority of countries, airlines which had stopped their flights to Iran began returning to the country (e.g. KLM, British Airways, Air France). In addition to hotel groups, the Lausanne Hotel School signed a deal in February 2016 to open a hotel school in

Table 1.6 Arrivals from select Western countries 2009–2017 (in 000s)

Trips	2009	2010	2011	2012	2013	2014	2015	2016	2017
France	8.0	6.1	6.0	5.9	7.3	7.4	12.95	19.96	41.43
Germany	18.1	18.5	16.9	18.0	21.2	21.9	32.86	50.37	61.54
Italy	11.0	9.2	10.0	9.6	13.0	13.2	25.28	24.23	38.13
Spain	2.5	2.5	2.7	2.3	3.6	3.7	6.8	7.22	9.76
United Kingdom	6.7	7.8	6.6	3.8	5.4	5.6	7.24	10.18	17.59

Source: ICHTO, 2017.

Isfahan as a hub for hotel education not only in Iran, but also throughout the entire region. The tourism industry in Iran has seen a sharp rise in the number of Western tourists visiting the country in the wake of this landmark deal. Given the positive prospects related to the recent lifting of economic sanctions on Iran, this flow of tourists is expected to increase steadily to reach 20 million by 2025 with the aim to achieve a US$30 billion tourism industry (Khodadadi, 2016a).

A threefold increase in the departure tax proposed by the government in 2017 prompted outrage among many Iranians (Bezhan, 2017). This skyrocketing increase in departure taxes may put a great deal of pressure on outbound tourists while it may increase the number of domestic travels.

The legal, regulatory and development framework

Tourism institutions

The Iran Cultural Heritage, Handcraft and Tourism Organization (ICHTO) which is the national tourism administration in Iran is a governmental administered and funded organization responsible for tourism planning and management in Iran. The overall responsibility of this organization is to safeguard the historical, archaeological, cultural, and religious sites under its jurisdiction as well as to regulate tourism entities and promote Iran regionally and internationally as a viable tourism destination (ICHTO, 2018). Construction, development, and functioning of touristic enterprises in Iran are being regulated by this organization as well. The organization is also responsible for reconstruction of recreational enterprises at the expense of direct investments or crediting private sector as well as licensing of touristic activities. ICHTO also controls functioning of hotels, restaurants, and touristic agencies, and also defines their qualifications.

Throughout the history, this organization has seen considerable changes to its name and structure. The first official attempt at formalizing tourism was marked by the establishment of Jalbe Sayahan e Khareji Va Tablighat Bureau in the Ministry of Interior in 1930s. The main purpose of this organization was to better introduce the country and its historical and national attractions to the world (Ghaderi, 2011). The Bureau was renamed the Higher Council of Tourism by 1940. By 1953 the Ministry of Interior had amended some laws in relation to tourist establishments (Alipour & Heydari, 2005).

In light of increasing tourist numbers in the 1960s, tourism gained special attention, and a new administrative body compromising 12 members from different ministries was given the responsibility for developing tourism policy. In order to better organize and administer tourism in the country, the semi-government 'Sazmane Jalbe Sayahan' (Organization of Tourism Affairs) was established under the auspices of the Ministry of Interior and under the direct control of the prime minister (Dibaei, 1993). The organization of tourism affairs consolidated with the Ministry of Information and was renamed the Ministry of Information and Tourism by 1975 resulting in an increase in inbound tourist numbers (Alipour & Heydari, 2005; Sheikhroodi, 2007). This administrative change resulted in an inbound tourist increase to Iran until the onset of the Islamic revolution in Iran in 1979. In 1979, in the wake of increasing numbers of inbound tourists, a Swiss consultant—Tourist Consult—was appointed to develop a comprehensive tourism plan for the country. Yet, as a result of the upheavals of the 1970s, the study could not be implemented properly (Zamani-Farahani & Henderson, 2010).

The post-revolutionary period in Iran brought fundamental changes in various forms and in numerous areas. The tourism sector also experienced restructuring as a new political structure replaced the old regime. After the revolution, the Ministry of Information and Tourism was combined with the Ministry of Culture and Arts to form the Ministry of Islamic Guidance. As a result of these structural changes in the administration, the Department of Pilgrimage and Travel was attached to this Ministry. This department was dealing with all matters related to Hajj and pilgrimage.

Following the decline in international tourist arrivals as a result of political instability, tourism responsibilities were transferred to the Iran Touring and Tourism Organization (ITTO) in 1980. ITTO was attached to the Ministry of Culture and Islamic Guidance.

In 2004, the Cultural Heritage Organization and ITTO were joined together to form the Iran Cultural Heritage and Tourism Organization (ICHTO) (Ghaderi, 2011). Only a few years later and in 2006 the Handcraft Organization which was separated from the Industry and Mining Ministry, was merged into ICHTO and renamed the Cultural Heritage, Handcraft and Tourism Organization with direct authority resting with the vice-president (O'Gorman et al., 2007; Zamani-Farahani & Henderson, 2010). As of 2018, formal responsibility for tourism lies with this organization which has six deputies, the three main ones being Handcrafts and Traditional Crafts, Tourism, and Cultural Heritage. Despite all these changes, the government has always played a determining role in the country's tourism arena.

The activity of ICHTO, based in Tehran, is structured around three main axes: cultural heritage, handcrafts, and tourism, and several offices, the most important of which are: General Administration of Museums, Training and Technical Support Office, National Ecotourism Committee, Office of Investment and Financing, and National Center for Tourism Studies and Research (Figure 1.3). ICHTO also has responsibility for monitoring and giving guidelines to the provincial tourism offices and receiving feedback from them. Provincial tourism offices communicate with the tourism committees at the sub-regional levels, which finally, engage with the tourist associations at the city and district levels (Alipour & Heydari, 2005). The 31 provincial ICHTO offices report directly to the main body organization and president of ICHTO. These offices are mainly responsible for implementing ICHTO's monitoring, inspection, and training roles, and for provincial tourism development functions under the auspices of the provincial governor.

The private sector's involvement in the country's tourism policy making is relatively weak, and tourism industry and tourism planning and strategy largely remain the domain of the public sector. Nonetheless, over the years, the private sector has expanded its role in the accommodation, travel agencies, and tour

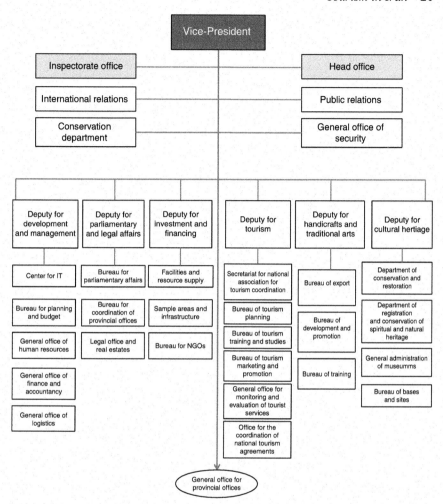

Figure 1.3 Structure of the Iran Cultural Heritage, Handcraft and Tourism Organization.

operation through forming some industry associations and unions (Alipour & Heydari, 2005). In some cases, these associations also have regional or provincial chapters. The key and recognized industry associations include: various hotel associations and unions, Apartment Hotels Association, Association of Air Transport and Travel Agencies, Iran Tourist Guides Association, and Board of Airline Representatives. At present the existing linkages between these private sector organizations and public sector tourism institutions at the national and provincial level tend to be mostly informal or based on a case-by-case function (Alipour & Heydari, 2005). The primary functions of the industry associations are to exchange information, ensure that their members follow ethical standards in business, in some cases to regulate the activities of their members (hotels,

apartment hotels, and travel agents associations), to discuss issues of general concern to their industry, and to put these to the relevant organizations (Alipour &
Heydari, 2005, p. 47).

Tourism policy

The planning and development of each country's tourism industry is influenced by
that country's overall political structure. With respect to Iran, the political structure of the country is unique and complex, with a blend of theocratic and democratic elements. The principles of popular sovereignty and separation of powers
are recognized within the Constitution (Katouzian, 2010). Following the fall of
the Pahlavi monarchy, a theocratic establishment was formalized in 1979 and the
Iranian religious and political landscapes were dramatically transformed with Shia
Islam becoming an inseparable element of the country's political structure. At the
top of Iran's power structure is the supreme leader who is selected by the Assembly
of Experts for a life term. The Assembly of Experts comprises 86 Islamic scholars
elected by the public, screened for piety by the Guardian Council. The Assembly
of Experts is responsible for appointing the supreme leader and supervising his
performance. The supreme leader is with broad powers, including command of the
armed forces, appointment of the head of the judiciary and of half of the Guardian
Council's members, and confirmation of presidential election results. He sets the
direction of the country's foreign policies (including the nuclear program) and is
extremely influential with respect to domestic policy as well. Moreover, he makes
final decisions about eligible presidential candidates, election results, and the cabinet posts of defense, foreign affairs, information, culture/Islamic guidance. He
also appoints the heads of judiciary and state broadcasting.

One of the most powerful forces in Iran's government is the Guardian Council,
which consists of 12 top Shia clerics. Six of the council members are appointed
by the supreme leader, while the remaining six are nominated by the judiciary
and then approved by parliament. The Guardian Council has the power to veto
any bill passed by parliament if it is judged inconsistent with the Iranian Constitution or with Islamic law. All bills must be approved by the council before they
become law. Another important function of the Guardian Council is the approval
of potential presidential candidates. The highly conservative council generally
blocks most reformists and all women from running. The president who is elected
directly by the people for a four-year term (no more than two consecutive terms) is
the head of the government and responsible for managing domestic policy. However, the supreme leader controls the armed forces and makes major security and
foreign policy decisions, so the power of the presidency is rather sharply curtailed.
The Guardian Council vets all potential presidential candidates and usually rejects
most reformers and all women.

Iran's unicameral parliament, called the *Majlis*, has a 290-member body of deputies representing all 30 of Iran's provinces. Members are directly elected every
four years, but again the Guardian Council vets all candidates. The Majlis proposes and passes legislation for approval by the Guardian Council. Parliament
also approves budgets submitted by the president. In addition, the Majlis has the

authority to impeach the president or cabinet members. The Expediency Council seeks to resolve conflicts between lawmakers and the Guardian Council. The Expediency Council is considered an advisory board for the supreme leader, who appoints its 20–30 members from among both religious and political circles. The Iranian judiciary ensures that all laws passed by the Majlis conform with Islamic law (*sharia*) and that the law is enforced according to the principles of sharia. The judiciary also selects six of the twelve members of the Guardian Council, who then must be approved by the Majlis. (The other six are appointed by the supreme leader.) The supreme leader also appoints the head of the judiciary, who selects the chief supreme court justice and the chief public prosecutor.

The formulation, development, and implementation of the rules of the constitution in the Islamic Republic of Iran on the basis of Islamic sharia along with religion-intervention principles have resulted in policies that affect tourism policy, marketing, development of tourism activities, attractions, and facilities (Zamani-Farahani & Henderson, 2010; Jafari & Scott, 2014; Henderson, 2014). Since the declaration of an Islamic Republic and a theocracy led by Ayatollah Khomeini in 1979, the state and religion are virtually indivisible (Zamani-Farahani & Henderson, 2010). Consequently, tourism policy is influenced by religion with a certain degree of restriction including customary restrictions on dress and a prohibition on alcohol. Food and beverages are halal (complying with Muslim dietary laws). Tourism industry employees must accord due respect to Islam in terms of dress code and behavior. With respect to domestic policy for tourism in Iran, after the war (from 1988-onward) a series of five-year development plans have been in place. However, tourism development has not given priority in the long-term development policies of the country and encouraging tourism in Iran has always been a hotly debated issue between two main factions in the ruling elite. One view sees tourism as a means to achieve economic benefits as well as a means to modernize and connect to the international community, where the second view, mainly in the clerical establishment as well as hard-liners, considers tourism as a means of globalization and a threat to the Islamic values and norms, and wish to prevent the erosion of religious devoutness and conventions (Alipour & Heydari, 2005; Morakabati, 2011; Zamani-Farahani & Henderson, 2010). Hence, in spite of its vast tourism resources and potential, Iranian tourism has experienced a tremendous setback due to the public sector's dominance over the major economic activities as well as policies. As (Zamani-Farahani, 2010, p. 209) noted,

> The institutional structure and organization of the tourism public sector in Iran displays a number of weaknesses. The selection of top-level managers and key figures in authority appears to be commonly decided based on candidates' devotion to Islam and Islamic appearance alongside political allegiance.

O'Gorman et al. (2007, p. 262) argued,

> the leadership of public sector tourism, both in promotional and operational roles, is rarely professional or long term. State and quasi-state tourism organizations do not operate under commercial criteria like profitability and are subject to poor and inconsistent management and high levels of political interference.

Males are more prevalent in top-level positions. Proximity to people of religious and political influence is another factor and the skills needed for effective management are secondary (Zamani-Farahani & Henderson, 2010). Tourism in Iran also faced interference by influential individuals from both the religious and political arena outside the tourism industry.

There is a lack of a clear national tourism development strategy. Government support to this sector is limited and appears not to be considered a priority for economic development and growth. However, there have been some efforts. For example, In Khatami's administration a comprehensive tourism master plan was prepared in cooperation with the UNWTO and the UNDP. More recently, in Rouhani's administration, tourism has also been given special attention and his administration has taken measures that mainly focus on creating better conditions to attract international tourists.

Iran aims to raise the number of international tourists to 20 million by 2025 with projected investment of over US$32 billion, with $5 billion from the government and the remainder from private enterprise (Faghri, 2007), which should potentially generate $25 to $30 billion as per the country's 2025 vision. Some policies have been implemented toward this goal including an on-arrival visa for more than 100 countries (except for nationals from the United States, the United Kingdom, Israel, Canada, Colombia, Somalia, Bangladesh, Jordan, Iraq, Afghanistan, Pakistan, and India) and has lifted the visa requirements for nationals of Azerbaijan, Bolivia, Malaysia, Sri Lanka, Syria, Turkey, and Venezuela. After the nuclear deal was reached, the government extended the tourist visa from two weeks to three months. However, American and British tourists are treated differently, and are only permitted to travel to the country in organized tours where they can be monitored.

In the wake of the 2015 nuclear agreement and the ensuing lifting of sanctions, improvements to the aging and underdeveloped infrastructure, particularly hotels and airplanes were given priority by tourism officials. The country has just over 130 four- and five-star hotels, while the industry suggests it needs at least 400 quality lodging facilities to accommodate the projected 20 million travelers. Iran offered 1,153 hotels, 2,007 hotel apartments, and 249 inns and budget accommodation properties in 2017, as well as many homestay facilities (more than 1,876) (ICHTO, 2018) which provide 271,989 available beds in total. However, many of these properties need to be modernized in light of current international requirements and service levels improved in order to be at par with standards in other successful destinations (ICHTO, 2018). In 2016, French group Accor Hotels became the first foreign branded hotel to open in Iran after the 1979 Islamic revolution when two hotels—Ibis and Novotel—were opened near Imam Khomeini International Airport, 30 km south of Tehran. Developments by other international hotel groups include the UAE-based Rotana group which is set to open three outlets by 2018 and Spain's Meliá Hotels International plans to open a five-star property called Gran Meliá Ghoo in a 130-meter tower in Salman Shahr, Mazandaran Province, on the Caspian

Sea which is Iran's first foreign-branded seaside hotel in nearly 40 years. Turkish and German investors have also planned to build hotels in major Iranian tourism destinations such as Tehran, Isfahan, Shiraz, Tabriz, and Mashhad which are suffering from insufficient lodging facilities. However, this could also place pressure on local independent hotels, most of which require renovation and improvements (Euromonitor International, 2015). But it could also encourage local players to invest in quality in order to able to cope with increased competition. However, US-based Hilton Worldwide Holdings are holding off investing in Iran as most American firms are still prohibited from exploring the Iranian market due to other sanctions imposed by Washington on Tehran.

With respect to the airlines, Iran's aging civilian air fleet is also being updated with the country ordering airplanes from the major aircraft producers such as Airbus, Boeing, and ATR. Over the past years and especially after political and economic sanctions against Iran, Iran Air has been unable to deliver the fleet size required to meet demand. Aging and outdated fleet, issues with fuel availability for Iranian aircraft on international flights, and increases in the foreign exchange rate are among the main reasons for the poor operation of Iran Air.

Other endeavors to encourage tourism

Special attention has been given to attracting the Iranian diaspora to come to Iran to visit family and friends which has improved domestic tourism as well as inbound. Although there is no clear information about the numbers of Iranians living abroad, it has been estimated that the total number is between 5 and 6 million, who mainly live in the United States, the United Kingdom, the United Arab Emirates, Canada, Germany, France, and Turkey (Ghaderi, 2015). Many of these people who are not refugees and are able to come to Iran to visit their family and friends do so at least once a year and make trips to other parts of the country to visit other tourist destinations. These Iranians usually have high income levels with strong purchasing power. When they come to Iran, they usually find it very affordable mainly due to the very favorable exchange rate. Besides its economic significance, VFR (visiting friends and relatives) travel has contributed to the solidarity and strength of the social foundations of Iranian communities (Ghaderi, 2015).

Another effort to encourage tourism is the development of computerized hotel reservations systems. ICHTO has signed several letters of understanding and bilateral tourism agreements with other states covering a range of issues, which include the exchange of tourists. Eight overseas tourism offices have been opened with private sector support and plans were announced to open Foreign Investment Offices in Malaysia, Turkey, China, and several Middle Eastern and European countries in a bid to raise investment in tourism from overseas (Zargam & Shalbafian, 2014).

Box 1.1: Tourism planning and policy before the 1979 revolution

Iran has faced different approaches to tourism planning and policy in its history, each of which is a function of political and socio-economic conditions. In the years before the 1979 revolution, Iran's development can be regarded as reflecting the modernization paradigm. In that period, Western lifestyles and culture enjoyed certain popularity (Devos & Werner, 2014), although the history of ancient Iran was also of particular importance, especially given its role in the promotion of national identity. The celebration of the 2,500-year-old kingdom of Iran, the construction and rebuilding of the prominent Iranian tombstones, often accompanied by the development of new museums, reflected the modernist paradigm (Grigor, 2014), and also strengthened nationalistic feelings. Recreation and entertainment also played important roles in the popularity of Western culture and were closely linked to new types of recreational activities in Iran (Devos & Werner, 2014).

Secular changes in that era created a culture of recreational activities that were unique to middle-class society. The opening of cinemas, clubs, bars, restaurants, parks, public sport facilities, swimming pools, and ski resorts, were among these new recreational activities (Grigor, 2014). Among the modernist architectural constructions were the Hilton Hotel in Tehran (Siebertz, 2014) and the Darband Hotel on the slopes of the Alborz Mountains, which were primarily accommodation for Europeans and the wealthy class of Iranian society (Grigor, 2014). However, such traveling opportunities were restricted to foreigners and the affluent of Iran society, and the majority of domestic travel was used to visit parents, friends, and relatives (Ghaderi, 2011).

The cultural policies of the Pahlavi era show the presence of a pragmatic attitude at that time (Devos & Werner, 2014). Presenting a modern image of Iran was extremely important for the authorities, to the extent that police officers had been trained to prevent photography by foreign tourists of dilapidated buildings and signs of traditional society, such as carrying loads with livestock (Devos, 2014).

Prior to the 1979 revolution, tourism planning was primarily initiated in order to help modernize and Westernize Iran. In the 1960s, a council of 12 people from different ministries was responsible for making decisions about the tourism sector (Alipour & Heydari, 2005). This council took charge of the policy making and implementation of the plans of the interior ministry's tourism office at the highest level of supervision (Shalbafian, 2016). As a result of these efforts and strong government interest in tourism, planning of tourism began in a coherent and structured way with the fourth (1967–1977) and the fifth (1973–1978) five-year development plans, which were previously called construction plans.

One of the most important governmental actions that took place in planning tourism in the years before the revolution was the 1971 Iranian Tourism Plan, which resulted in the preparation of a master plan by foreign consultants, in which the resources and facilities for developing tourism were identified (Dibayee, 1992). In addition to this master plan, several other tourism projects were identified regionally in Iran before the 1979 Islamic revolution, but virtually none of them were executed. These included (Ebrahimzadeh, 2007):

- Tourism Master Plan of Caspian Sea Seashore;
- Tourism Centers in Kelardasht and Dasht Nazir;
- Tourism Centers in Karand;

- Mineral Water Springs Master Plans in Sarein and Larijan;
- Tourism Master Plans of Kish and Minoo Islands;
- Tourism Master Plan of Latian Dam.

In addition to these, other studies were carried out by the research office of *Jalb-e-Sayahan*. The most important of these was the identification of different cities' needs to establish accommodation and hospitality along the main road transport routes.

The global energy crisis of the early 1970s proved a boon to Iran's energy sector and the country's economy therefore faced unprecedented growth. As a result of this economic boom, the tourism industry in Iran flourished for two reasons (Khaksari, 2012). First, the increasing per capita income of the Iranian people. Between 1960 and 1977, per capita GDP of Iran increased due to the rise of oil revenues at a high rate of 9.6% per year (Farzanegan & Alaedini, 2016), which expanded domestic tourism as well as the desire of Iranians to make international trips. Second, increase in investment of tourism's infrastructure of the country led to the construction and development of tourism infrastructure, including hotels, roads, airports, restaurants, and more. During this period, domestic tourism in the country was given special attention along with growing interest in promoting Iran as an international destination with the country joining the World Tourism Organization in 1975 (Khaksari, 2012).

Generally, the top-down planning for tourism development in pre-revolutionary Iran was deemed as misshapen by some critics, in that the traditional and devout community of the country, which consisted of the majority of the Iranian population, was not prepared to support this modernization process including the presence of foreigners and even nationals who did not adhere to the traditions and religion of the country. Added to this is the poverty in the undeveloped parts of the country that was sharply juxtaposed with the heavy investments on modern facilities for tourism development and which was considered to be the rulers' attempt at face-saving in the world. The 'modernization' approach to non-inclusive development led to widespread discontent and reinforced the observation that political leaders, who had not taken measures to ensure public support, may jeopardize the tourism industry (Richter, 1999).

The approach to tourism development underwent fundamental changes with the 1979 revolution. Indeed, this revolution was a revolution in values and had a significant impact on attitudes toward tourism and heritage. After the 1979 revolution, caring for Iranian national and historical symbols and values, and modernization in development, was replaced by reliance on Islamic values (Baum & O'Gorman, 2010). As a result, the international image of a recently modernized ancient Iran rapidly faded from view and was replaced by that of a conservative Islamic state (Butler, O'Gorman, & Prentice, 2012).

Niloofar Abbaspour and Marjan Abdi

Constraints facing the Iranian tourism industry

The image of Iran

The overall instability in the region and the growth of radicalism and Islamic extremism has created perceptions of insecurity (Isaac et al., 2015; Avraham, 2015; Tomazos, 2017) and has influenced the long-term prospects of the tourism industry, tourism investment's opportunities, and tourist flows to the region (Morakabati, 2013). Even if they are often exaggerated, these perceptions obviously affect the marketability of Iran as a tourist destination. Recently, the risk and political instability of countries such as Iraq and Syria created a halo effect in surrounding countries and had a significant impact on the tourism industry in this region. Iran has long been regarded as an international pariah state in some parts of the international community and has been better known for its nuclear program, anti-West conspiracies, restrictive rules on female clothing, flag-burning tradition, and human rights violations than for its hospitality to tourists. However, its negative image in many countries disguises its long history of tourism and its rich cultural and natural heritage (Seyfi et al., 2018). The Iranian tourism industry, despite enormous potential, has therefore suffered significantly ever since the establishment of the theocratic Islamic Republic of 1979. However, following the election of a moderate administration in Iran in 2013, the country has welcomed foreigners as part of an effort to improve its international image and boost an economy battered by low oil prices and years of crippling international sanctions imposed over Iran's contentious nuclear program.

Following the nuclear agreement of 2015, Iran has witnessed a significant increase in international tourists. The number of visitors to Iran increased from 2.2 million in 2009 to 5.2 million in 2015. Nevertheless, certain domestic and foreign political groups have been trying to tarnish Iran's image as a safe and tranquil tourism destination. The number of arrivals, that it was hoped would increase following the nuclear agreement between Iran and P5+1, has declined because of domestic pressure group 'The Concerned,' who want to create obstacles for the government by not permitting it to forge improved international ties. Moreover, the Trump administration and the potential re-imposition of sanctions along with domestic tensions between the state and the fundamental clerical establishment have all affected the image and outlook of the country.

With regard to domestic policy and willingness for tourism development, foreigners, who have previously been seen as 'aliens' and potential 'spies' by domestic security and intelligence organizations, need to be welcomed. To improve the international image of the country better communication is needed about its cultural and natural assets. Participation in all major international trade fairs and use of UNESCO as a channel to advertise the heritage of Iran are promising avenues. However, since the resolution of the nuclear dispute and shifts in perceptions of Iran from that of a 'pariah' state to an emerging tourism destination, Rouhani's administration (2013–ongoing) has been placing increasing attention and priority on tourism, even as conflict, political instability, and xenophobic rhetoric from the ruling elite and religious establishments have presented significant challenges to the country's tourism image.

Policy constraints

Iran's over-reliance on oil and gas is regarded as one of the main reasons for the lack of government support of the tourism industry (Alipour & Heydari, 2005). According to the World Bank (2018), Iran is one of the world's largest producers of oil and gas with 10% of the world's petroleum reserves together with the world's second largest reserves of natural gas after Russia (15% of the world's total). Income from oil and gas exploitation is one of the most important features of the Iranian government's revenues and economic policy settings.

> The twentieth century was a period of profound transformation for the Iranian economy. After centuries of under-development and economic stagnation with only a marginal role in the world markets, the economy of Iran began to change in terms of structure, productivity, and international impact.
>
> (Esfahani & Pesaran, 2009, p. 177)

Oil revenues are still the growth engine of the Iranian economy, but easy access to these revenues crippled the development of other sectors and replaced the development of productive industries (e.g. agriculture) with the increase in imports. Iran's economy is dominated by oil and gas production and exports, which is about 85% of the country's annual budget. According to the Organization of Petroleum Exporting Countries (OPEC, 2013), the country's total revenue from petroleum exports—even under heavy international sanctions—was more than $100 billion in 2012, roughly ten times greater than tourism's contribution to its GDP. Therefore, tourism is neglected by the state and given a low priority, thereby limiting the industry's contribution to the country's economic growth and GNP (Zamani-Farahani & Henderson, 2010). Consequently, given the state's monopoly of ownership of oil and gas resources and revenues, and the rentier mentality that prevails in natural resources-dependent economies, other sources of income that require long-term development planning and vision have been neglected. With respect to investment, the share of tourism from the government budget is estimated to be substantially less than that received by the clergy and religious institutions. While the government has significantly cut spending for infrastructure projects and cash subsidies, allocations for religious seminaries and similar entities has increased (Radio Farda, 2018). Many of these wealthy religious foundations are tax exempt. The share of religious foundations from the budget was widely debated in the country as many people were upset over appropriations for religious and revolutionary institutions while other areas of the budget were cut. This has led to recent protestation in the country. While the protests that swept Iran in 2009 were led by the urban middle class, the more recent protests have been largely driven by disaffected young people in rural areas, towns, and small cities who showed their frustrations with the political elite (Nasr, 2018).

US-led international sanctions along with domestic policies and tensions in Iran have also reduced foreign investment in tourism development which has created obstacles to the promotion of the international tourism market in Iran. Moreover, customs regulations, administrative difficulties in obtaining a visa, and use of credit cards have long been among the constraints. Notwithstanding Iran's long struggle with a series of chronic and severe macroeconomic problems, such as high rates of unemployment, increasing levels of debt, and relatively high inflation and interest rates compared to other countries in the region, tourism's economic role has occasionally been allocated greater priority particularly when oil prices drop, and it is seen as a potential means of reducing oil dependence. Nevertheless, the history of tourism planning in Iran is characterized by a high degree of state and religion intervention. A series of so-called five-year socio-cultural and economic development plans have been in operation since 1979. However, the efficacy of the plans is debatable and tourism's contribution to the economy remains relatively minor (Alipour & Heydari, 2005). The ongoing political instability in the Middle East region has also long influenced the long-term prospects of the tourism industry.

Lack of infrastructure

Tourism infrastructure in Iran is relatively underdeveloped and suffers from poor service quality at hotels and other service providers within the sector. One reason for this situation is that the centralized government system in Iran and lack of coordination among different organizations leads to imbalance in infrastructure development. On the one hand, big cities like Tehran, Mashhad, Isfahan, and Tabriz are developed and modern, but on the other hand, other cities and areas are deprived and marginalized (Alipour & Heydari, 2005). Roads and railways were also not built on the basis of development needs. Considering the current limitations of the transportation network accompanied by sharp growth in the population rate (from 37 million in 1979 to over 80 million in 2018), there is a great shortfall in transport, mainly rail and air transport, throughout the country. The shortage of hotel rooms coupled with the low quality of accommodation, the lack of trained drivers and tour leaders and the shortage of rest areas on roads could also hold back the growth of the country's budding tourism sector. More importantly, Iran has no connection to international payment networks such as Visa and MasterCard. In this regard, Iran's banking system, due mostly to international sanctions, has remained an isolated island with few connections to the outside world. Domestic banks have failed to provide services to foreign clients. It is rarely possible for visiting foreigners to have access to their original accounts since sanctions have restrained international banking operations in Iran. As a result, most visitors have no alternative but to carry cash with them. In the wake of the lifting of nuclear-related international sanctions, the country has been working toward improving the quality of its lodging facilities and services and attracting foreign investment to expand the variety of hotels and other infrastructure based on quality and price to meet the needs of a wider range of travelers, but progress has been slow. According to the World Travel and Tourism Council (WTTC, 2017) Iran ranks 119th among 141 countries in terms of tourism service infrastructure, while for other countries in the region, the United Arab Emirates ranks 27th, Turkey 42nd, and Egypt 93rd (see Table 1.5).

Lack of investment

Other challenges that have negatively influenced the growth of Iran's tourism sector have been a lack of investment in the sector and the absence of a long-term national vision with respect to the tourism and hospitality industry.

Although, there was increased investment in the sector in Khatami's administration (2000–2008) and from 2013 onward, as evidenced by the opening of new hotels and updating of the aging air fleet. Nevertheless, Iran has invested less than its neighbors in its tourism industry. The capital investment in tourism for Iran in 2016 was 3.3% of total investment (US$3.5 billion), while for Turkey it was 12.3% of total investment, and for the United Arab Emirates was 7% of total investment (WTTC, 2017). More importantly, due to the US and international sanctions imposed on the country, billions of dollars in Iran's oil revenues have been blocked in the country's accounts in foreign banks. Since the softening of sanctions, Rouhani's administration has provided some incentives to gain foreign investment. For example, new hotels and tourism infrastructure in less developed areas will receive a 100% exemption on income tax if a license is issued by the ICHTO. Hotels and tourism projects in developed towns and areas will also benefit from 50% income tax exemption (Khodadadi, 2016c). Despite many international sanctions being lifted, foreign companies still have concerns over investment in Iran. Moreover, the existing sanctions along with the tensions between Iran and the Trump administration prohibited some international financial institutions from having relationships with Iranian banks, with negative consequences for the Iranian government. The Trump administration's desire to pull out of the nuclear deal and re-impose sanctions against Iran over the nuclear agreement, and that Iran's hard-liners call for the dismantlement of this deal have also hampered Iran's efforts to rebuild foreign trade and lure investment (Khodadadi, 2018; Sharafedin, 2018).

Lack of hands-on training

Beyond a weak strategic approach for tourism planning in Iran, staff training in the tourism sector is also lacking (Zargam & Shalbafian, 2014; Seyfi et al., 2018). The employment of unqualified staff in tourist resorts has had negative impacts on the visitor experience (Alipour & Heydari, 2005). It has also been asserted that there is a lack of cooperation between the tourism higher education program and the tourism industry in spite of their role as the main supplier to the industry's labor pool (Ziaee et al., 2012; Ziaee, 2004; Zargam, 2004). Tourism programs at undergraduate level lack diversity with the focus being on either tourism management or hotel management. Most curricula is similar without distinctive contents and requirements. Other specializations including airlines and travel agency management, food and beverage management, and event management are neglected in higher education. There is evidence of a lack of communication and cooperation between tourism enterprises and training institutions making it difficult for training institutions to encourage students to enhance their learning in a real service environment, such as a hotel. While tourism and hospitality education has a short history, the lack of qualified professors and educators, as well as an absence of specific technical infrastructure, provide a less-than-ideal education (Ziaee et al., 2012). This lack of cooperation and communication has also resulted in a lack of trust from the private sector toward graduates due to the fact that they have limited practical knowledge (Zargam, 2004; Ziaee, 2004). Therefore, while new graduates enter the professional working environment, they often either fail to make use of what they were taught; or they adapt ineffectively to the working situation. As a result, many students have insufficient skills and opportunities to get a job. Greater acknowledgment of the role of stakeholders in the education process may assist the process of adaptation to the rapidly changing environment. Moreover, the curriculum for tourism has not been updated since its establishment in 1995. Criticisms had been raised about the curricula used in the tourism program in higher education. There have been ongoing debates and discussions among academics as well as between academics and industry practitioners about the improvement of the curriculum of the tourism degree program.

Structure of the book

Tourism in Iran represents major challenges as well as hopes for future development. This book aims to outline many of the major issues facing tourism in Iran to an international audience as well as detail some of the complexity that characterizes tourism development in the country. The book therefore highlights a range of approaches and concerns that reflect the different ways in which research on tourism in Iran is examined. The book consists of 14 chapters divided into four main sections. Part I includes this introduction (Chapter 1) and chapters on domestic tourism and the effects of sanctions. Part II consists of three chapters that tackle pilgrimage and religious tourism, which is a major market in Iranian tourism and which is arguably the most acceptable form of tourism for the country's religious leaders. Part III consists of four chapters that examine various dimensions of heritage tourism in the country which is significant for national identity as well as for domestic and international tourism. Part IV looks at emerging tourisms and has chapters on the empowerment of women, community-based tourism and health tourism. The conclusion (Chapter 14) highlights some of the issues that need to be addressed if international tourism is to make a greater contribution to Iran's economy and society.

This book began at a time of greatly increased optimism for tourism in Iran and is being completed when much of that positivity about the role of tourism in Iranian economy and society has been overshadowed by the Trump administration's antagonistic attitude to the nuclear agreement, and ongoing political and military tension in the region in which Iran, among other regional and international powers, is engaged. Nevertheless, hopefully the book will help illustrate the way in which tourism serves to reveal that Iran is not a one-dimensional state, despite how it is often presented in the West, and indicates the wealth of hospitality and significance of travel in Iranian society.

References

Alavi, J. & Yasin, M. M. (2000). A systematic approach to tourism policy. *Journal of Business Research, 48*(2), 147–156.

Alipour, H. & Heydari, R. (2005). Tourism revival and planning in Islamic Republic of Iran: Challenges and prospects. *Anatolia, 16*(1), 39–61.

Almuhrzi, H., Alriyami, H., & Scott, N. (Eds.). (2017). *Tourism in the Arab world: An industry perspective.* Bristol: Channel View Publications.

Avraham, E. (2015). Destination image repair during crisis: Attracting tourism during the Arab Spring uprisings. *Tourism Management, 47,* 224–232.

Bassil, C. (2014). The effect of terrorism on tourism demand in the Middle East. *Peace Economics, Peace Science and Public Policy, 20*(4), 669–684.

Baum, T. G. & O'Gorman, K. D. (2010). Iran or Persia: What's in a name, the decline and fall of a tourism industry? In R. Butler & W. Suntikul (Eds.), *Tourism and political change* (pp. 175–185). Oxford: Goodfellow Publishers.

Bezhan, F. (2017). *Flight fight: Proposed tripling of 'departure tax' roils Iranians.* Retrieved from https://www.rferl.org/a/iran-skyrocketing-departure-tax-proposal-anger-tourism/28914103.html

Bizaer, M. (2016). 'Can Iran go around Turkey to reach Europe?' *Al-Monitor,* August 9. Retrieved from http://realiran.org/can-iran-go-around-turkey-to-reach-europe/

Bureau of Statistics and Marketing. (1978). *Tourist arrivals in Iran.* Tehran: Statistic Center of Iran.

Butler, R. & Suntikul, W. (Eds.). (2017). *Tourism and political change* (2nd ed.). Oxford: Goodfellow Publishers.

Butler, R., O'Gorman, K. D., & Prentice, R. (2012). Destination appraisal for European cultural tourism to Iran. *International Journal of Tourism Research, 14*(4), 323–338.

Chehabi, H. E. (1993). Staging the emperor's new clothes: Dress codes and nation-building under Reza Shah. *Iranian Studies, 26*(3–4), 209–233.

Cohen, E. & Cohen, S. A. (2015). A mobilities approach to tourism from emerging world regions. *Current Issues in Tourism, 18*(1), 11–43.

Dabashi, H. (2011). *The green movement in Iran.* Abingdon: Routledge.

Devos, B. (2014). Engineering a modern society? In B. Devos & C. Werner (Eds.), *Culture and cultural politics under Reza Shah; The Pahlavi state, new bourgeoisie and the creation of a modern society in Iran* (pp. 266–287). Abingdon: Routledge.

Devos, B. & Werner, C. (2014). Introduction. In B. Devos & C. Werner (Eds.), *Culture and cultural politics under Reza Shah; The Pahlavi state, new bourgeoisie and the creation of a modern society in Iran* (pp. 1–15). Abingdon: Routledge.

Dibaei, P. (1993). *International tourism.* Tehran: Allameh Tabataba'i University Press [in Persian].

Dibayee, P. (1992). *Understanding tourism.* Tehran: Allameh Tabataba'i University [in Persian].

Ebadi, M. (2017). *Iran.* In L. Lowry (Ed.), *The Sage international encyclopedia of travel and tourism* (pp. 671–674). Thousand Oaks, CA: Sage.

Ebrahimzadeh, I. (2007). Tourism development and its practical changes in transitory Iran. *Journal of Geographic Sciences, 6*(8–9), 97–117 [in Persian].

Ehteshami, A. & Zweiri, M. (2007). *Iran and the rise of its neoconservatives: The politics of Tehran's silent revolution.* London and New York: I. B. Tauris.

Esfahani, H. S. & Pesaran, M. H. (2009). The Iranian economy in the twentieth century: A global perspective. *Iranian Studies, 42*(2), 177–211.

Esposito, J. L. (Ed.). (1990). *The Iranian revolution: Its global impact.* Gainesville, FL: Florida International University Press.

Euromonitor International (2015). Travel and tourism in Iran report. Retrieved from https://www.portal.euromonitor.com/

Faghri, R. (2007). *Tourism planning and policy making of the Islamic Republic of Iran: Analysis of the four five-year development plans.* Unpublished master's thesis. Lulea University of Technology, Sweden.

Farzanegan, M. & Alaedini, P. (2016). Introduction. In M. Farzanegan & P. Alaedini (Eds.), *Economic welfare and inequality in Iran; Developments since the revolution* (pp. 1–13). New York, NY: Palgrave Macmillan.

Ghaderi, E. (2017). *An introduction to tourism geography of Iran.* Tehran: Mahkame Publications [in Persian].

Ghaderi, Z. (2011). Domestic tourism in Iran. *Anatolia, 22*(2), 278–281.

Ghaderi, Z. (2015). Visiting friends and relatives (VFR) travel: The case of Iran. In E. Backer & B. King (Eds.), *VFR travel research: International perspectives* (pp. 109–120). Bristol: Channel View Publications.

Ghirshman, R. (1951). *L'Iran, des origines à l'Islam.* Paris: Payot.

Ghods, M. R. (1991). Iranian nationalism and Reza Shah. *Middle Eastern Studies, 27*(1), 35–45.

Grigor, T. (2014). The king's white wall; Modernism and bourgeois architecture. In B. Devos & C. Werner (Eds.), *Culture and cultural politics under Reza Shah; The Pahlavi state, new bourgeoisie and the creation of a modern society in Iran* (pp. 95–118). Abingdon: Routledge.

Hall, C. M. (2019). The physical geography of the Middle East in the Anthropocene. In D. Timothy (Ed.), *The Routledge handbook of tourism in the Middle East.* Abingdon: Routledge.

Hall, C. M. & Page, S. (2017). Developing tourism in south and central Asia. In C. M. Hall & S. Page (Eds.), *The Routledge handbook on tourism in Asia* (pp. 223–240). Abingdon: Routledge.

Hazbun, W. (2004). Globalisation, reterritorialisation and the political economy of tourism development in the Middle East. *Geopolitics, 9*(2), 310–341.

Hazbun, W. (2008). *Beaches, ruins, resorts: The politics of tourism in the Arab world.* London: University of Minnesota Press.

Heidari, M. & Najafipour, A. (2014). Study of war tourism in the world; a solution for developing war tourism in Iran, *Holy Defense Quarterly, 49*(3), 117–152.

Henderson, J. C. (2014). Global Gulf cities and tourism: A review of Abu Dhabi, Doha and Dubai. *Tourism Recreation Research, 39*(1), 107–114.

Hinnebusch, R. (2010). *The international politics of the Middle East.* Manchester: Manchester University Press.

Hourani, A. (1992) *A history of the Arab peoples.* New York, NY: Warner Books.

Iran Cultural Heritage, Handcraft and Tourism Organization (ICHTO). (2018). *Tourism statistics of Iran.* Retrieved from http://bogendesign-vr.ir/gardeshgari2/19.php

Isaac, R. K. (2013). Palestine: Tourism under occupation. In R. Butler & S. Wantanee (Eds.), *Tourism and war* (pp. 143–158). London: Routledge.

Isaac, R. K., Hall, C. M., & Higgins-Desbiolles, F. (Eds.). (2015). *The politics and power of tourism in Palestine.* Abingdon: Routledge.

Jafari, J. & Scott, N. (2014). Muslim world and its tourisms. *Annals of Tourism Research, 44*, 1–19.

Jalilvand, M. R. & Samiei, N. (2012). Perceived risks in travelling to the Islamic Republic of Iran. *Journal of Islamic Marketing, 3*(2), 175–189.

Katouzian, H. (2010). *The Persians: Ancient, mediaeval and modern Iran.* New Haven, CT and London: Yale University Press.

Kazemi, F. (2003). The precarious revolution: Unchanging institutions and the fate of reform in Iran. *Journal of International Affairs, 51*(1), 81–95.

Khaksari, A. (2012). Tourism development planning in Iran: the role of tourism develop-ment planners in Islamic countries. *Quarterly Journal of Social Science*, *58*, 1–33 [in Persian].

Khodadadi, M. (2016a). A new dawn? The Iran nuclear deal and the future of the Iranian tourism industry. *Tourism Management Perspectives*, *18*, 6–9.

Khodadadi, M. (2016b). Return to glory? Prospects of Iran's hospitality sector post-nuclear deal. *Tourism Management Perspectives*, *19*(Part A), 16–18.

Khodadadi, M. (2016c). Challenges and opportunities for tourism development in Iran: Per-spectives of Iranian tourism suppliers. *Tourism Management Perspectives*, *19*(Part A), 90–92.

Khodadadi, M. (2018). Donald Trump, US foreign policy and potential impacts on Iran's tourism industry: Post-nuclear deal. *Tourism Management Perspectives*, *26*, 28–30.

Khodaei, A. (2017). *More western tourists, less Arab ones visiting Iran*. Retrieved from http://ifpnews.com/exclusive/more-western-tourists-visit-iran/

Majidyar, A. (2018). *Iran's visa waiver proposal worries some Iraqis*. Retrieved from http://www.mei.edu/content/io/iran-s-visa-waiver-proposal-worries-some-iraqis

Mansfeld, Y. (1999). Cycles of war, terror, and peace: Determinants and management of cri-sis and recovery of the Israeli tourism industry. *Journal of Travel Research*, *38*(1), 30–36.

Matthee, R. (1993). Transforming dangerous nomads into useful artisans, technicians, agri-culturists: Education in the Reza Shah period. *Iranian Studies*, *26*(3–4), 313–336.

McSmith, A. (2016). *Iran is world's biggest emerging market since collapse of Soviet Union, says Lord Lamont*. Retrieved from http://www.independent.co.uk/news/world/middle-east/iran-is-worlds-biggest-emerging-market-since-collapse-of-soviet-union-says-lord-lamont-a6831636.html

Mirzaei, R. (2013). *Modeling the socioeconomic and environmental impacts of nature-based tourism to the host communities and their support for tourism: Perceptions of local pop-ulation, Mazandaran, North of Iran* (Doctoral dissertation). Retrieved from http://geb.uni-giessen.de/geb/volltexte/2013/10085/pdf/MirzaeiRoozbeh_2013_09_25.pdf

Moghimehfar, F. & Nasr-Esfahani, M. H. (2011). Decisive factors in medical tourism des-tination choice: A case study of Isfahan, Iran and fertility treatments. *Tourism Manage-ment*, *32*(6), 1431–1434.

Molavi, A. (1999). *Iran mends ties with Europeans*. Retrieved from https://www.wash-ingtonpost.com/archive/politics/1999/12/10/iran-mendsties-with-europeans/20181acc-b706-4909-8440-7c72dc6b3365/?utm_term=.b40fb5875372

Morakabati, Y. (2011). Deterrents to tourism development in Iran. *International Journal of Tourism Research*, *13*(2), 103–123.

Morakabati, Y. (2013). Tourism in the Middle East: Conflicts, crises and economic diversifi-cation, some critical issues. *International Journal of Tourism Research*, *15*(4), 375–387.

Mozaffari, A., Karimian, R., & Mousavi, S. (2017). The return of the 'Idea of Iran' (2005–2015). In R. Butler & W. Suntikul (Eds.), *Tourism and political change* (2nd ed., pp. 186–199). Oxford: Goodfellow Publishers.

Nasr, V. (2018). *What the Iran protests were not*. Retrieved from https://www.theatlantic.com/international/archive/2018/01/iran-economic-protests-urban-rural-divide/550211/

O'Gorman, K. D. (2009). Origins of the commercial hospitality industry: From the fanci-ful to factual. *International Journal of Contemporary Hospitality Management*, *21*(7), 777–790.

O'Gorman, K. D., McLellan, L. R., & Baum, T. (2007). Tourism in Iran: Central control and indignity. In R. Butler & T. Hinch (Eds.), *Tourism and indigenous peoples: Issues and implications* (pp. 251–264). Oxford: Butterworth-Heinemann.

Organization of the Petroleum Exporting Countries (OPEC). (2013). *World oil outlook.* Retrieved from http://www.opec.org/opec_web/static_files_project/media/downloads/publications/WOO_2013.pdf

Pierret, T. (2017). Shi'ism and politics in the Middle East. *Iranian Studies, 50*(3), 471–474.

Pratt, S. & Alizadeh, V. (2017). The economic impact of the lifting of sanctions on tourism in Iran: A computable general equilibrium analysis. *Current Issues in Tourism.* https://doi.org/10.1080/13683500.2017.1307329

Radio Farda. (2018). *Clergy secures millions of dollars in Iran's budget bill.* Retrieved from https://en.radiofarda.com/a/iran-clergy-secures-millions/28920567.html

Richter, L. K. (1999). After political turmoil: The lessons of rebuilding tourism in three Asian countries. *Journal of Travel Research, 38*(1), 41–45.

Rule, S. (1989). Iran breaks off relations with Britain. *New York Times.* Retrieved from http://www.nytimes.com/1989/03/08/world/iran-breaks-off-relations-with-britian.html

Saeidi, A. A. (2002). Dislocation of the state and the emergence of factional politics in post-revolutionary Iran. *Political Geography, 21*(4), 525–546.

Seyfi, S., Hall, C. M., & Kuhzadi, S. (2018). Tourism and hospitality research on Iran: Current state and perspectives. *Tourism Geographies.* https://doi.org/10.1080/146166 88.2018.1454506

Shalbafian, A. (2016). *With representatives of the people in tenth parliament (introducing tourism).* Tehran: Research Center of the Iranian Parliament [in Persian].

Sharafedin, B. (2018). Iran says may withdraw from nuclear deal if banks continue to stay away. *Reuters.* Retrieved from https://www.reuters.com/article/us-iran-usa-nuclear/iran-says-may-withdraw-from-nuclear-deal-if-banks-continue-to-stay-away-idUSKCN1G610S

Sheikhroodi, B. (2007). *The evolution of the tourism organization in Iran.* Retrieved from https://e-turism.persianblog.ir

Siebertz, R. (2014). Depicting power. In B. Devos & C. Werner (Eds.), *Culture and cultural politics under Reza Shah; The Pahlavi state, new bourgeoisie and the creation of a modern society in Iran* (pp. 266–287). Abingdon: Routledge.

Statistical Center of Iran (SCI). (2018). *History of production of population data.* Retrieved from https://www.amar.org.ir/english/Statistics-by-Topic/Population#288289-definitions-concepts

Stone, P. R. (2006). A dark tourism spectrum: Towards a typology of death and macabre related tourist sites, attractions and exhibitions. *Tourism: An International Interdisciplinary Journal, 54*(2), 145–160.

Tomazos, K. (2017). Egypt's tourism industry and the Arab Spring. In R. Butler and W. Suntikul (Eds.), *Tourism and political change* (2nd ed., pp. 214–229). Oxford: Goodfellow Publishers.

United Nations Educational, Scientific and Cultural Organization (UNESCO). (2018). *Iran (Islamic Republic of).* Retrieved from http://whc.unesco.org/en/statesparties/ir

United Nations World Tourism Organization (UNWTO). (2017). *UNWTO Tourism highlights,* 2016 edition. Madrid: UNWTO. Retrieved from http://mkt.unwto.org/publication/unwto-tourism-highlights-2016-edition

World Bank. (2018). *Iran overview.* Retrieved from http://www.worldbank.org/en/country/iran/overview

World Travel and Tourism Council (WTTC). (2015). *Travel and tourism economic impact 2015 Iran.* London: WTTC.

World Travel and Tourism Council (WTTC). (2017). *Travel and tourism economic impact 2017 Iran.* Retrieved from https://www.wttc.org/-/media/files/reports/economic-impact-research/countries-2017/iran2017.pdf

Yarshater, E. (1989). Persia or Iran. *Iranian Studies, 22*(1).

Zamani-Farahani, H. (2010). Iran: Tourism, heritage and religion. In N. Scott & J. Jafari (Eds.), *Tourism in the Muslim world* (vol. 2, pp. 205–218). Bingley: Emerald Group Publishing.

Zamani-Farahani, H. & Henderson, J. C. (2010). Islamic tourism and managing tourism development in Islamic societies: The cases of Iran and Saudi Arabia. *International Journal of Tourism Research, 12*(1), 79–89.

Zamani Zenouzi, E. (1980). *A summarized report on the role of tourism in Iran.* Tehran, Iran: Planning and Budget Organization, Department of Guidance, Culture, and Arts.

Zargam, H. (2004). Career path and the need for manpower training in the hospitality and tourism industry. *Tourism Studies, 2*(6), 1–18.

Zargam, H. & Shalbafian, A. (2014). *National tourism policies (a comparative study).* Tehran: Mahkame Publications.

Ziaee, M. (2004). Education and human resource condition in tourism segment (emphasis upon Tehran Province). *Tourism Studies, 2*(6), 19–37.

Ziaee, M., Saeedi, A., & Torab Ahmadi, M. (2012). Exploring the state of tourism in Iran's higher education. *Tourism Studies, 7*(17), 61–86.

2 Domestic tourism in Iran: development, directions, and issues

Siamak Seyfi, Adel Nikjoo, and Mohammad Sharifi-Tehrani

Introduction

The tourism industry has been regarded by many countries as a source of economic prosperity and foreign exchange earnings (Telfer & Sharpley, 2016; Hall & Page, 2017). However, there is significantly less focus devoted to domestic tourism. As Kang, Kim, & Nicholls (2014) suggest, governments place more emphasis on inbound tourism due to its more significant economic output at the national level. This might be because of the greater appeal of international tourism in terms of its more lucrative nature, huge intercultural influences, and the availability of more data and statistics compared with domestic tourism flows (Tsui, 2017; Hall, 2015; Kang et al., 2014).

Domestic tourism throughout the world is a significant yet often a somewhat invisible portion of economic activities in the tourism industry. However, recognizing the enormous amount of domestic tourism activities is indispensable for tourism patterns and flows (Hall, 2015) as domestic tourism is estimated to represent approximately 80% of world tourism flows (Hall, 2015; Canavan, 2013). Research on domestic tourism is of primary importance in order to gain a better understanding of its local and regional economic and cultural impacts on destinations, its potential to contribute to sustainable regional development, the preferences of domestic travelers (e.g. medium quality or low-priced accommodation), and coherent policies for improving it (Kang et al., 2014; Bel, Lacroix, Lyser, Rambonilaza, & Turpin, 2015).

In Iran, domestic tourism has been given less attention in the literature as well, although at least when quantity is taken into account, its domestic tourists far outnumber foreign tourists (Ghaderi, 2011). For example, in 2017, the country attracted around 5 million inbound tourists, while more than 65 million domestic tourists traveled throughout the country (Statistics Center of Iran (SCI), 2017). This could be attributed to several factors, discussed in the following.

Domestic tourism was a savior of the country's tourism industry when its inbound tourism was affected by tough sanctions imposed on the country over the decades. One of the consequences of the sanctions was exchange rate fluctuations, starting in 2012, triggering a reduction of outbound tourism (Mozaffari, Karimian, & Mousavi, 2017). Despite that, due to the significance of inbound tourism as a source of foreign currency earnings, job generator, and its contribution to GDP, this segment of the tourism market was deemed to be of significantly greater value. This persuaded the government to give priority to inbound tourism (Alipour, Kilic, & Zamani, 2013; Ghaderi, 2011) and the improvement of facilities and services appropriate for domestic tourists was ignored. This is also the case in academia in the sense that despite the steady growth and significance of Iranian domestic tourism, there is a dearth of research on the characteristics of this segment of the tourism market.

Drawing on the presentation and analysis of recently collected data from within Iran compiled by the Academic Center for Education, Culture and Research's (ACECR) institute for tourism research in 2017, accompanied by studies on domestic tourism conducted by the Statistics Center of Iran (SCI), this chapter therefore aims at introducing features of the domestic tourism market in Iran and the challenges it has had to deal with over the course of time and under different governments' development plans. The chapter's analysis relies mainly on official government sources, including data gathered from policy statements, development plans, and archives. It is noteworthy that uniform statistics are not always available in Iran and various statistical sources in Iran represent to some extent contradictory information and facts about tourism (Financial Tribune, 2016b).

Historical perspective

The inherent causes for and conditions generating growth and decline in domestic tourism are linked to patterns of development in Iran's economy during different periods and administrations. There is a long history of organized travel on the plateau of Iran (Ghaderi, 2017). The Royal Road built by the Persian king Darius the Great (Darius I) in the fifth century BC as an ancient highway with its numerous royal outposts (Caravanserai) facilitated communication and travel throughout his large empire from Susa to Sardis (2,699 km). Although the Silk Road as an ancient network of trade routes contributed to travel and trade flows along various countries including Iran, the construction of a short suburban railway south of Tehran in the second half of the nineteenth century during the reign of Nasser-al-Din Shah, can be viewed as one of the primary attempts for building a modern travel related infrastructure in Iran (Ghaderi, 2017).

The Tabriz–Jolfa line (146 km) inaugurated in 1914 was the first railway in Iran, while the first national airline of Iran was founded in 1944 with the first passenger flight from Tehran to Mashhad. Such measures contributed to the improvement of domestic tourism in the early modern Iran. However, even though there is no reliable statistical information about domestic movements during this period and the Pahlavi dynasty founded by Reza Shah in 1925, what is clear is that at that time, tourism was a privilege of the upper class and affluent individuals, and rarely affordable to the middle class, and leisure-based travel constituted a small proportion of mobility at the time.

Following the overthrow of the Western-supported Pahlavi monarchy and the establishment of a theocratic Islamic republic in 1979, Iran's tourism industry faced abrupt and profound deterioration (Khodadadi, 2016a; Morakabati, 2011, 2013; Baum & O'Gorman, 2010). For example, in this period of revolutionary zeal, tourism development was not encouraged and funded by the authorities, partially because a great number of tourist ancient sites belonged to the pre-Islamic era and were inconsistent with Islamic values. Further, a majority of residential facilities, primarily in coastal destinations, in addition to well-known international chain hotel brands such as Hyatt, Sheraton, Hilton, and Intercontinental were confiscated and forced to close down (Ghaderi, 2017; Mirzaei, 2013). This was also the case for many amusement and entertainment centers that were considered against Islamic norms and values which were ostensibly the rationales behind the revolution. The challenges facing the country's tourism industry were further aggravated just one year after the revolution by the eight-year war with Iraq (1980–1988).

In the second presidential election after the revolution, one year after the end of the Iran–Iraq war, Hashemi Rafsanjani took office (two terms, 1989–1997). During his presidency, the administration focused on the restructuring of the economy by advocating a free market policy (transition from a state-controlled economy to a market-based one) and pursuing an economic liberalization policy. He also tried to represent a moderate position internationally, seeking to avoid conflict with the United States and the West as well as regional countries.

In light of relieving the isolation from the West following years of deterioration in foreign relations under Ayatollah Khomeini's leadership (the architect of the 1979 Islamic revolution), tourism was seen as a great source of revenue for government. Therefore, hotels started to open again. In this period, several offshore free economic zones were established in the Persian Gulf islands of Qeshm, Kish, and Chabahar Port. They were intended to prepare the country for a shift from the closed wartime economic system to a more open one, which at the same time facilitated domestic travel to these islands.

Because of Rafsanjani's economic reforms and liberalization policy, many Iranian industries were revived and the country invested heavily on building domestic capacity (Khajehpour, 2013). Following investment in the national automotive industry, the number of cars produced soared from 51,000 in 1977 to 278,000 in 1997 (Mehri, 2015). This combined with improved economic conditions and standards of living as well as infrastructure development encouraged the revival of domestic tourism. The system of rationing which covered basic goods, fuel, and home appliances which had been put in place by successive administrations during the war was scrapped in this period (Affianian, 2017).

Gradually, with the establishment of infrastructure (e.g. railways, roads, budget hotels) and through the emergence of cheaper transportation, accompanied by increased availability of accommodation and increasing disposable income, tourism became popular with the middle class. The emergence of the middle class in this period increased the demand for outbound tourism as well. The picture for domestic tourism during this period is sketchy due to the lack of detailed reliable data in the archives. However, what is clear is that leisure travel for the poor and the middle classes consisted primarily of pilgrimages to sacred Shi'ite sites mainly in Mashhad and Qom and visiting friends and relatives in urban and rural areas (Ghaderi, 2011).

During Khatami's administration (two terms, 1997–2005), a new chapter was opened in the contemporary history of the country in the sense that the political relationships between Iran and the West and subsequently the country's image substantially improved (Mozaffari et al., 2017). His administration actively promoted Iran as a travel destination. The government was making rapid progress in achieving its goals of building infrastructure, accumulating foreign capital, and stabilizing the economy (Amuzegar, 1999). Khatami's economic policies followed the previous government's commitment to industrialization and liberalization (Behdad, 2001). At a macro-economic level, Khatami continued the liberal policies that Rafsanjani had embarked on in the state's first five-year economic development plan (1990–1995). However, after the reduction of oil prices, the country's economy experienced a period of instability and unemployment (Behdad, 2001), with implications for domestic tourism.

In 2003, the Domestic Tourism Bureau was founded. In the climate of normalizing the relationship with Western countries, the Khatami administration took some measures to renovate the Iranian air fleet by buying new passenger planes, though the US economic sanctions disrupted the sales process. Sanctions imposed on the country since the revolution of 1979 had created a major obstacle forcing Iran's Civil Aviation Organization (CAO) to turn to Russian planes. Iran also has an aging fleet of US-made Boeings purchased before the 1979 Islamic revolution. The United States has refused to provide spare parts for Boeing planes as part of its wide-ranging economic sanctions against Iran, leading finally to many crashes with hundreds of fatalities.

A notable domestic tourism development in the period was the development of battlefield or dark tourism (Mirisaee & Ahmad, 2018). In 1997 Rahian-e Noor tours first took visitors to areas that were once the heart of the battle during the Iran–Iraq war. It was meant to commemorate martyrs of the Iran–Iraq war, a product that became popular for domestic travelers. During Khatami's presidency, special attention was given to attract the Iranian diaspora visiting family and relatives in Iran which also provided a stimulus for domestic trips as well as inbound tourism.

During the presidency of Mahmoud Ahmadinejad (2005–2013), in the climate of rising international tensions, the country's image once again became negative and a round of sanctions was imposed on the county, crippling the economy (Pratt & Alizadeh, 2017). In 2007, a gasoline rationing plan was introduced in order to reduce the country's fuel consumption. This policy negatively affected domestic tourism as each private vehicle could only obtain a limited amount of gasoline with government subsidies. Further fuel amounts than the predetermined ration could be purchased at higher rates. This policy increased domestic travel expenses dramatically (Ghaderi, 2011).

The rapid inflation rate and the subsequent increase in the cost of housing also led to higher prices of accommodations across the coastal resorts and thus reduction of second-homers (see Box 2.1). Another big challenge facing the domestic tourism was the Subsidy Reform Plan in 2010 which was the most important part of a broader Iranian economic reform plan. This plan was introduced as the 'biggest surgery' to the nation's economy during the past half-century. The main goal of the plan was to replace government subsidies on food and energy (80% of total) with targeted social assistance, in accordance with the Five-Year Economic Development Plan and a movement toward free market prices (Associated Press, 2010). As a result of this plan, prices of petrol along with goods dramatically increased, affecting domestic travel (Yong, 2011). However, supporting data and statistics to clarify the extent to which domestic tourism was affected are not available.

With respect to domestic politics, during Ahmadinejad's presidency, which was known as a 'new conservative era,' hardliners blocked any relaxation of the Islamic social rules and social constraints on travel were increased. As an example, the Guidance Patrol (also known as the morality police) was established in 2005 to arrest those women and men who were deemed improperly dressed. This could affect domestic tourism, especially in coastal areas. At the same time, because of intensifying sanctions along with the huge fluctuations in exchange rates, outbound tourism experienced a sharp decline. However, there was an overall rise in domestic tourism (Figure 2.1). This may be attributed, at least in part, to the political restrictions forced by Ahmadinejad's administration on travel to some destinations such as Turkey and Thailand that affected outbound tourism and increased domestic tourism (Mozaffari et al., 2017).

In Rouhani's administration (2013–ongoing), tourism became a major priority for the government in light of the easing of sanctions following the nuclear deal of 2015. The government started to renovate the aging air fleet and several investors such as French Accor, UAE-based Rotana, Spanish Meliá, and other Turkish and German companies invested in building hotels in the country (Khodadadi, 2016b).

The price of domestic flights has fluctuated substantially for consumers. However, given the renovation of the air fleet and the capacity to purchase spare parts for older planes, the number of domestic flights has been increased. In addition, resuming direct flights and trains has helped Iranians to eliminate the charges of mediators, leading to a fall in flight prices. During this period, the tourism orga-

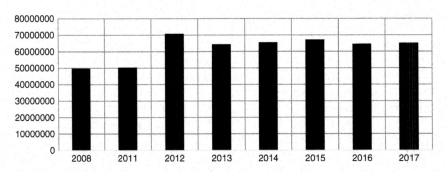

Figure 2.1 Number of domestic trips in Iran.

Source: ICHTO, 2017.

nization has stepped up efforts to improve the quality of countrywide eco-lodges. The number of eco-lodges throughout the country has witnessed a sharp increase (from 30 in 2012 to over 500 in 2018). The government has given special attention to such hospitality services as a means of generating employment, reviving rural areas and helping to develop local economies. All these improvements have played important roles in the growth of domestic tourism. More recently, a three-fold increase in the departure tax proposed by the government in 2017 may also increase the number of domestic trips (Bezhan, 2017).

Research on domestic tourism

In reporting research on domestic tourism in Iran, it should be noted that there are no concrete statistics regarding the domestic segment of tourists in Iran, as different organizations publish somewhat contradictory statistics, leading to substantial uncertainty regarding the volume and characteristics of domestic tourism in the country (Ghaderi, 2011, 2015; Alipour et al., 2013). Initial large-scale efforts to gather information about domestic tourism in Iran dates back to 2008 when the Institute of Statistics conducted research in six selected provinces. Prior to this survey, there was no coherent and reliable information in regard to domestic travel within the country. However, in some cases, the official statistics of visitors to the historical museums and monuments gathered by the Iran Cultural Heritage, Handcraft and Tourism Organization (ICHTO) were published in the Statistical Yearbooks. More recently, the Statistics Center of Iran (SCI) has conducted investigations on domestic tourism twice a year incorporating both urban and rural areas.

With respect to the measurement of domestic tourism, the Statistics Center of Iran (SCI) compiles data based on a household survey which takes place in spring and summer. This survey aims to understand the profile of domestic visitors, their expenditure pattern, and purpose of destination of travel. The study population of this survey is 5,000 households in major provinces of Iran.

Features of domestic tourism in Iran

Size and structure

In Iran, domestic tourists far outnumber inbound tourists. For example, in 2017, the country attracted around 5 million inbound tourists, while more than 65 million domestic tourism trips were made throughout the country (SCI, 2017). The reasons for the substantial gap between international and domestic tourism numbers may be attributable to several factors, discussed below.

In the wake of the post-revolutionary upheaval, Iran's population experienced a rapid growth from 35 million inhabitants in 1979 to 54 million in 1989 due to the adoption of a government-spurred baby boom policy and the suspension of family planning programs (Alipour et al., 2013). During the first two decades after the revolution, by 1996, the population reached about 60 million people. In 2018, the total population of Iran is estimated to amount to approximately 82 million inhabitants of which over 60% are under 30 years old. The population's growth coupled with an increase in the migration to urban areas (around 6 million people migrated from rural to urban areas, mainly Tehran, from 1977 to 1987) and the development of transportation systems (Alipour et al., 2013).

The transition in the country's demographic profile, as well as the country's economic and political trajectory, has implications for tourism (Sheykhi, 2008). Long vacations, such as a two-week vacation for New Year, and a wide range of religious public vacations have also helped spur the growth of Iran's domestic tourism. However, the growth of so many public holidays, as many as 22 days in a year has been an ongoing subject of economic concern for many years (Financial Tribune, 2016a).

Different administrations in Iran have recognized the need for the development of domestic tourism as a response to the inadequate number of international tourist arrivals (Ghaderi, 2011; Alipour et al., 2013). Although domestic tourism has witnessed significant growth over the years, low purchasing power is one of the negative factors influencing development of domestic tourism (Ghaderi, 2011). In 2017, Iran's per capita GDP ($4,526) is below the global average ($10,562, ranked 103rd) and the average monthly income ($470 month) is low as well. The economic divide between different regions and societal classes is also huge. Hence, the length of domestic trips is often short and travelers stay with friends and relatives, also contributing to low domestic tourism expenditures (Ghaderi, 2011). Luxury travel is still out of the reach of most domestic tourists, and many Iranians with higher incomes prefer to spend their money outside of Iran where they can escape obligatory Islamic dress codes (Nikjoo & Ketabi, 2015).

With respect to the travel mode, over 98% of Iranians travel independently and only 1.47% use package tours bought through travel agents. This may be attributed, in part, to socio-cultural norms that can effectively require domestic travelers to stay with family and friends (Pearce & Moscardo, 2006). These family trips are often undertaken with personal vehicles rather than public transport (ACECR, 2017). The relatively low cost of fuel, low average income, and poorly developed public transportation in Iran, as well as the Iranian tendency to travel in family groups, may be the main reasons for traveling by personal vehicle, although traveling with friends is a growing trend among young Iranians. This group plans their trip on their own instead of using a package tour, travel agents, or tour operators. Day excursions, especially to nature and mountain resorts, in the vicinity of the larger cities have become popular, with these excursions often being run by travel agencies. However, the clerical establishments believe that these tours, which are often mixed-gender tours, have resulted in the violation of religious and revolutionary values and they have imposed strict obstacles on these tours and travel agencies with some destinations being closed to tourists following some 'non-Islamic behavior' by excursionists. As an example, in 2015, the Maranjab Desert and Nushabad underground city were closed to all domestic tours for several months (Radio Zamaneh, 2015).

With respect to accommodation (Table 2.1), significant numbers of people stay with friends and relatives with only small numbers staying in commercial

Table 2.1 Type of accommodation used by domestic tourists

Type of accommodation	%	Type of accommodation	%
Friends and relatives	48.0	Guesthouses	5.8
Villa and apartment rental	11.1	Organizational establishments	5.2
Tent and personal camp	8.1	Second home (villa or apartment)	5.2
Hotel	7.2	Schools and mosques	2.5
Hotel apartment	5.8	Other types of accommodation	1.2

Source: ACECR, 2017.

Table 2.2 Mode of transportation of domestic tourists

Type of transport	%
Personal vehicles	71.9
Bus	15.9
Airplane	4.5
Train	3.7
Car rental (including taxi)	3.3
Others	0.7

Source: ACECR, 2017.

accommodation establishments such as hotels and apartments in their destinations. The majority of hotel beds in major cultural cities, such as Isfahan and Shiraz, are normally booked by foreign and business tourists. The southern islands in the Persian Gulf, such as Kish, are regarded as luxury domestic travel given the expensive price of flights and accommodation facilities in these islands. Northern coastal resorts are much more popular as they offer low-cost residential facilities along with easy accessibility. In sacred cities, such as Mashhad, which are mainly visited by pilgrims, the 'unofficial' accommodation available in privately owned houses are offered to domestic tourists at a low price compared to the commercial accommodation. During the peak seasons, with increasing numbers of domestic tourists, schools are also used by low-budget domestic tourists.

With respect to mode of transportation, as Table 2.2 indicates, more than half of domestic tourists travel using their personal vehicles. This may be attributed to the fact that public transport is insufficient to handle the enormous domestic demand during the peak seasons. Given the lack of a developed railway system throughout the country, rail travel is limited and its share is less than 4% of all travel. A sharp increase in the number of passengers in peak seasons makes it difficult for the transport sector to accommodate all the domestic tourists and there is often a huge surge in prices for tickets for planes, trains, and buses. The airline network has not been expanded to reach most major destinations. The price of flight tickets therefore rises drastically during peak seasons. However, air travel is beyond the reach of most domestic travelers. Despite improvements with respect to the expansion of public transportation, especially to facilitate vacation travel, travel by personal vehicle is by far the favorite means of transportation.

Although Iran has one of the highest car crash rates in the world (BBC, 2012), more than 70% of Iranian domestic travel is undertaken by personal cars. Traveling by bus is the preferred mode of budget travel and is flexible and convenient due to Iran's extensive bus network. Traveling by bus is sometimes the only available option to travel to remote towns which are not connected to the country's railroad or aviation network.

Travel intentions and motivations

In summer, northern coastal destinations are normally occupied with leisure-pleasure tourists who spend their vacations in coastal accommodation or in their second homes. In winter, recreational travelers mostly choose southern islands such as Kish and Qeshm where they can enjoy the weather, beaches, entertainment, and shopping. The Iranian New Year, Nowruz begins in mid-March and many people undertake domestic or international travel during these two weeks of holiday. This is the highest travel season in Iran.

Along with the significant expansion of demand segments, travel motives have also become more varied. Traditionally, more affluent people have traveled to coastal resorts, while the middle and lower classes often made religious pilgrimages to Shia sacred sites in Mashhad and Qom for religious events such as death of Imam Reza, the eighth Imam of Shia or Ashura, the ceremony for the death of the third Imam. For many Iranians, especially in small towns or remote villages, traveling to sacred places such as Mashhad to make a pilgrimage has long been a dream. Pilgrimage has been encouraged by the ruling religious and political elite and the biggest clerical establishments are situated in the holy cities such as Qom and Mashhad (Zamani-Farahani, 2010; see also Chapter 4, this volume).

As Table 2.3 shows, 36% of domestic tourists traveled for the purpose of visiting friends and relatives (VFR). The VFR market is the largest market but it is also the most unknown travel segment in Iran and is often overlooked by tourism stakeholders (Ghaderi, 2015). Nevertheless, this is a significant share of the country's tourism market as almost half of all domestic trips were conducted for the purpose of VFR during the summer. VFR trips in Iran are typically undertaken in the peak seasons (during summer and school holidays), when a large volume of people from metropolitan areas travel to see their friends and relatives and also

Table 2.3 Purpose of domestic travel

Travel intention	%
Sightseeing and entertainment	37.9
Visiting friends and relatives (VFR)	36
Pilgrimage	17.3
Business	4.9
Medical	3.9

Source: ACECR, 2017.

stay with them. They usually visit their ancestors' heritage. This market is very large in Tehran, as more than 5 million people living in Tehran come from other provinces (Ghaderi, 2011). This mass market tends to return to their birthplace during holidays, with a seemingly large part of the VFR market being the Iranian diaspora living abroad (Ghaderi, 2015).

The major destinations for the domestic leisure vacation market in Iran are the coastal areas of the Caspian Sea in the north of the country, the southern coastal areas in the Persian Gulf and the Sea of Oman, as well as urban centers such as Shiraz, Isfahan, and Hamadan (Figure 2.2). Another large market is travel associated with pilgrimage to sacred places. Mashhad and Qom are the most familiar destinations for this market. However, pilgrimage is often combined with other activities. Given that small cities and villages are not well developed in terms of hospital and medical care, a majority of people living in these areas travel to larger

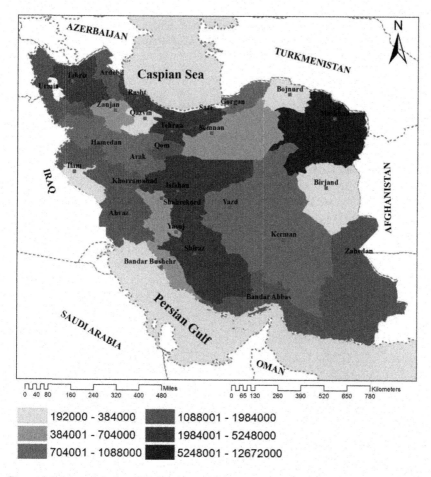

192000 - 384000	1088001 - 1984000
384001 - 704000	1984001 - 5248000
704001 - 1088000	5248001 - 12672000

Figure 2.2 Most visited regions by domestic tourists.

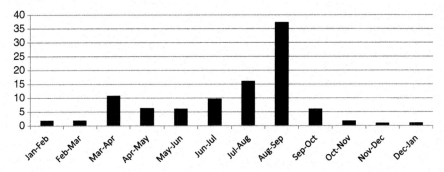

Figure 2.3 Distribution of domestic travel throughout the year (%).
Source: ACECR, 201.

cities for treatment. Tehran, Mashhad, Shiraz, and Isfahan are centers for health and medical services. Tehran, Isfahan, Mashhad, Shiraz, Kish, and Tabriz are the main destinations for business and meetings, incentives, conferences, and events (MICE) markets.

Seasonality

The domestic tourism market in Iran is highly seasonal (Figure 2.3). Most workers and civil servants have a one-month vacation. A large part of this period is used for family visits, especially at Iranian New Year. Large numbers of university staff and students also travel during the Nowruz and summer holidays. During these peak periods, infrastructure is insufficient to meet demand. The public and private sectors have attempted to cope with the problem of seasonality in Iran. The government has tried to encourage leisure travel at weekends and has sought to gradually decrease the summer holiday period and eliminate some one-day holidays in order to provide some longer holidays at other times of the year. Hotels and travel agencies also offer competitive prices to attract more tourists to use their services in low seasons. The government is not able to eliminate one-day religious holidays which have been supported by clerical establishments.

Generating areas and destinations

Over the decades, the spatial mobility of the Iranian people has changed. On the whole, domestic travel activities are highly concentrated and urban-oriented. The principal generating markets are concentrated in the large metropolitan areas such as Tehran, and the provinces, such as Khorasan, Isfahan, Shiraz, and East and West Azerbaijan. Underpinning such a basic pattern of domestic tourist demand are the disparities in living standards at both regional and household levels. For instance, Tehran is the largest generator of domestic tourism as its residents have higher incomes than most Iranians and show a strong interest in travel to other parts of the country. With respect to the preferred destinations for domestic tourists, as Figure 2.2 indicates, Mashhad, Tehran, Shiraz, Rasht, and Isfahan along with the northern coastal areas and Persian Gulf islands (i.e. Kish) are the most visited destinations among domestic tourists.

Box 2.1: Second-home tourism in Iran

The history of second homes in the area covered by present-day Iran goes back to ancient Persia, Egypt, and classical Rome when ancient wealthy aristocracy and royalty had second homes and villas available for seasonal use (Coppock, 1977; Dadvar-Khani, 2012). In the present-day, in many countries, including Iran, second-home tourism and lifestyle migration has become the vehicle of globalization of the countryside and rural areas (Dadvar-Khani, 2012; Hall and Müller, 2018).

The phenomenon of second-home tourism in Iran has experienced significant growth in a number of areas of the country, particularly as a result of international travel constraints arising from international sanctions. Growth is especially notable in the Caspian Sea region of Iran, in the municipalities of Noshahr, Mahmudabad, and Nur, as well as surrounding villages. These areas are located in the province of Mazandaran, a major tourism destination for Iranians and international visitors. However, most of the second-home developments in the province are growing spontaneously without any clear policy and adequate planning mechanisms. Even though the economic benefits of tourism and second homes are recognized in the province, ecological, social, and cultural conflicts have occurred resulting in conflict between the indigenous inhabitants and second-home owners/visitors (Dadvar-Khani, 2012).

In the case of the Caspian Sea region of Iran, the close proximity of Tehran, the rapidly growing capital city of Iran, to the region, has exacerbated development pressures and intensified demand for second homes. Real estate developers and construction companies have moved in to the region to try and meet demand for second homes with much of the second-home development being uncontrolled and unplanned. Although potentially beneficial to some aspects of conservation, second-home development has the potential to transform the cultural landscape of destinations. As Fatimah (2015, p. 569) noted, tourism can be seen as both "an agent of rural economic regeneration and as a way of valorizing conservation." However, the sustainability of the value systems as cultural assets in, for example, a rural setting is a significant issue. The process of second-home development not only is devoid of a clear policy and planning framework, it has also generated a heated debate among some elements in the public sector, the media, environmentalists, and indigenous residents, pertaining to the negative social, cultural, and ecological impacts.

Unfortunately, there are no available statistics on second-home numbers in Iran, while studies on second-home tourism in Iran are scant, as in most developing countries. Most of the research on this topic has been conducted in Europe and North America (Hall & Müller, 2018). However, in the case of Iran, second-home tourism is becoming part of a new leisure lifestyle for Iranians (Rezvani & Safaee, 2005; Anabestani, 2014). With further improvements in mobility, second-home phenomena are likely to experience even more growth, particularly in regions which are endowed with major pull factors such as geographic proximity to major urban areas, travel enabling infrastructure, growth in domestic tourism demand, rapid urbanization, and rural to urban migration.

Notwithstanding the spread of second-home development in rural areas, the Caspian Sea region of Iran is spatially the favored region for second-home development due to its environment, cultural, and natural heritage, and sun, sea, and sand tourism resources. The region's proximity to Tehran, which is experiencing population explosion, especially during the post-Islamic revolution (Moeini, 2012), exacerbated the flow of recreationalists to the region. Second-home tourism is also associated with negative and positive impacts. Although there are not many studies on this subject, some scholars have raised concerns regarding unplanned and uncontrolled second-home development in Iran. Rezvani and Safaee (2005) and Nowzari (2007) examined second-home development and its impact in rural areas and concluded that second-home development has resulted in negative impacts on water resources, damage to the natural landscape, destruction of green spaces, and land use violation. The lack of strategic planning and direction by the public sector, especially at local levels, has been indicated as a major cause of negative impacts. Nevertheless, their studies also revealed some positive impacts in terms of the economy, job creation, and enhanced general welfare of rural people in locations where second homes were developed or purchased. Nevertheless, it is recognized that second-home development can affect the housing market which has benefited second-home developers and some property owners, while also potentially applying pressure on local residents as this form of leisure might distort the housing prices and generate land speculation. The present trajectory of second-home development in Iran is therefore filled with spatial problems which subordinate environmental and social issues to the economic/market realm and which present major long-term planning issues for government authorities seeking to balance local and second-home interests.

Habib Alipour, Bahareh Hassanzadeh, and Hamed Rezapouraghdam

Conclusion

In one of the earliest studies, Archer (1978, p. 127) stressed the positive impacts of domestic tourism on "a spatial redistribution of spending power" as well as "an intermingling of people from diverse social and cultural backgrounds." Since then, a number of tourism researchers have issued calls for more scholarly attention to domestic tourism (Kang et al., 2014; Bel et al., 2015). Notwithstanding, there is seemingly an inclination in the literature and among practitioners to focus more on international tourism (Tsui, 2017; Kang et al., 2014).

This study examined domestic tourism in Iran by discussing key features of this segment of the market and the ways different governments have dealt with domestic tourism over time. Like many countries, various Iranian administrations tend to support inbound tourism due to its capacity to generate foreign exchange. However, some administrations in Iran have also recognized the need for the development of domestic tourism, as a response to the inadequate number of international arrivals caused by sanctions and the country's negative image (Morakabati, 2011, 2013).

Since the overthrow of the Pahlavi monarchy and the establishment of a theocratic Islamic republic, domestic tourism has been a contentious issue at times, with some citizens demanding recreation and leisure as their human right, while some officials, mainly clerical establishments, perceive it as a luxurious decadence associated with the Western way of life and materialism. Over recent decades, due to various factors such as the increase in disposable income, leisure, desire for travel, and improved infrastructures, domestic tourism has grown dramatically. Nevertheless, at the same time this growth has created concerns over negative impacts on the environment and sustainability issues. Such concerns are not irrelevant as consumption of resources in top destinations in the country are believed higher than their carrying capacity, leading to soil erosion, environmental pollution, and deterioration of local cultures (Ghaderi, 2011). For instance, the concentration of tourism and second-home developments on the central banks of the Mazandaran Sea has caused almost irreparable environmental damage to the region, including the destruction of forests for the construction of villas and the change in the use of agricultural land for the construction of villas. Iran ranked 119th in the world in terms of environmental sustainability (World Economic Forum, 2017). Many famous villages which have long attracted domestic tourism (e.g. Masouleh, Kandavan) have become overloaded with travelers.

A second major issue is that due to Iran's unique centralized structure, many authorities involved in the planning and management of tourism are not giving much consideration to including local people in their decision-making. Rural destinations visited by domestic tourists are clear examples of destinations which have been developed without considering the basic principle of sustainable development, as put forward by Hall, Gossling, and Scott (2015) and Mowforth and Munt (2015), that tourism development inevitably requires more involvement among local residents in the planning and management of tourism.

Of the major constraints for development of domestic tourism in Iran is low per capita GDP and economic divide between different regions (Ghaderi, 2011). The travel preferences of domestic tourists cover a complete spectrum from traditional low budget pilgrimage to special interest tourism with higher expenditure. With increasing incomes, the travel preferences of traditional Iranians are shifting from pilgrimage areas (e.g. Mashhad and Qom) to cultural areas (e.g. Isfahan, Shiraz, Yazd, Kerman) and coastal regions (e.g. Kish, Gheshm, Mazandaran). Special tourism programs such as eco-tourism and sports tourism have emerged, and folk tourism, recreation, and educational tourism are also on the rise.

Finally, key to the future trajectory of domestic tourism in Iran will be the development of new transport and tourism infrastructures. Although flexible flight fares have benefited both passengers and travel agencies during periods of peak demand, prices still fluctuate significantly. In light of the softening of sanctions in recent years, domestic airlines are renovating their aging fleet which has led to more flights throughout the country. However, the underdeveloped railway system is one of the most significant transport issues in Iran. Although the establishment of the first railway in Iran dates to 1914, many major cities are not connected to the railway network yet (Yaghini, Sharifian, & Akhavan, 2012). There is no high-speed train in Iran and the long duration of trips causes many Iranians to avoid train travel. The government is trying to establish high speed trains on the Tehran–Isfahan and Tehran–Mashhad routes that may decrease the travel duration between Tehran and Isfahan from five to two hours and between Tehran and Mashhad from twelve to six hours. Following the nuclear deal of 2015, the national administration for railways has signed an agreement with Italy's state railway to construct two high-speed links in Iran. Moreover, an $8 million contract has been signed with the French company AREP to modernize three train stations, in Tehran, Qom, and Mashhad. The country plans to invest $25 billion over the next ten years in the modernization and expansion of its railway network, increasing its railroad network to 25,000 km by 2025 from under 15,000 km at the start of 2018. Significantly, the country's transport expansion plans will potentially contribute to international as well as domestic tourism as they include aligning the Iranian network with the regional rail networks in the Persian Gulf, the subcontinent, and Central Asia (PressTV, 2017), leading to a significant realignment of the region's tourism system.

Acknowledgments

The authors would like to cordially thank Mr. Mehdi Kazemi Biniaz for helping with the design of Figure 2.2.

References

Academic Center for Education, Culture and Research (ACECR). (2017). *A Survey on Iranian tourist behavior* (Unpublished report).

Affianian, M. (2017). *Hero of construction: A glance at Rafsanjani's economic legacy.* Retrieved from https://financialtribune.com/articles/economy-business-and-markets/57238/hero-of-construction-a-glance-at-rafsanjanis-economic

Alipour, H., Kilic, H., & Zamani, N. (2013). The untapped potential of sustainable domestic tourism in Iran. *Anatolia, 24*(3), 468–483.

Amuzegar, J. (1999). Khatami and the Iranian economy at mid-term. *The Middle East Journal, 53*(4), 534–552.

Anabestani, A. (2014). Effects of second home tourism on rural settlements development in Iran (case study: Shirin-Dareh Region). *International Journal of Culture, Tourism and Hospitality Research, 8*(1), 58–73.

Archer, B. (1978). Domestic tourism as a development factor. *Annals of Tourism Research, 5*(1), 126–141.

Associated Press. (2010). *Iran doubles the price of bread with subsidy cut.* Retrieved from http://newsok.com/article/feed/228800

Baum, T. G. & O'Gorman, K. D. (2010). Iran or Persia: What's in a name, the decline and fall of a tourism industry? In R. Butler & W. Suntikul (Eds.), *Tourism and political change* (pp. 175–186). Oxford: Goodfellow Publishers.

BBC. (2012). *Iran comes top in the number of global road accident deaths.* Retrieved from http://www.bbc.com/news/av/world-middle-east-18023809/iran-comes-top-in-the-number-of-global-road-accident-deaths

Behdad, S. (2001). Khatami and his 'reformist' economic (non-)agenda. *Middle East Report Online, 21*. Retrieved from http://www.merip.org/mero/mero052101

Bel, F., Lacroix, A., Lyser, S., Rambonilaza, T., & Turpin, N. (2015). Domestic demand for tourism in rural areas: Insights from summer stays in three French regions. *Tourism Management, 46*, 562–570.

Bezhan, F. (2017). *Flight fight: Proposed tripling of 'departure tax' roils Iranians.* Retrieved from https://www.rferl.org/a/iran-skyrocketing-departure-tax-proposal-anger-tourism/28914103.html

Canavan, B. (2013). The extent and role of domestic tourism in a small island: The case of the Isle of Man. *Journal of Travel Research, 52*(3), 340–352.

Coppock, J. T. (1977). Second homes in perspective. In J. T. Coppock (Ed.), *Second homes: Curse or blessing?* (pp. 1–15). Oxford: Pergamon Press.

Dadvar-Khani, F. (2012). Participation of rural community and tourism development in Iran. *Community Development, 43*(2), 259–277.

Fatimah, T. (2015). The impacts of rural tourism initiatives on cultural landscape sustainability in Borobudur area. *Procedia Environmental Sciences, 28*, 567–577.

Financial Tribune. (2016a). *Iran tops in school holidays.* Retrieved from https://financial-tribune.com/articles/people/56383/iran-tops-in-school-holidays

Financial Tribune (2016b). *Tourism statistics 'unreliable'.* Retrieved from https://financial-tribune.com/articles/people-travel/44820/tourism-statistics-unreliable

Ghaderi, E. (2017). *An introduction to tourism geography of Iran.* Tehran: Mahkame Publications [in Persian].

Ghaderi, Z. (2011). Domestic tourism in Iran. *Anatolia, 22*(2), 278–281.

Ghaderi, Z. (2015). Visiting friends and relatives (VFR) travel: The case of Iran. In E. Backer & B. King (Eds.), *VFR travel research: International perspectives* (pp. 109–120). Bristol: Channel View Publications.

Hall, C. M. (2015). On the mobility of tourism mobilities. *Current Issues in Tourism, 18*(1), 7–10.

Hall, C. M. & Müller, D. (Eds.). (2018). *The Routledge handbook of second home tourism and mobilities.* Abingdon: Routledge.

Hall, C. M. & Page, S. (2017). Developing tourism in south and central Asia. In C. M. Hall & S. Page (Eds.), *The Routledge handbook on tourism in Asia* (pp. 223–240). Abingdon: Routledge.

Hall, C. M., Gössling, S., & Scott, D. (Eds.). (2015). *The Routledge handbook of tourism and sustainability.* Abingdon: Routledge.

Iran Cultural Heritage, Handcraft and Tourism Organization (ICHTO). (2018). *Tourism statistics of Iran.* Retrieved from http://bogendesign-vr.ir/gardeshgari2/19.php

Kang, S., Kim, J., & Nicholls, S. (2014). National tourism policy and spatial patterns of domestic tourism in South Korea. *Journal of Travel Research, 53*(6), 791–804.

Khajehpour, B. (2013). The future of the petroleum sector in Iran. *Legatum Institute.* Retrieved from https://lif.blob.core.windows.net/lif/docs/default-source/future-of-iran/the-future-of-iran-(economy)-future-of-the-petroleum-sector-in-iran-pdf.pdf?sfvrsn=0

Khodadadi, M. (2016a). A new dawn? The Iran nuclear deal and the future of the Iranian tourism industry. *Tourism Management Perspectives, 18*, 6–9.

Khodadadi, M. (2016b). Return to glory? Prospects of Iran's hospitality sector post-nuclear deal. *Tourism Management Perspectives, 19*, 16–18.

Mehri, D. B. (2015). *The rise of Iran auto: Globalization, liberalization and network-centered development in the Islamic Republic.* (Doctoral dissertation). Retrieved from http://digitalassets.lib.berkeley.edu/etd/ucb/text/Mehri_berkeley_0028E_15123.pdf

Mirisaee, S. M. & Ahmad, Y. (2018). Post-war tourism as an urban reconstruction strategy case study: Khorramshahr. *International Journal of Tourism Cities, 4*(1), 81–97.

Mirzaei, R. (2013). *Modeling the socioeconomic and environmental impacts of nature-based tourism to the host communities and their support for tourism: Perceptions of local population, Mazandaran, North of Iran* (Doctoral dissertation). Retrieved from http://geb.uni-giessen.de/geb/volltexte/2013/10085/pdf/MirzaeiRoozbeh_2013_09_25.pdf

Moeini, S. M. (2012). Attitudes to urban walking in Tehran. *Environment and Planning B: Planning and Design, 39*(2), 344–359.

Morakabati, Y. (2011). Deterrents to tourism development in Iran. *International Journal of Tourism Research, 13*(2), 103–123.

Morakabati, Y. (2013). Tourism in the Middle East: Conflicts, crises and economic diversification, some critical issues. *International Journal of Tourism Research, 15*(4), 375–387.

Mowforth, M. & Munt, I. (2015). *Tourism and sustainability: Development, globalisation and new tourism in the third world* (4th ed.). Abingdon: Routledge.

Mozaffari, A., Karimian, R., & Mousavi, S. (2017). The return of the 'Idea of Iran' (2005–2015). In R. Butler & W. Suntikul (Eds.), *Tourism and political change* (2nd ed., pp. 186–199). Oxford: Goodfellow Publishers.

Nikjoo, A. H. & Ketabi, M. (2015). The role of push and pull factors in the way tourists choose their destination. *Anatolia, 26*(4), 588–597.

Nowzari, H. (2007). *The role of second homes on land use change and economic development of Kordan County*. Unpublished master's thesis. Tehran University, Tehran, Iran.

Pearce, P. L. & Moscardo, G. (2006). Domestic and visiting friends and relatives tourism. In D. Buhalis & C. Costa (Eds.), *Tourism business frontiers: Consumers, products and industry* (pp. 48–55). Amsterdam: Elsevier.

Pratt, S. & Alizadeh, V. (2017). The economic impact of the lifting of sanctions on tourism in Iran: A computable general equilibrium analysis. *Current Issues in Tourism*. https://doi.org/10.1080/13683500.2017.1307329

PressTV. (2017). *Italy, Iran sign $1.3 billion high-speed rail deal*. Retrieved from http://217.218.67.231/Detail/2017/07/12/528200/Iran-Italy-railway-deal-FS-France-AREP

Radio Zamaneh. (2015). *Isfahan court bars mixed-gender tourist groups in Maranjab*. Retrieved from https://en.radiozamaneh.com/featured/isfahan-court-bars-mixed-gender-tourist-groups-in-maranjab/

Rezvani, M. & Safaee, J. (2005). Second home tourism and its impact on rural areas: Opportunity or threat. *Journal of Geographical Research, 37*, 109–121.

Sheykhi, M. (2008). Domestic tourism in Iran. *Tourismos, 4*(1), 109–123.

Statistics Center of Iran (SCI). (2017). *Results of survey on domestic tourism*. Retrieved from https://www.amar.org.ir/Portals/0/News/1396/gardesh%201-95.pdf

Telfer, D. J. & Sharpley, R. (2016). *Tourism and development in the developing world* (2nd ed.). Abingdon: Routledge.

Tsui, K. W. H. (2017). Does a low-cost carrier lead the domestic tourism demand and growth of New Zealand? *Tourism Management, 60*, 390–403.

World Economic Forum (WEF). (2017). *The travel & tourism competitiveness report 2017. Paving the way for a more sustainable and inclusive future*. Gland: WEF. Retrieved from http://www3.weforum.org/docs/WEF_TTCR_2017_web_0401.pdf

Yaghini, M., Sharifian, S., & Akhavan, R. (2012). Reengineering the locomotive operation management process in the railways of Iran (RAI). *Procedia-Social and Behavioral Sciences, 43*, 86–97.

Yong, W. (2011). *Politically confident, Iran cuts subsidies on prices*. Received from https://www.nytimes.com/2011/01/17/world/middleeast/17iran.html

Zamani-Farahani, H. (2010). Iran: Tourism, heritage and religion. In N. Scott & J. Jafari (Eds.), *Tourism in the Muslim world* (pp. 205–218). Bingley: Emerald Group Publishing.

3 Sanctions, the 2015 agreement and Iran's tourism industry

Zahed Ghaderi, Sahar Soltani, Joan Henderson and Afsaneh Zareei

Introduction

Iran has been subject to sanctions by individual nations and international bodies since the 1979 revolution which established the Islamic Republic. These were initially designed to effect political and social change, but have been targeted at its nuclear capabilities most recently until the 2015 deal which saw agreement about the ending of specific sanctions. The tourism industry has been negatively impacted by sanctions and other internal and external factors in ways indicated by the limited number of international arrivals and lack of foreign investment in facilities and infrastructure. It is, however, identified as having potential for growth and an instrument of economic diversification deemed necessary to reduce dependence on oil and gas revenues. Many within the country and outside believed that the situation would improve after 2015 due to greater accessibility and more favourable views of Iran among travellers and the tourism industry worldwide as a place to visit and invest. There was a mood of optimism about the future and anticipation of a revival of tourism, ideas about which are explored in this chapter.

The implications of sanctions have inevitably been of critical interest to the tourism industry and received attention in the media and academic literature, but the latest events have not been widely studied and especially with regard to activity and investment by overseas businesses. The research project reported on in this chapter attempts to fill the gap and enhance knowledge and understanding of Iran's experiences. It investigates the perceived effects of sanctions and the 2015 agreement on the nation's tourism, focusing on the commercial perspective. A qualitative approach was adopted involving semi-structured interviews with ten selected representatives from the public and private tourism sectors. Responses of these experts are discussed after accounts of sanctions and their interactions with tourism in general and the nature and consequences of those imposed on Iran in order to set the scene.

Sanctions and tourism

Sanctions are defined by the Oxford Dictionary (2017) as 'measures taken by a state to coerce another to conform to an international agreement or norms of

conduct, typically in the form of restrictions on trade or official sporting participation'. They have also been described in terms of the 'planned actions by one or
more governments to place pressure on and limit relations to a country for political or economic purposes' (Galtung, 1967, as cited in Pratt & Alizadeh, 2017,
p. 1). Purported human rights abuses are a further cause of sanctions and they can
become highly politicised, employed as a tool in pursuit of broader agendas. Puni-
tive steps include tariffs, export controls, import and trade embargoes, banking
and other financial restrictions, travel bans, asset freezing, cutting aid and block-
ades (Ivanov, Sypchenko, & Webster, 2017; Pratt & Alizadeh, 2017). Diplomatic
ties may be affected, marked by the closure of embassies, and participation in
international agencies and negotiations denied.

Effects of sanctions have been categorised as macroeconomic, direct, indirect
and induced (Pratt & Alizadeh, 2017). Demand and supply can be damaged by a
prohibition on foreign investment and imported goods as well as access to export
markets. Business and consumer confidence can be undermined with a reduction
in spending and job losses, thereby inhibiting economic growth. National currencies too may weaken, compounding economic problems. In addition, reputation
and image risk tarnishing from the harmful publicity and negative associations
accompanying being the recipient of sanctions. A country may be left isolated
and possibly alienated from the global community. Sanction measures all have
ramifications for the economy and business operations, but their ability to produce
the desired results is debatable. A frequent criticism which has been applied in the
context of Iran is that they punish a nation's citizenry rather than its government
while costs may be incurred by the sanctioning country (Tarock, 2016). It should
also be recognised that policing is not always easy and efforts to evade sanctions
through various methods do occur and can be successful.

Tourism is inextricably linked to domestic and global economics and politics
and is international in its activities. The presence of sanctions thus creates challenges for the industry in destination and generating countries, but especially the
former. Transport and accommodation sectors could all be directly hit by a decline
in foreign visitors together with attractions and intermediaries as well as enterprises which support the work of these suppliers. Sanctions against the former
military government of Myanmar (Burma) are found to have depressed tourist
arrivals and revenues, at least from Western generators, over an extended period
(Andreasson, 2008) while Cuba had to contend with the banning of travel there for
citizens of the United States (Dowell, 2011). Russian hoteliers registered a contraction in demand attributed to sanctions (Ivanov et al., 2017) which also harmed
Serbia's tourism industry (Popesku & Hall, 2004). Similarly, outcomes have been
noticed in Iran (Farahani & Shabani, 2013; Khodadadi, 2016a; Pratt & Alizadeh,
2017) which is perhaps an exceptional case.

Sanctions against Iran and its tourism

The Islamic Revolution in 1979 deposed the incumbent Shah who was regarded
as pro-Western and a close ally of the United States. The event prompted a series

of sanctions against Iran initiated primarily by the United States, United Nations Security Council and European Union which have persisted intermittently thereafter. The American–Iranian relationship has been particularly tense (Tarock, 2006) and the United States introduced further sanctions in the Iran–Iraq war and its aftermath and then following the 2001 terrorist attacks (Pratt & Alizadeh, 2017), having previously condemned the Iranian state for sponsoring terrorism. Attention later concentrated on Iran's nuclear energy programme which incorporates uranium enrichment (Tarock, 2006, 2016). Objectors claimed that it was directed at weapons production in violation of the Nuclear Non-Proliferation Treaty, leading to more sanctions (Jacobson, 2008) which included bans on Iranian oil exports, banking transactions, the national airline and shipping companies. There is some disagreement about whether sanctions have 'crippled' the economy as advocates assert (Torchia, 2013), but there is no doubt that it has deteriorated as a consequence and standards of living have fallen for many residents.

The eleventh presidential election in 2013 initiated an apparent move towards economic liberalism and social reform (Ansari, 2016). The trend looks set to continue given the re-election of President Hassan Rouhani in May 2017, although resistance is expected from more conservative elements in the administration (Economist Intelligence Unit, 2017). A new willingness to engage internationally is reflected in the agreement reached in July 2015 between Iran and the five United Nations Security Council permanent members (China, France, Russia, the United Kingdom and the United States) and Germany, known as P5+1, alongside the European Union. Negotiations had been lengthy, and the arrangement was that sanctions would cease if Iran allowed closer inspection of its nuclear sites by international monitors. The decision was generally welcomed, yet it was not without controversy within and outside the country. There were hopes of a recovery in Iran's economy and improved quality of life for its people as the country was readmitted into the international community. While optimism about the deal which is formally known as the Joint Comprehensive Plan of Action (JCPOA) persists, its future is in some doubt under the presidency of Donald Trump and revisions or even abandonment are possibilities (Kahan, 2017). It must also be remembered that some American unilateral sanctions remain in force and hinder global financial exchanges with Iran (Economist Intelligence Unit, 2017).

As stated in the introduction, the JCPOA was hailed as a turning point affording new opportunities for tourism which was seen to have been impeded by sanctions. Certain positive outcomes of sanctions have, however, been suggested; for example, domestic tourism was boosted because foreign destinations became more expensive and difficult for Iranians. Travel from within the Middle East region is important, and it is less affected by sanctions (Farahani & Shabani, 2013), albeit sensitive to struggles among regional powers and shifting international allegiances. Much inbound tourism is motivated by religion, undertaken by Muslims keen to visit the sites which are holy to Muslims from the Shia branch of Islam who form the majority in Iran, and it too is resilient. At the same time, exclusion from the main Western generators of international tourism has been a serious constraint (Khodadadi, 2016a). However, numerous forces are at work in determining flows of tourists to Iran which demonstrates other weaknesses as an international destination. Inefficient transport and communications infrastructures, visa regulations, lack of resources and poor governance are all deficiencies which have to be addressed (Ghaderi & Henderson, 2012; Khodadadi, 2016b; Morakabati, 2011; O'Gorman, McLellan, & Baum, 2007).

Nevertheless, the country does possess many natural and cultural heritage attractions in addition to those with great religious significance. It has appeal as an exotic destination to those from outside the region and is in a position to exploit the search for novelty which characterises contemporary tourism. There are already signs of heightened interest in visiting among prospective tourists (Khodadadi, 2016b) and investment by the tourism industry, notably in hospitality (Khodadadi, 2016c). Increases in arrivals have been formally reported since 2013 which accelerated after the 2015 agreement with a steady rise in European visitors (Iran Front Page, 2017). Growth is predicted, but the official aim of 20 million tourists and US$30 billion in revenues annually by 2025 is somewhat ambitious in view of current estimates of between 4 and 5 million (Porter, 2015). The remainder of this chapter is devoted to expert opinions on Iran's tourism which reveal thinking about sanctions, their consequences and future prospects.

A study of expert opinion

The study comprised semi-structured interviews with key figures in Iran's tourism sector. Participants were selected through the snowball sampling technique based on personal contacts and all had worked in tourism for more than a decade. A total of ten individuals agreed to take part from public bodies, private enterprises and academic institutions. The Iran Cultural Heritage, Handcraft and Tourism Organisation (ICHTO) has formal responsibility for tourism and was represented. Interviews were conducted in the capital of Tehran and in Mashhad, the second largest city and location of some of the most sacred Shia shrines. Other venues were Isfahan and Shiraz, both popular historic centres. The Persian language (Farsi) was used and the material later translated into English in order to reach a wider audience. The sessions lasted from 30 minutes to two hours and were tape recorded except for two instances which were manually recorded at the request of interviewees. Thematic analysis of collected data was then completed, as recommended for such an exercise (Braun & Clarke, 2006), to reveal any patterns. The emergent themes are now considered.

The impact of sanctions and their relaxation on tourism arrivals

Interviewees strongly agreed that sanctions had adversely affected tourism businesses in Iran over preceding decades. Problems related to restrictions on banking and trade and lack of access to overseas finance, foreign exchange and insurance coverage. Hostile propaganda emanating from Western nations resulted in negative associations and destination images. Also mentioned were the ban on aircraft part sales and declining investment as well as more general economic consequences of unemployment and inflation. The removal or partial lifting of these obstacles was clearly to be celebrated and heralded a potential new beginning for Iran's tourism industry, although such thoughts were accompanied by an awareness that critical issues had yet to be resolved and challenges ahead were formidable.

A key perceived benefit was the chance to enhance the standing of Iran globally and overturn misconceptions of the country in international markets. There was a consensus that curiosity had been stimulated due to what could be interpreted as the opening of its doors. As one interviewee observed, 'after lifting sanctions, many foreign tourists decided to choose Iran as their holiday destination, the nation's image became relatively positive and we now see more international visitors in the country'. The anecdotal evidence about growth in arrivals is supported by the aforementioned official figures, yet interruptions to the trend were noted. A dip in tourists during 2016 was explained by deteriorating relations with certain Arab countries such as Saudi Arabia and Bahrain. According to a respondent, 'when the country had a frosty relationship with some neighbouring countries, we lost almost 90% of tourists from these markets. They were quite rich, and their length of stay was one or two months'.

Questions of the uneven spatial distribution of tourism were raised by a senior official. Locations within Iran would not gain equally from any boom in tourists who already were concentrated in a small number of more famous sites. It seemed that 'post sanctions, international tourists were more interested in visiting Isfahan, Shiraz and Yazd' and other provinces were overlooked. The tendency was, however, apparent before 2015 when organised itineraries featured well-known places which were presented as repositories of culture and traditions.

New business opportunities?

Despite the 2015 deal, several respondents from the private sector maintained that impediments were still present. A tour operator/travel agent commented that 'sanctions have not been lifted in our business, nothing important has happened for our work' and 'we still have challenges related to sanctions'. Others believed that things had advanced, but the industry was not always able to take advantage of improvements. One spoke of 'many opportunities for tourism businesses, but so far we did not use such an opportunity because our view was not international'. A representative of ICHTO was more positive, saying that 'lifting sanctions opened up unique opportunities to modernise our tourism infrastructure, establish new facilities and invite foreign investors' partly because 'Iran's image was changed in the international arena'. His opinion was echoed by an accommodation proprietor who stated that 'now it's our turn to get ultimate rewards from this immense opportunity. Iran is one of the safest countries in the Middle East and we have to use this chance to find our position in international markets'.

However, even the optimists were worried about attitudes to the JCPOA in the American Congress and White House. They feared opposition and delays whereby foreign companies would be discouraged and, at worse, prevented from doing business in Iran by the re-imposition of sanctions. An Iranian-German who was exploring five-star hotel investment prospects remarked that

> we know that our home country is suitable and safe for investment and several companies have asked me to investigate if they could enter the tourism market, but we always have a real concern that sanctions will come back … I think we need to wait until a clear decision is taken by the US and European Union.

There were also complaints about shortcomings in internal structures and processes with a feeling that an absence of coherence and coordination among relevant departments and agencies could lead to missed opportunities. A tourism official proclaimed that

> after lifting sanctions, many foreign investors announced their readiness for investment at a seminar we held in Tehran. However, the administrative framework to allow communication and collaboration amongst tourism related organisations has not yet been established. For example, there are still issues between us (ICHTO) and the Ministry of Economic Affairs and Finance and we have not yet come together to make it faster. If we are not ready enough, then the opportunity will become a threat.

Obstacles to foreign investment

It was appreciated that foreign businesses probably saw Iran as a very risky investment in light of myriad uncertainties about the future. There were possibilities that the JCPOA would not be fully implemented or Iran might violate its terms. Political instability in response to what was described as repressive domestic policies and tensions between moderates and hardliners within government could also disrupt progress. In addition, it was mentioned that most of the economy is controlled by the state with complicated legal and trade regulatory systems and weak labour laws. The conclusion was that overall economic, social and political circumstances might be unappealing to investors who could find a more promising commercial climate in other countries.

Persistent barriers were identified as constraints on banking and financial transactions and excessive bureaucracy. Foreigners were believed to lack confidence in the safety and security of investments and to be fearful of what might lie ahead. An interviewee working with a foreign company which had already started a hotel business in Mashhad complained about facing

> very difficult and complex challenges, but currently our main problem is banking and legal issues. Iranian banks are still under sanctions and we are unable to use loans and credits. We have a big problem in what we see as discrimination between local and foreign investors. There are no transparent regulations regarding land and property ownership and foreigners' rights.

He also averred that 'authorities did not live up to their promises. They asked us to bring our investment and when we did, they were unsupportive'.

Respondents felt that investors needed reassurance and guarantees, otherwise they would not be prepared to take the manifest risks; for example, an interviewee in Mashhad said that 'when an investor comes to Mashhad, he should find the place safe enough for his investment. Unfortunately, this safety hardly exists'. Tourism officials disagreed, asserting that

> we have a law to encourage and support foreign investment which applies to all foreign investors who would like to come to Iran and work in the field of tourism. Under this law, these investors enjoy all the rights, benefits, incentives and support from government of domestic investors. The government's backing of the domestic investor applies equally to the foreign investor.

It was observed that fluctuations in the value of the national currency were occurring and substantial falls had been recorded. Volatility in the exchange rate acted as a further perceived deterrent with one respondent commenting that 'the exchange market is not stable and investors face significant losses due to the unclear market situation. We do not even know what will be the rate for American dollars tomorrow'. High interest rates of between 10 and 20% on loans and credits and only a short period before instalment payments commenced was another consideration which made Iran uncompetitive compared to Europe and North America. A respondent spoke of Iran as a 'very special country. Banks offered us very high interest rates and there is no monetary assistance from the government. We do not have such issues in Dubai and Canada'.

The actions and rhetoric of the new Trump administration were referred to as a cause of more unease. As well as raising questions about the success of the JCPOA, there was apprehension that existing difficulties of doing business with Iran generally would be worsened for American enterprises. It was stated that 'although European countries attempt to live up to the historic deal and stay in Iran's rich market, Trump and his aggressive stance on Iran exacerbates the situation and creates an unstable environment for investors'. This in combination with the other obstacles would slow down the pace of investment in tourism and economic recovery as a whole. Even companies from Europe which now had legal permission might be reluctant to enter the market.

Interest in accommodation

Irrespective of investor caution, respondents had seen how firms were travelling to Iran to assess commercial prospects. In the field of tourism, these were primarily hospitality groups. An ICHTO employee recalled that

> many companies from Turkey, Germany, Spain and France came here with the hope to invest in the accommodation sector. For example, the French Accor opened a hotel in Imam Khomeini International Airport and we have

also signed a memorandum of understanding with Steigenberger Hotels Group in Germany for building ten hotels of five-star quality.

Middle Eastern and American chains had also expressed interest. He added that investment permission had been granted for 21 plans submitted by ventures from assorted countries including Afghanistan, Iraq, Turkey and Venezuela. North Americans of Iranian origin were involved in a further three proposals. The potential for accommodation development was confirmed by a respondent from a private holding company who explained how

> foreign investors were extremely eager to invest in Iran's travel sector, especially hotels. We realised this and have devised a specific plan called One Hundred Hotels, One Hundred Businesses. We have conceptualised almost 205 projects which caught the attention of international investors, especially Europeans.

When asked about reasons for foreign emphasis on the accommodation industry, a respondent replied that it was 'more profitable, especially in touristic cities like Tehran, Isfahan, Shiraz and Yazd'. The 'government's flexibility in licensing hotel apartments and the possibility of changing the licence of residential buildings into service buildings' was additionally cited. Another spoke about endeavours to lower legal barriers to the purchase of land and securing planning permission with financial incentives playing a part. New hotels and tourism infrastructure in developed areas are eligible for a 50% reduction in income tax and there is a full exemption elsewhere, conditional on a licence issued by ICHTO. An interviewee thought that the 'presence of many famous hotel companies here is not for the reason of investing in hotel construction with their own capital, but they are here to sell their brand'. The franchising and management contract arrangements they engaged in minimised costs and risks.

Summary and conclusions

The study outlined in this chapter investigated the effects of sanctions on Iran and the 2015 agreement to lift a package of them within the context of tourism from the perspective of a group of experts. Events were seen to be a source of great opportunity for attracting visitors and investment from overseas. While the JCPOA was hailed as an historic breakthrough, initial hopes of an immediate increase in activity by international companies and investors had not yet been realised. Foreign business interests in Iran were believed to still confront serious obstacles arising from sanctions and their legacy together with other unfavourable conditions in the wider economic and political environments. Those expecting dramatic changes after the nuclear deal were disappointed, feeling that little headway had been made, and there were doubts about whether the deal would be honoured by both parties.

The findings are a reminder that not all restrictive measures against Iran have been revoked and some sanctions and their ramifications are still operative. In addition, internal weaknesses in Iranian governance are suggested which may frustrate the ability of the country's tourism industry to capitalise on any improvements. It seems that progress towards recovery and rehabilitation as an international tourist destination will be slower than anticipated with reluctance among many foreign businesses to take the necessary risks. Nevertheless, there are opportunities and these extend beyond accommodation to food service, leisure amenities and infrastructure. Such chances are perhaps more likely to be seized by European investors who are now less constrained than their counterparts in the United States. It would appear to be some time before familiar American brands such as Hilton, Starbucks and McDonalds are found in the streets of Tehran.

The results of the study also indicate areas for action by government to help the tourism industry at home and overseas surmount the obstacles, maximise opportunities and minimise risks. There is scope for better communication and cooperation among relevant agencies to coordinate policies and harmonise goals. Dedicated zones could be introduced in cities such as Tehran, Isfahan and Shiraz to create space for new projects accompanied by a streamlining of processes and procedures to facilitate investment and development. Attention needs to be given to the legal framework and demonstrating clarity, consistency and transparency. Relaxation of the banking and financial restrictions is an urgent priority and the government must take the lead in negotiations with international banks and credit providers. It is also important to avoid over-emphasis on hotels and try to ensure that other vital components of the tourism industry receive due consideration.

Calling for fundamental reforms within Iran may be unrealistic, but steps can be taken to offer better support for tourism at this critical stage. Whether the country can realise its tourism potential is a matter of debate and its experiences merit monitoring and further study. The case serves as an illuminating example of the impact of sanctions specifically and the manner in which politics and tourism interact more generally.

Acknowledgements

The authors would like to thank the study's respondents, especially Mr Molaie and Mr Sharifi from the department of investment of ICHTO for their great cooperation in completing this research.

References

Andreasson, G. (2008). *Evaluating the effects of economic sanctions against Burma.* Retrieved from http://lup.lub.lu.se/luur/download?func=downloadFile&recordOId=1335119&fileOId=1646821

Ansari, A. (2016). Iran's eleventh presidential election revisited: The politics of managing change, *LSE Middle East Centre Paper Series, 17*. London: Middle East Centre, LSE.

Braun, V. & Clarke, V. (2006) Using thematic analysis in psychology. *Qualitative Research in Psychology, 3*(2), 77–101.

Dowell, L. M. (2011). *The potential impact of United States tourists on the Cuban market if travel sanctions are lifted; as well as the identification of their push–pull travel motivational factors*. Retrieved from http://scholarworks.umass.edu/cgi/viewcontent.cgi?article=1030&context=gradconf_hospitality

Economist Intelligence Unit. (2017). *Country report: Iran*. London: Economist Intelligence Unit.

Farahani, B. M. & Shabani, M. (2013). The impact of sanctions on Iran's tourism. *International Journal of Resistive Economics, 1*(1), 44–54.

Galtung, J. (1967). On the effects of international economic sanctions, with examples from the case of Rhodesia. *World Politics, 19*(3), 378–416.

Ghaderi, Z. & Henderson, J. C. (2012). Sustainable rural tourism in Iran: A perspective from Hawraman Village. *Tourism Management Perspectives, 2–3*, 47–54.

Iran Front Page. (2017). *Figures say number of foreign tourists to Iran peaked in 2016*. Retrieved from http://ifpnews.com/exclusive/figures-say-number-foreign-tourists-iran-peaked-2016/

Ivanov, S., Sypchenko, L., & Webster, C. (2017). International sanctions and Russia's hotel industry: The impact on business and coping mechanisms of hoteliers. *Tourism Planning & Development, 14*(3), 430–441.

Jacobson, M. (2008). Sanctions against Iran: A promising struggle. *Washington Quarterly, 31*(3), 69–88.

Kahan, J. H. (2017). Revisiting the Iran nuclear deal. *Orbis, 61*(1), 109–124.

Khodadadi, M. (2016a). A new dawn? The Iran nuclear deal and the future of the Iranian tourism industry. *Tourism Management Perspectives, 18*, 6–9.

Khodadadi, M. (2016b). Challenges and opportunities for tourism development in Iran: Perspectives of Iranian tourism suppliers. *Tourism Management Perspectives, 19*(Part A), 90–92.

Khodadadi, M. (2016c). Return to glory? Prospects of Iran's hospitality sector post-nuclear deal. *Tourism Management Perspectives, 19*(Part A), 16–18.

Morakabati, Y. (2011). Deterrents to tourism development in Iran. *International Journal of Tourism Research, 13*(2), 103–123.

O'Gorman, K. D., McLellan, L. R., & Baum, T. (2007). Tourism in Iran: Central control and indignity. In R. Butler & T. Hinch (Eds.), *Tourism and indigenous peoples: Issues and implications* (pp. 251–264). Oxford: Butterworth-Heinemann.

Oxford Dictionary. (2017). *Sanction*. Retrieved from https://en.oxforddictionaries.com/definition/sanction

Popesku, J. & Hall, D. (2004). Sustainability as the basis for future tourism development in Serbia. In D. Hall (Ed.), *Tourism and transition: Governance, transformation and development* (pp. 95–104). Wallingford: CABI Publishing.

Porter, L. (2015). Iran hopes to welcome 20 million tourists a year following nuclear deal. *The Telegraph*. Retrieved from http://www.telegraph.co.uk/travel/destinations/middle-east/iran/articles/Iranians-more-than-eager-to-welcome-tourists/

Pratt, S. & Alizadeh, V. (2017). The economic impact of the lifting of sanctions on tourism in Iran: A computable general equilibrium analysis. *Current Issues in Tourism*. http://dx.doi.org/10.1080/13683500.2017.1307329

Tarock, A. (2006). Iran's nuclear programme and the West. *Third World Quarterly, 27*(4), 645–664.

Tarock, A. (2016). The Iran nuclear deal: Winning a little, losing a lot. *Third World Quarterly, 37*(8), 1408–1424.

Torchia, A. (2013). Analysis: Iran economy far from collapse as sanctions tighten. *Reuters*. Retrieved from https://www.reuters.com/article/us-iran-economy-sanctions-idUSBRE 91J0SM20130220

Part II

Pilgrimage and religious tourism

4 Islamic pilgrimage tourism in Iran: challenges and perspectives

Mahmood Ziaee and Somayeh Amiri

Introduction

Holy sites and religious rituals have always been important tourism attractions and an important travel motivation. Pilgrimage continues to be a major travel activity, while secular trips to thousands of religious buildings that are visited mainly due to their historical and cultural, rather than religious, values, also reinforce the relationship between religion and tourism (Tohidlou, 2011; Jafari & Scott, 2014). Religion is an element of cultural tourism and religious tourism is a common form of tourism in developing countries. Spiritual tourism is generally defined as any type of tourism that is driven entirely, or in part, by religious tourism values. Religious tourism refers to visiting tangible heritage or religious rituals (intangible heritage) (UNWTO, 2011). Various writers define religious tourism in terms of pilgrimages, religious events (major gatherings for important religious occasions and anniversaries), tours, and visits to important religious sites (Timothy & Olsen, 2006). Pilgrimage is a journey for religious reasons (acts of worship) to holy places. During the past five decades, religious trips and, in particular, pilgrimages have had an enormous growth (Butler & Suntikul, 2018; Jafari & Scott, 2014), while tourism itself is often regarded as a form of modern pilgrimage (Timothy & Olsen, 2006).

Each year about 300–330 million tourists visit religious sites with about 40% of religious oriented trips being in Europe and about half in Asia (Scott & Jafari, 2010; Jafari & Scott, 2014). Religious tourism has a high growth potential since 60% of the world's population follow a religion (UNWTO, 2011; Butler & Suntikul, 2018). Islam is the foundation of society and order of law in Muslim nations and plays a determining role in tourism policy-making, destination development, management, marketing, and the operation of the industry. The religion also plays a significant role in the socio-political and cultural landscapes of Muslim countries. However, given interpretations of Islam, adherence to Islam as well as the level of state intervention varies among Muslim countries (Zamani-Frahani & Henderson, 2010), tourism has been developed differently in Muslim countries and each country has its own level of development, and national development priorities and policies (Almuhrzi, Alriyami, & Scott, 2017). "In Iran, the land of Shia pilgrimage, religious elements are found in its architecture, history, festivals,

70 *Mahmood Ziaee and Somayeh Amiri*

rituals, and lifestyles" (Zamani-Farahani, 2010, p. 214), and the state institutions and value systems are closely linked to Islam and based on Sharia law. Given the dominant role of Iran as the biggest Shia country in the world and the political objectives of the clerical establishments in the country toward exporting the "revolution" (Esposito, 1990), Shia pilgrimage is recognized and favored by the ruling elite. This is because it is regarded as contributing significantly to the achievement of major national socio-economic development objectives and, more importantly, as not being detrimental to the erosion of religious devoutness and conventions. Against this backdrop, this chapter examines religious tourism of Iran through a systematic approach, by taking into consideration the dimensions of supply, demand, and effects, but with a focus on Islam. The comments are derived from the analysis of published materials supplemented by observations and the authors' personal experiences.

Iran: religion and tourism

Iran is among the most attractive Asian countries and one of the most important destinations for religious tourists in Asia. Asia is a cradle of religions and a region with the largest number of pilgrims and travelers for religious events (UNWTO, 2011). More than 60% of the world's 1.5 billion Muslim population lives in Asia. The followers of Islam across the world are in two different groups: Sunni (87%) and Shia (13%). Iran is the largest Shiite country in the world and it has a rich history and a culture originated from the geographical location and tourism resources of different historical periods. Iran also has many Shiite religious attractions which has made it unique among the Islamic tourism destinations of the world (UNWTO, 2017).

Iran has experienced different religions in various historical periods. From the main religions of the world, Islam is the dominant religion of Iran and three religions—Zoroastrian, Judaism, and Christianity—are recognized in Iran as minority religions (Zamani-Farahani, 2010). The total population of 79,926,270 people in Iran in 2016 consisted of about 99.38% Muslim; 0.1% Assyrian or Chaldean Christianity; 0.06% Christian; 0.01% Jewish; 0.03% Zoroastrian; and 0.42% other or unspecified religions (Statistical Center of Iran (SCI), 2016).

The Zoroastrian religion that dates back to the seventh century BC was the official religion of Iran during the Sassanid period, had a great influence on Christianity and Islam and is still alive in Iran, India, and Central Asia (Esfandiar, 2015). Today, Zoroastrian has about 200,000 followers in the world. But the origin of Zoroaster is Iran, where, according to official statistics, it has 25,271 followers (SCI, 2016). Iran's Zoroastrians are mostly inhabitants of Yazd province, then Tehran and Kerman. Before the Muslim conquest of Persia (also known as the Arab conquest of Iran), monotheistic religion was practiced by Iranians. The Iranian prophet and religious reformer Zarathustra, more widely known outside Iran as Zoroaster, the Greek form of his name—is traditionally regarded as the founder of the religion. This religion has a long history and is rooted in Persian history, heritage, and culture. In the wake of the foundation of the Islamic republic in

1979, the country has seen the rise of political Islam and the practice of Sharia law (Zubaida, 2000).

Jews have lived in Iran for more than 2,700 years. In 2012, 8,756 Jews lived in Iran, mainly in Tehran (60%), Shiraz (30%) and Isfahan (7%) (Tehran Jewish Committee, 2017). Notwithstanding, as Iran has refused to recognize Israel and given the highly tense political relationship between Iran and Israel, there is the issue of accessibility of sites for Jews outside of Iran.

The official appointees of Christianity in Iran include the Armenian and Assyrian Christians who entered the country from the time of the Parthian Empire. Armenians in Iran are both religious and ethnic minorities. Of the total population of 1.5 million Assyrian Christians in the world, more than 30,000 live in Iran. A total of 117,704 Christian Iranians live in all 31 provinces of the country. However, due to challenges facing the recognition of converting to Christianity in Iran, there is no precise estimate of its followers.

Although potentially one of the largest religious minorities, the Bahá'í Faith is not recognized by the Iranian government and no official statistics are available on the religion.

Islam came to Iran in the seventh century AD, and Shia was recognized as the official religion during the Safavid period. The Islamic Republic of Iran dates from the 1979 revolution when the Pahlavi monarchy was toppled and Ayatollah Khomeini (the architect of the revolution) installed Islamic rule and the religious and political landscapes were dramatically transformed. According to the constitution, the official religion of Iran is Islam of the Twelver Shia denomination. The term Twelver refers to its followers' belief in 12 divinely ordained leaders, known as the Twelve Imams. While Shiites make up only 10–13% of the total Muslims in the world (UNWTO, 2011), 89% of Iran's 99% Muslim population are Shiites. Of the four Sunnite schools, Hanafi has the highest population in Iran and they live in north-eastern, eastern, and south-east areas.

The supply side of religious tourism

Iran has a substantial number of sites and attractions that can contribute to religious tourism. There are about 33 tombs of prophets, 8,919 religious holy places including shrines, husseiniyas, mosques, religious schools, and seminaries, churches, synagogues, fire temples, and sanctuaries of different religions, 4,319 of which are nationally registered. Of the 1,539 nationally registered Imam Zadeh and holy places, Tehran (11%), Khorasan Razavi (10.9%), Fars and Isfahan (8.5%), Mazandaran and Yazd (5.9%), and Semnan (4.8%) have the largest shares.

Tourism capacities of Islam

As the centers of Islamic civilization in Iran, Mashhad, Qom, Shiraz, and Rey contain a large proportion of Islamic heritage (Heidari, 2012). Pilgrimage is the main form of religious tourism in Iran (see also Chapters 5 and 6, this volume) and is focused on Shiite pilgrimages primarily to Mashhad as the most important pilgrimage center of Islam after Mecca and secondly to Qom, as the center of Shia religious scholarship and theology and home to some of the country's most influential clerics (UNWTO, 2011). Table 4.1 indicates tangible and intangible attractions of religious tourism in Iran.

Tourism capacities of Shiism: tangible heritage

The only Shiite Imam buried in Iran, the eighth Imam, is Imam Reza in Mashhad, which is the second religious metropolis of the Islamic world after Mecca, and the second largest metropolis in the country, hosting pilgrims across Iran and other Muslim countries (Badri & Tayyebi, 2012). After the Islamic Revolution of Iran of 1979, Mashhad became more important and the number of cultural-religious tourists increased. Mashhad has 42% of train passengers in Iran, about 12% of passengers on domestic flights, about 55% of public accommodation, almost 50% of hotel capacity (Ghadami, 2011) and 16% of hotels by number (Tohidlou, 2011). Mashhad Seminary, the largest and most important Shiite seminary after Qom Seminary, was established in the early centuries of Islam and has a large number of seminary students studying there.

Qom, the spiritual capital of the Islamic revolution is an important hub of religious tourism due to the shrine of Masumeh, the sister of Imam Reza, and Jamkaran mosque, which annually attracts thousands of visitors. Qom is the city of 'piety science' and has 544 Imamzadeh (a shrine-tomb of the descendants of Imams who are directly related to Muhammad) and sacred sites (Karimi Alavijeh, Ahmadi, & Nazari, 2016).

Important Imamzadehs include the tomb of Mir Seyed Ahmad known as Shah Cheragh in Shiraz; Imamzadeh Saleh in Tajrish, Tehran; and the tomb of Abdul Azim in the town of Rey, known as 'the mother of Tehran.' Since the shrine of Imam Khomeini, the International Airport, and Tehran Refinery are all located near Rey, its geographical, economic, and social importance has been doubled. In the shrine of Imam Khomeini, located south of Tehran, the tombs of former Iranian president Ali Akbar Hashemi Rafsanjani and Khomeini's first child are also buried. The anniversary of his passing, along with some religious and revolutionary events, are held in this tomb and are attended by thousands of people.

The most prominent, largest, and complete Sufi monastery is the tomb of Sheikh Safi Ardebili in Ardebil, the founder of the Safavid dynasty. This place is a center of Sufi pilgrimage and a manifestation of sacred art and architecture of the fourteenth to eighteenth centuries. Its architecture and art have universal values and indicate the fundamental principles of Sufism (Esfandiar, 2015).

Muslim mosques can sometimes act as museums, gathering places for Muslim arts and crafts, and as places for congregational prayer (Aghajani & Farahani Fard, 2015). Among the 70,000 mosques in Iran (UNWTO, 2017), the most famous is Jamkaran in Qom at which Imam Mahdi (the savior and last Imam in Shiite Islam) is believed to have appeared. Other famous mosques include Goharshad in Mashhad, Masjed Jama, Shah, and Sheikh Lotfollah mosque in Isfahan, which is recognized internationally for its Islamic cultural value, and the Blue Mosque of Tabriz.

Table 4.1 Islamic religious tourist attractions in Iran

Religious attraction	Type of attraction	Location	Official heritage status	Pilgrimage period
Imam Reza Shrine	Shrine	Mashhad	Tentative World Heritage	During the year
Fatima Masumeh Shrine		Qom	National	During the year
Shah-e-Cheragh Shrine	Imamzadeh	Shiraz	National	
Shah Abdol Azim Shrine		Shahr-e Rey		
Imamzadeh Saleh		Tehran		
Shah Nematollah Vali		Kerman		
Sultan Ali ibn Muhammad Baqer		Kashan		
Imamzadeh Davood		Tehran		
Imam Khomeini Tomb	Shrine	Tehran		
Jamkaran	Mosque	Qom	National	During the year
Majed Imam Isfahan		Isfahan	World Heritage	
Sheikh Lotfolah Mosque		Isfahan	World Heritage	
Goharshad Mosque		Mashhad	National	
Blue Mosque		Tabriz	National	
Sanandaj Jame Mosque		Sanandaj	National	
Sheikh Safi Tomb	Tomb	Ardebil	World Heritage	
Bayazid Bastami Tomb		Bastam	National	
Sheikh Ahmad Jami Tomb		Torbate Jam	National	
Khaled Nabi Tomb		Golestan	National	
Tsua's and Ashoura	Event	IRAN		9th and 10th Moharram
Mourning ceremonies in Husseiniya A'zam Zanjan – Muharram 8th		Zanjan	National	8th Moharram
Nakhlgardani Rirual		Yazd	National	9th and 10th Moharram, End of Safar

(*Continued*)

Table 4.1 (Continued)

Religious attraction	Type of attraction	Location	Official heritage status	Pilgrimage period
Bam ritual of Tasua and Ashoura		Kerman	National	9th and 10th Moharram
Shabanie Eids		Iran	National	Mid-Sha'ban
Tazieh		Iran	World Heritage	Tasua, Ashura and Arbaeen
Fatima Birthday		Iran	National	
Ghadr nights		Iran		Ramadan month
Eid-al-Ghorban		Iran	National	
Eid-al-Fitr		Iran	National	End of Ramadan
Ghadire Khom Eid		Iran	National	
Ghalishooee Ritual Ardahal		Kashan	World Heritage	Second Friday of autumn
Imam Khomeini mourning		Tehran	National	
Pir Shaliar's ritual		Uraman Takht	National	Middle of spring and winter

In some religious traditions, the path leading to the shrine can be as enlightening and spiritually moving as the shrine itself. Every year in Iran, from the first days of Safar, many people from all over the country and even neighboring countries travel on foot via various routes to attend the mourning ceremony of Imam Reza's martyrdom, a trip than can take between 3 and 28 days. The same is also done on the birthday of this Imam.

Rahian-e-Noor is a pilgrimage trip to the border area of Iran and Iraq (Khuzestan), in which many people were regarded as martyred in the eight-year war between the two countries. Supported by the government, these trips are aimed at introducing the importance of sacrifice to students and other visitors. Every year around 6 million people visit this area (Iran Daily, 2013). Since Jihad is a religious act of Islam, and martyrdom during Jihad is regarded as spiritually valuable and the place of martyrdom is holy, traveling to these areas is a kind of pilgrimage and spiritual journey which also overlaps with war tourism and dark tourism.

Tourism capacities of Islam: intangible heritage

The most important celebrations of Muslims in Iran are Eid Fitr (end of Ramadan), Eid Qorban (sacrifice during Hajj), Eid Ghadir (special significance for Shiites) and the birth of Prophet Muhammad and also his first revelation which are all official holidays in the country and cause a large volume of domestic travel.

The most important events of Islam are during Muharram, Safar, and Ramadan, which are held in pilgrimage centers and mosques. Muharram is the month of Imam Hussein's martyrdom and has certain rituals associated with it, including mourning and votive food. Safar is the month of Imam Reza's martyrdom, Prophet Muhammad's death, and the fortieth day of Imam Hussein's martyrdom (Arbaeen). In Ramadan, the rituals of Ghadr nights and the feast of Eid Fitr at the end of the month have a great significance.

Ashura mourning has different styles in different parts of Iran because of the diversity of languages, dialects, ethnicities, and climates, and experiences with local communities can be attractive for domestic and foreign tourists. Religious carnivals and the rituals of Ashura and the first ten days of Muharram appear of interest to European tourists. Since Tasua and Ashura are public holidays on the calendar of Iran, substantial numbers of domestic trips occur on these days with people tending to travel to their hometowns.

The historic city of Yazd is a World Heritage site, registered by UNESCO in 2017, and is a prominent religious city in which to commemorate Muharram. Palm-carrying is one of the most important mourning rituals in the first days of Muharram and last days of Safar (UNWTO, 2017). As the symbol of Imam Hussein's coffin, the palm is moved around the town square as part of the mourning procession. Religious tourism in Zanjan is also substantial due to the great Husseiniya (congregation halls) as well as mourning rituals on different occasions, especially during Muharram.

Ramadan and its associated customs including Eid Fitr and Qadr nights are other tourist attractions of Islam in Iran. The International Holy Quran Exhibition is also held in this month.

The midpoint of Sha'ban coincides with the birth of the last Imam of Shia. Many religious pilgrimages to holy Islamic places happen at this time, the most important being the Jamkaran mosque in Qom. Streets are illuminated, and many wedding parties are held to coincide with this celebration.

There are also other opportunities for further promotion for religious tourism. The carpet-washing ceremony in Mashhad Ardehal, Kashan shows the martyrdom of Sultan Ali ibn Muhammad Baqir, a descendant of Imam Muhammad Baqir, the fifth Imam of Shiites and his burial by residents of Fin in Mashhad Ardehal. It is performed each year on the first Friday of October. Taziyeh is one of the most prominent Iranian performing arts depicting the epic tale of Ashura, relying on dramatic structure and poetry and utilizing a variety of local and traditional arts. Taziyeh is a symbol of love and devotion to Imam Hussein and is considered as worship and has potential for development as a form of religious tourism (Heidari, 2012).

Sunni tourism capacities

The most important religious centers of Sunnis are Sheikh Ahmad Jami tomb in Torbat-e Jam in Khorasan and Masjed Jama Sanandaj in Isfahan. The Khalid Nabi cemetery in the north-east of Iran is notable for its transformation from an unknown tomb into a place for weekly gatherings and is visited especially by the

Turkmen population, one of the Iranian ethnic minorities. Despite being located in an isolated area, it receives an estimated 90,000 visitors each year, with 66% of these visitors being Sunni Turkmen pilgrims. In his study, Ebadi (2015) believes 67% of non-Turkmen visitors are secular.

The tombs of Bayazid Bastami and Shaikh Abul-Hassan Kharaqāni are important to Sufis and are potential candidate World Heritage sites (UNESCO, 2017). The tomb of Abul-Hassan Kharaqāni at Qaleh Now-e Kharaqan near Bastam is a religious destination for Sunnis and especially the Turkmen people.

Pir Shaliar's ritual includes pilgrimages, wedding ceremonies, mystical ceremonies, and cooking votive potage. This ritual is held in the village of Oraman Takht in Iranian Kurdistan twice a year, in the middle of the spring and 45 days after the beginning of winter, which is held simultaneously with Sadeh celebration of the Zoroastrians (Hanifi, Ebrahimi Dehkordy, & Beladi Dehbozorg, 2016). Notwithstanding, unlike the Shia pilgrimage which has been given a special priority and is favored by the Shiite ruling elite, Iran has not placed a deal of attention to the Sunni tourism market despite its potential given the long-running Shia–Sunni conflict and sectarian division (Zamani-Farahani & Musa, 2012), regional rivalry, as well as the Shiite-centric policies in Iran toward the Sunni minority (Aman, 2016).

The demand side of religious tourism

Religious tourism of Iran is focused primarily on Shiite and particularly on Mashhad and Qom. With 5.3% growth during 2011–2015, 28,452,421 domestic and 845,525 international tourists visited Mashhad in 2016 with 15,766,051 overnight stays. Some 26% of pilgrimage visas issued were for travel to Mashhad in 2016 (ICHTO, 2016). Pilgrims to Mashhad are mainly from the Middle East (Afghanistan, Pakistan, Iraq, Kuwait, Lebanon, Syria, and the United Arab Emirates) (ICHTO, 2016) and Central Asia (Turkmenistan, Uzbekistan, Tajikistan, Kyrgyzstan, and Kazakhstan) (Tohidlou, 2011). Mashhad is the primary destination for pilgrimage in all religious ceremonies over the year, and the number of travels to Mashhad is consistent throughout the year and it peaks in holidays (Tohidlou, 2011). More than 80% of Mashhad tourists arrive in four months of the year. Nowruz (the Persian New Year) is one of the peak times. In 2016, 16% of registered stays occurred in Nowruz and 67% in the summer (ICHTO, 2016). Due to the difference in length of the Islamic calendar and the Solar Hijri calendar, the dates of religious ceremonies are not consistent over the years, and this displaces the peak times of travel to Mashhad.

Qom receives approximately 20 million domestic and 2.5 million international tourists annually. According to the latest statistics, most tourists of Qom were from Iran and they were from Tehran, West Azerbaijan, Isfahan, and Khorasan respectively (Deputy of Planning and Information Technology Development Center of Jamkaran Mosque, 2014). The pattern of tourism in Qom is based on short trips. The average stay of foreign tourists in Qom is two–three days, and the average stay of domestic visitors is less than one day and about nine hours (Heidari, 2012), because the proximity of Qom to some cities in the country, especially Tehran, Isfahan, Arak, Kashan, Yazd, and Saveh as well as the improvement of routes and transportation to these cities have shortened the average length of stay in Qom. The spatial and climatic location of Qom, the single-product tourism (pilgrimage as the only attraction of travel), and the weaknesses and limitations of facilities has shortened the period of travel to this city.

A total of more than 20 million domestic pilgrims also visited Jamkaran in 2014 with 13,540,000 pilgrims visiting in the first half of the year including Nowruz, Sha'ban, and Ramadan and 6,798,000 pilgrims in the second half. The travels to Qom and Jamkaran are mostly family trips and 80% of them had previously traveled to Qom. The domestic trips to Qom and Jamkaran are mainly by road and personal vehicle. Interestingly, in Mid-Sha'ban (the birth of Imam Zaman), 2.5% of visitors travel to Jamkaran on foot (Deputy of Planning and Information Technology Development Center of Jamkaran Mosque, 2014). The highest number of pilgrims in Jamkaran visit for Mid-Sha'ban. Most pilgrims were from Qom, Tehran, Khorasan Razavi, and Isfahan.

Typology of religious tourists in Iran

The motives of religious tourism in Iran can be summarized in three categories: pilgrimage, visiting religious architecture and art, and travel for religious ceremonies (Zamani-Farahani, 2010). Studies suggest that more than 40% of international tourists arrive in Iran with pilgrimage motives, the most important of which is the pilgrimage of Imam Reza. However, visitation to religious sites is not necessarily for religious reasons and can also be for historical, cultural, and heritage values. A study of spiritual tourism in Yazd found that more than 80% of the tourists participating in Ashura rituals were primarily interested in visiting cultural-religious rituals of Muharram, Mid-Sha'ban celebrations, and other Shiite ceremonies, and then visited the mosques and Imamzadeh shrines (Bahadori et al., 2018). Many mosques, churches, and other holy places that tourists are interested in visiting are World Heritage sites and are included in foreign tourists' itineraries (ICHTO, 2016).

The impacts of religious tourism

The most prominent positive economic function of religious-cultural tourism in Mashhad is job creation and foreign exchange earnings (Alipour, Olya, & Forouzan, 2017; see also Chapters 5 and 6, this volume). Mashhad is the most important city in terms of religious tourism and the city's economy is largely based on tourism (see also Chapter 13, this volume, on health tourism in Mashhad). One of the important revenues from pilgrimage is votive offerings and charity that is devoted to public-benefit affairs and the development of religious sites (Badri & Tayyebi, 2012).

Accommodation is the largest share in total expenditure by pilgrims during their stay in Mashhad, and as a result, Mashhad's tourist income is derived primarily from the hotel sector. Nevertheless, Mashhad has also increased tourism income by diversifying its tourism product to include shopping and leisure centers. Domestic tourists indicate that shopping centers are the second priority in terms of tourism attraction after the pilgrimage of the Imam Reza. Given that shopping accounts for 33% of visitor spending (Soltani & Shahnoushi, 2012), this represents a significant positive economic impact to the region.

Tourism and spatial development

Other effects of religious tourism include its physical effects, and its role in the social and spatial development of urban centers. Cities such as Mashhad, Qom, Rey, Ardabil, and Mahan formed, grew, and developed because of the presence of some tombs (Aghajani & Farahani Fard, 2015). Major tombs offer a range of facilities for pilgrims including markets, restaurants, parking lots, and shopping malls that residents can utilize as well. The effects of spatial development caused by religious tourism in Mashhad include the development of the Razavi area; the streets leading to the shrine of Imam Reza; markets, parks, and hotels; road, air, and rail transport infrastructure; and flow-on benefits to other economic sectors. However, despite economic benefits, there are also concerns about other impacts (Aminian, 2012). In Mashhad, the largest amount of accommodation is located in the Samen region. The high volumes of pilgrims have meant associated problems such as traffic, noise, and environmental pollution, and negative social behavior at times (Alipour et al., 2017). The high number of pilgrims and tourists in Mashhad has meant an increase in the visitor to resident ratio over the years, to the extent that there were 8.6 tourists in the city per inhabitant in 2016.

Management and planning issues

In recent years, the importance of tourism to the socio-economic development of the country has been recognized. Iran's government is actively emphasizing tourism development as an effort for regional development and preserving cultural and Islamic heritage. The growth of tourism in the state budget allocation from 2013 to 2017 reflects the government's increasing attention to tourism (Khodadadi, 2016) and improved competitive position (World Economic Forum (WEF), 2017).

Pilgrimages and pilgrimage cities such as Mashhad, Qom, and Shiraz were considered for the first time in the Fifth Five-Year National Development Plan of the country. The first chapter of the Fifth Development Plan has pointed out the support of the Government and ICHTO for tourism development, including religious tourism and pilgrimage. Article 12 of the chapter states that in order to deepen the values, beliefs, and culture based on Islamic identity and promotion of the tradition of Ahl al-Bayt (the family of the Islamic prophet Muhammad) and the optimal use of the spiritual capacity of pilgrimage places, government should act:

• To accurately identify the needs and problems of pilgrims;
• To plan and develop mechanisms for organizing the work of pilgrims; and

- To provide the necessary infrastructure by supporting municipalities and non-governmental sectors as well as developing facilities, cultural activities, and pilgrimage services at pilgrimage and religious tourism centers and providing desirable settings for pilgrimage and implementation of required infrastructure projects in the form of an annual budget.

Under the country's 20-Year National Vision Plan (2005–2025), Astan Quds Razavi will be introduced as the highest cultural center of the Shiite world with respect to the culture and tradition of Imam Reza, in order to attract religious tourists (Astan Quds Razavi, 2018). According to the targets for tourism development in the fifth program, Iran's share of world tourists should increase to 1.5% (about 20 million tourists) and Iran's share of tourism income should increase to 2% (about US$25 billion) in 2025 (the last year of the 20-year outlook) (see also Chapter 1, this volume).

The challenges of development and management of religious tourism in Iran

Factors such as poor management, lack of proper planning, a lack of a dedicated organization for domestic pilgrimage, cultural barriers, and the weakness of welfare and urban infrastructure contribute to the lack of development of religious tourism capacities. Although there is the Hajj and Pilgrimage Organization, it mainly deals with the pilgrimage and travel to Hajj and the shrines of Iraq and Syria. Travel agencies, who operate exclusively in the Hajj and pilgrimage area, receive their license from the Hajj and Pilgrimage Organization and not from the Tourism Organization. Other challenges include:

- Lack of proper advertising, marketing, and appropriate media productions to introduce Iran's attractions;
- Limited accommodation facilities at luxurious and medium level;
- Lack of information centers;
- Lack of feasibility and scientific studies and planning for developing the holy places;
- Lack of accurate statistics of tourists;
- Negative images regarding religious tourism in Iran in some markets;
- Lack of trained tour guides to guide religious tourists;
- Seasonality issues that leave many tourism and residential facilities unable to use their full capacity during low periods of demand;
- The negative impact of political relations with Saudi Arabia on the market of religious tourism. The attack on the Saudi embassy and consulate in 2015 in response to the death penalty for Shiite cleric Sheikh Nimr, in addition to undermining Iran's general image in the world, led to the loss of two-thirds of the Arab tourists of Mashhad, who mainly travel from Persian Gulf countries for pilgrimage and negative flow-on effects to hotels in Khorasan Razavi province, especially in Mashhad (Khodaei, 2017);
- Negative balance of Iran's tourism with international outbound greater than inbound.

Conclusion

The most obvious and clearest focus of religious tourism of Muslims in Iran is on Mashhad and then Qom. For Imamzadeh shrines, Fars is the leading province after Mashhad and Qom. The historic city of Yazd was listed as a UNESCO World Heritage site in 2017. This city has many attractions of Islam and Zoroastrianism. In Isfahan, which has several mosques and World Heritage sites, the culmination of Armenian architecture and decorative arts can be seen especially in Jolfa churches. However, many of Iran's religious centers are registered as World Heritage sites because of their architectural, cultural, and religious values, providing a range of reasons for visiting them.

Religious tourism in Iran is mainly domestic, and pilgrimage to destinations in Mashhad and Qom are the most important form. Mashhad is the foremost Islamic religious destination of Iran, and Imam Reza's shrine is one of the most prominent holy places in Iran. There are also various religious ceremonies and events that may be attractive to non-Muslim tourists. The most important ceremonial destinations of Iran are Yazd and Zanjan and they provide an opportunity to learn about Iranian culture and heritage. Religious tourism may also be a means of positively changing perceptions of Iran as an unsuitable destination for travel, while it may also potentially contribute to addressing seasonality issues at the national scale.

Iraq should be considered as the first target country of religious tourism in Iran, considering its large Shiite population, the cultural and religious similarities, and the already significant number of Iraqi tourists in Iran. The selection of Tabriz as the tourism capital of Islamic countries in 2018 and the direct flight from Najaf to Tabriz, and the religious similarities between Iran and Iraq, has created a great opportunity for the tourist exchange in cultural and religious areas.

The growth of religious tourism in Iran, partly due to the development of transportation infrastructure, the issuance of online and airport visas, and the increased period of visa validity, has had significant flow-on economic and social effects, especially in creating employment and income, and developing urban facilities and infrastructure, although there are also negative effects arising from large numbers of tourists in some locations. Nevertheless, if Iran, through its religious tourism potential, can attract 1% of the global Shiite population as tourists, over a million religious tourists could potentially arrive in Iran annually, whose revenues would then have significant benefits for the Iranian economy.

Iran's religious tourism is mainly centered on attracting Shiites while holy Islamic sites appeal to non-Muslims as well. Given the huge share of the Shia pilgrimage in the national tourism market and the concentration of pilgrimage tourism activity in only a few cities, it seems that a large part of the tourism potential of other attractions for Sunnis and other religious tourists, such as Jews and Christians, remains unutilized. Hence, significant investment in the exploitation of religious heritage along with its valorization is sought so as to help meet the expectations of religious tourists to the country (Heydari Chianeh, Del Chiappa, & Ghasemi, 2018). Tourism is highly vulnerable to changes in political arrangements and controls (Hall, 2010), and there is uncertainty about the future of pilgrimage tourism in Iran given the ongoing instability and insecurity in the region and escalation in tensions with Saudi Arabia and other Persian Gulf states; the number of religious tourists to Iran has dramatically dropped and has had a negative impact on the economy. Moreover, this political crisis coupled with President Trump's withdrawal of the United States from the nuclear agreement has led to ongoing concerns that Iran will be pushed back toward isolation.

References

Aghajani, M. & Farahani Fard, S. (2015). Religious tourism and effective factors on it (Case study Iran). *Quarterly Journal of the Macro and Strategic Policies, 3*(9), 43–66 [in Persian].

Alipour, H., Olya, H. G., & Forouzan, I. (2017). Environmental impacts of mass religious tourism: From residents' perspectives. *Tourism Analysis, 22*(2), 167–183.

Almuhrzi, H., Alriyami, H., & Scott, N. (Eds.). (2017). *Tourism in the Arab world: An industry perspective*. Bristol: Channel View Publications.

Aman, F. (2016). *Iran's Uneasy Relationship with its Sunni Minority*. Retrieved from http://www.mei.edu/content/article/iran%E2%80%99s-uneasy-relationship-its-sunni-minorities

Aminian, A. (2012). Environmental performance measurement of tourism accommodations in the pilgrimage urban areas: The case of the holy city of Mashhad, Iran. *Procedia-Social and Behavioral Sciences, 35*, 514–522.

Astan Quds Razavi (2018). *Astan Quds Razavi 20-year vision plan*. Retrieved from https://rezvan.aqr.ir

Badri, S. A. & Tayyebi, S. (2012). Factors affecting the costs of religious tourism: A case study of Mashhad, Iran. *Journal of Tourism Planning and Development, 1*(1), 153–177 [in Persian].

Bahadori, R., Farsani, N., Sadeghi, R., Shafiei, Z., & Mortazavy, M. (2018). A study on religious tourists' motivations: the case of the Muharram event (Yazd, Iran). *Revista Turismo & Desenvolvimento, 2*(27/28), 129–132.

Butler, R. & Suntikul, W. (Eds.). (2018). *Tourism and religion, Issues and implications*. Bristol: Channel View Publications.

Deputy of Planning and Information Technology Development Center of Jamkaran Mosque. (2014). *Report on the results of the census of pilgrims of the Holy Mosque of Jamkaran in 2014*. Qom: Planning Department of Jamkaran Mosque.

Ebadi, M. (2015). Forms of pilgrimage at the Shrine of Khāled Nabi, Northeastern Iran. *International Journal of Religious Tourism and Pilgrimage, 3*(1), 66–78.

Esfandiar, K. (2015). *English for Iranian tourist guides* (2nd ed.). Tehran: Mahkameh [in Persian].

Esposito, J. L. (Ed.). (1990). *The Iranian revolution: Its global impact*. Gainsville, FL: Florida International University Press.

Ghadami, M. (2011). Assessment and Strategy Formulation in destination in the framework of tourism sustainable development (Case study the city of Mashhad). *Journal of Urban – Regional Studies and Research, 3*(9), 59–82 [in Persian].

Hall, C. M. (2010). Politics and tourism: Interdependency and implications in understanding changes. In R. Butler & W. Suntikul (Eds.), *Tourism and political change* (pp. 7–19). Oxford: Goodfellow Publishers.

Hanifi, P., Ebrahimi Dehkordy, A., & Beladi Dehbozorg, S. E. (2016). Recognition cultural-religious landscape of Hooraman with emphasis on pilgrimage celebrations of Pir-e-shalyar *Journal of Urban Landscape Research, 2*(4), 47–58 [in Persian].

Heidari, M. (2012). *The role of Islamic civilization in the development of religious tourism of religious destinations. Case study of the Holy City of Qom.* Unpublished master's thesis. Tehran: Allameh Tabataba'i University, Tehran, Iran.

Heydari Chianeh, R., Del Chiappa, G., & Ghasemi, V. (2018). Cultural and religious tourism development in Iran: Prospects and challenges. *Anatolia.* https://doi.org/10.1080/1 3032917.2017.1414439

Iran Cultural Heritage, Handcraft and Tourism Organization (ICHTO). (2016). *Iran highlights of tourism statistics.* Tehran: ICHTO.

Iran Daily (2013). *Rahian-e Noor. Promotes tourism, economy.* Retrieved from http://old. iran-daily.com/1392/9/7/MainPaper/4662/Page/6/MainPaper_4662_6.pdf

Jafari, J. & Scott, N. (2014). Muslim world and its tourisms. *Annals of Tourism Research, 44,* 1–19.

Karimi Alavijeh, M., Ahmadi, M., & Nazari, M. (2016). Investigating the effects of traditional values and Islamic values on the tourists' satisfaction and loyalty in Qom. *Journal of Tourism Management Studies (Tourism Studies), 10*(32), 21–42 [in Persian].

Khodadadi, M. (2016). Challenges and opportunities for tourism development in Iran: Perspectives of Iranian tourism suppliers. *Tourism Management Perspectives, 19*(Part A), 90–92.

Khodaei, A. (2017). *More Western tourists, less Arab ones visiting Iran.* Retrieved from http://ifpnews.com/exclusive/more-western-tourists-visit-iran/

Scott, N. & Jafari, J. (Eds.). (2010). *Tourism in the Muslim world.* Cheltenham: Emerald Group Publishing.

Soltani, S. & Shahnoushi, N. (2012). Prioritizing the major tourist attractions of Mashhad from the perspective of domestic tourists. *Tourism Studies Quarterly, 1*(1), 5–17 [in Persian].

Statistical Center of Iran (SCI). (2016). General population and housing census 2015. Retrieved from http://www.amar.org.ir

Tehran Jewish Committee (2017). *Jewish in Iran.* Retrieved from http://www.iranjewish. com/worldyahood/yahood%20Iran.htm

Timothy, D. J. & Olsen, D. H. (Eds.). (2006). *Tourism, religion and spiritual journeys.* London: Routledge.

Tohidlou, M. (2011). *Defining an effective management model for religious destination, case of Mashhad.* Unpublished master's thesis. Allameh Tabataba'i University, Tehran, Iran.

United Nations Educational, Scientific and Cultural Organization (UNESCO). (2017). *Bastam and Kharghan.* Retrieved from http://whc.unesco.org/en/tentativelists/5198/

World Economic Forum (WEF). (2017). *The travel & tourism competitiveness report (2017). Paving the way for a more sustainable and inclusive future.* Gland: WEF. Retrieved from http://www3.weforum.org/docs/WEF_TTCR_2017_web_0401.pdf

World Tourism Organization (UNWTO). (2011). *Religious tourism in Asia and the Pacific.* Madrid, Spain: UNWTO.

World Tourism Organization (UNWTO). (2017). *Contribution of Islamic culture and its impact on the Asian tourism market.* Madrid, Spain: UNWTO.

Zamani-Farahani, H. (2010). Iran: Tourism, heritage and religion. In N. Scott & J. Jafari (Eds.), *Tourism in the Muslim world* (pp. 205–218). Bingley: Emerald Group Publishing.

Zamani-Farahani, H. & Henderson, J. C. (2010). Islamic tourism and managing tourism development in Islamic societies: The cases of Iran and Saudi Arabia. *International Journal of Tourism Research, 12*(1), 79–89.

Zamani-Farahani, H. & Musa, G. (2012). The relationship between Islamic religiosity and residents' perceptions of socio-cultural impacts of tourism in Iran: Case studies of Sare'in and Masooleh. *Tourism Management, 33*(4), 802–814.

Zubaida, S. (2000). Trajectories of political Islam: Egypt, Iran and Turkey. *The Political Quarterly, 71*(s1), 60–78.

5 The mutual relationship between women's pilgrimage tourism and the religious city: a case study of Mashhad, Iran

Nina Khamsy and Fatemeh Vossughi

Introduction

In contemporary Iran, the ingrained traditional practice of pilgrimage and tourism, or *Jahangardi va ziyarat*, has been rising steadily during the last three decades, due to Iran's rapid population growth accompanied by the country's increased communication and transportation sectors, as well as the apparition of new leisure activities, causing wide-ranging socio-economic impacts on women working in both sectors. This is particularly seen in the religious city of Mashhad, arguably the epicentre of Shiia *Ziyarat* pilgrimage, which is a voluntary movement to pay respect to a person or shrine, whose authority is thereby acknowledged (Tapper, 1990). One of the main impacts of the increase in women's pilgrimages is the presence of a higher proportion of women within the labour force of the shrine in Mashhad (*Haram*), and in the industries linked to tourism, which poses a fresh challenge to the common view that Islamic practices such as pilgrimage result in the exclusion of women from public life. To solve this seeming dilemma, questions relating to the way the religious-tourism nexus plays out in Iranian society and the opportunities that *Jahangardi va ziyarat* creates for women, remain to be explored.

This chapter explores key issues of the relationship between women performing pilgrimage tourism on one hand, and women who are involved in the religious city, as workers or volunteers, on the other. This 'mutual relationship' refers to how women pilgrims relate and perceive the city of Mashhad other than a destination for pilgrimage to visit the Shrine of Imam Reza. By examining the other activities undertaken under the theme of *Jahangardi* (tourism), the wide range of opportunities for women in the tourism industry become clearer.

A variety of profane and spiritual motivations explain a trip to Imam Reza's Shrine. In turn, scholars have shown that tourism can offer an avenue to women such as leadership in community and political life as well as vital employment and entrepreneurial opportunities (Figueroa-Domecq, Pritchard, Segovia-Pérez, Morgan, & Villacé-Molinero, 2015). It can be a tool of economic development from a gender perspective (Swain, 1995). Little research has been conducted on women's *Jahangardi* linked to pilgrimage in Iran. A closer look at women's own perception is essential to understand the extent of opportunities this industry is offering to women and how they make use of it.

An expanding body of knowledge is addressing the issues of Muslim women's pilgrimage (Adelkhah, 1999, 2009; Ghadially, 2005; Honarpisheh, 2013) but very limited literature has articulated the links between pilgrimage and tourism (e.g. Adelkhah, 1999, 2009). Questions linked to the impact of religion on Islamic women's labour market participation and their employment in the touristic industry have largely been overlooked (Jafari & Scott, 2014; Sönmez, 2001). This chapter is an attempt to fill this void with a new angle to the study of the complex pilgrimage–tourism relationship by tackling how Islamic women relate to *Jahangardi va ziarat* in Iran.

Through theoretical and empirical analyses of the case study of the religious city of Mashhad, it becomes clear that pilgrimage sites, far from perpetuating strict doctrinal practices and women's exclusion, are places enabling women to travel for pilgrimage and leisure activities. Human mobility for leisure and religious purposes in Iran carves new socio-economic spaces for women and can lead to their economic empowerment. Pilgrimage tourism has resulted in the inclusion of more women into public life through their employment or participation in organising the pilgrimage. However, these processes have only slightly led to the enhancement of their economic status and participation in decision-making processes.

The study

This study is based on fieldwork conducted by both authors in the city of Mashhad, using semi-structured interviews with women performing their pilgrimage, volunteer women in Mashhad working in the Shrine and women involved in the tourism sector. The authors also carried out participant observation among the managers, volunteers and pilgrims within the shrine and *imamzadehs* (shrine-tombs of a descendant or relative of a Shiia Imam) in the context of their daily lives. The fieldwork lasted from May to July 2017 and the research was supplemented with a two-year-long study of urban planning patterns and tourism in Mashhad with the Amir Kabir Research Center. Informants are from a range of socio-economic backgrounds but almost all of them attended higher education. These samples cannot lead to established frequencies but they do show the range of responses.

The analysis of the data was concentrated mainly on two issues: first, the motivations of women pilgrims visiting Mashhad and of women involved in delivering activities linked to tourism and pilgrimage; and, second, the way pilgrimage and tourism are interlinked in their practices. The authors faced challenges in this research regarding the access to precise data on the exact numbers of women embarking on these journeys to Mashhad, gender division of labour and the evolution of the gender repartition over time. This chapter is to be considered as an introduction to further thorough investigations on the opportunities of *Jahangardi va ziarat*.

Islamisation and female employment in Iran

The relation between Iranian society's Islamisation and women's employment enables a contextualisation of women's role as workers in tourism and pilgrimage sites. The Pahlavi regime's (1925–1979) perception of women was engrained in the process of Western-inspired modernisation. These policies were mostly favouring women from privileged social backgrounds but did little for working-class women as well as for those with a degree of religious adherence (Velayati, 2012). In contrast, post-revolutionary Islamisation policies on women have emphasised women's modesty, chastity and dignity in conformity to the traditional norms and conceptions of morality (Velayati, 2012). The implementation of gender segregation is aimed to protect these values. Some scholars see these policies as a repressive mechanism excluding women from the public sphere, especially from the labour market (Afshar, 1985, 1997; Hoodfar, 1999; Moghadam, 1999; Poya, 1999). A more nuanced view posits that women's involvement in politics and their new reading of gender relations have led to reforms in law, education and employment (Kian, 1997). Islamisation coincided with women's higher access to education and involvement in the public sphere, especially for women from low-income or religious backgrounds (Bahramitash & Esfahani, 2011). Different political gender policies, depending on the support of religious ideologies, play a crucial role 'in the expansion or contraction of potential opportunities for women, and their socioeconomic status within their family and the wider society' (Velayati, 2012, p. 130). Women's involvement in the tourism industry is linked to contemporary gender policies.

The conditions of entry of Iranian women on the tourism industry can face challenges. Gender is a notable form of division between workers, with visible differences in the way women and men are involved in the production and consumption of tourism (Apostolopoulos, Sönmez, & Timothy, 2001; Swain, 1995), as well as receipt of economic benefits (Harvey, Hunt, & Harris, 1995), long recognised. In Iran where gender segregation is encoded, these differences are more pronounced. The conformity of the activity with the rule of women's modesty are required. In addition, the encoded gendered division of labour creates categories of jobs exclusively to be exercised by women, with a set of opportunities and challenges.

Contextualising *Jahangardi va Ziyarat*

A substantial literature has discussed the links between tourism and spirituality, but these links prove misleading when applied to a particular Muslim context, such as that of Iran. There are two main perspectives on the relationship between tourists and pilgrims in Western academic literature (Timothy & Olsen, 2005). The first approach points to their interconnectedness, while the other points to their divergence.

The first perspective on pilgrimage tourism does not conceive pilgrims as tourists. This perspective divides travellers 'whose motivations are deeply spiritual from those motivated by pleasure, education, curiosity, altruism, and relaxation'

(Timothy & Olsen, 2005, p. 6). While pilgrims are associated with humble and sensitive values, tourists are seen as hedonistic, consuming more services and expressing more needs (Cohen, 1992). The insistence of the seeming opposition between 'tourism and faith/religion/spirituality' has delayed adequate research on the mutual relationship of pilgrimage and tourism (Stausberg, 2014, p. 349). The second perspective is more widely shared: tourists and pilgrims as similar, embodied in the same individual. Smith suggests the existence of a continuum or range of nuances varying between religion and tourism with ranging degrees of secularity or religiosity (Smith, 1992). Her pilgrim–tourist continuum, which has been widely reflected upon by other scholars, replicates the traveller's purpose, with 'pious pilgrim' and 'secular tourist' at the two poles, within different levels of religious–secular combinations. Smith's (1992) classification helps account for the numerous hybrid practices of mobility, yet the categories of 'secular' and 'religious', and the tensions they raise when they are combined vary greatly from one cultural context to another.

There are at least three shortcomings with both views. First, as noted by Jafari and Scott (2014), these topics are mostly discussed without reference to a particular religion. Therefore, 'there is an implicit assumption that the study of spirituality or pilgrimage does not require a detailed understanding of the religion in which they are embedded' (Jafari & Scott, 2014, p. 1). Second, this body of work often does not discuss the non-pilgrimage travel behaviour by the faith's adherents. Third, in the secular–religious nexus on which both approaches rely, these concepts are presenting without contextualising the meaning that they dialectically have in their specific socio-cultural environment. Secularism needs to be contextualised by looking at the politics in place, and understanding the secular domain as the ground from which the religious domain emerges provides a normative conception of religion as well as politics (Asad, 2003; Mahmood, 2009). In the case of the Islamic Republic of Iran, the state and the religious authority are central in defining the form of secularism, and the restrictions of tourism/secular practices.

As presented, the study of Islam challenges these academic works. In the Islamic faith, the hybridity of pilgrim–tourism is accentuated since 'the boundaries of the spiritual and secular are transcended' (Jafari & Scott, 2014, p. 1). The holy book *Quran* provides guidance in all aspects of human activity (Aziz, 2001), and tackles travelling as a way to reach God (Quran 29, pp. 19–20). Travel is encouraged both physically and conceptually (Aziz, 2001). The Quran not only promotes travel for pilgrimage, but also as a mean to trade, explore and learn (e.g. 62:10, 16:14, 5:96). For both individuals and governments, religion is the main influence of tourism choices and the different forms of practising it (Jafari & Scott, 2014). The motivations of the faith's adherent who is performing 'tourism' can be rooted in religious incentives.

In the Iranian context, as noted by Adelkhah (2016), tourism and pilgrimage (*Jahangardi va ziyarat*) is commonly used by travellers who combine devotion and secular activities. Similarly, *Jahangardi* (tourism) and *tejarat* (trade) are commonly performed together (Adelkhah, 2016). Travelling is central to the Islamic faith, yet pilgrims' motivations are not purely based on the strict following of dogmatic rules. As Eickelman and Piscatori (1990, p. xiv) suggest, pilgrims' motivations 'are inevitably mixed – a combination of holy reason and social, economic, and political concerns'. A study of the historical context and how individuals perceive opportunities is therefore to be taken into account.

Interestingly, the academic debate about whether pilgrimage and tourism are dichotomous or interconnected is echoed in the domestic Iranian context. Mostly coming from conservative clerics, tourism can be viewed as embedded in negative influences and depravity, while pilgrimage is seen as pure and in need of protection (Alamolhoda, 2016). This discourse resonates with the revolutionary rhetoric whereby 'secularity' is associated with the pejorative term of 'Westernisation' and is antagonistic to Islamic values. Other clerics consider the opportunities that tourism brings for pilgrimage. Since tourism is a significant international economic activity encouraging mobility, tourism should be developed according to religious and temporal requirement (Tasnim News, 2016). This shows that secularism, religiosity and their interface are constantly re-defined and negotiated as a matter of contemporary politics.

These disagreements have practical effects on the management of tourism and pilgrimage in Mashhad. Even though tourism is unanimously held as having high economic spinoffs by the interviewees, the collaboration between organisations related to tourism is greatly lacking. This is due to a lack of a systematic approach, weak legal structure, poor planning, a lack of integrated tourism management and a weak policy-making system (Azizpour & Fathizadeh, 2016). An integrated approach is required to use all the opportunities.

Ziyarat is a form of pilgrimage enabling a great degree of flexibility, and performing it in Mashhad is seen as almost equivalent to *Hajj* for many Iranians. Whereas *Hajj* to the *Kaba* (House of God) is the most sacred form of pilgrimage for Muslims guided by normative rules and fixed rituals, *ziyarat* is a voluntary movement practised in a variety of forms with unwritten rules, reflecting the cultural diversity of Islam and the influences of geography, domestic custom, as well as religious tradition (Tapper, 1990; Khosronejad, 2012; Ebadi, 2015). *Ziyarat* has a significant socio-economic role in Shiia societies. In many parts of Iran, pilgrims visiting Imam Reza and Mashhad enjoy a particular social prestige when they come back to their hometown. In many areas, *Mashhadi*, as a nickname, is given to someone undertaking Imam Reza's pilgrimage. This is a replication of the custom to assign the denomination *Hajji* to someone who comes back from a pilgrimage to Mecca. *Mashhadi* can be added at the beginning or at the end of the pilgrim's name. The flexible yet important character of *ziyarat* enables a dynamic evolution of women's role in these rituals.

The study of women enables us to shed a particular light on the pilgrimage–tourism relationship. In Iranian pilgrimage sites and religious rituals, women make up a substantial number of believers and play a central role (Adelkhah, 2009; Betteridge, 1992; Honarpisheh, 2013; Kamalkhani, 1993; Tapper, 1990; Torab, 1996). Visits to pilgrimage sites go with pilgrim women asserting themselves in public spaces, where they 'acquire specific expertise; develop specific forms of socialising … The pilgrimage … becomes the visible aspect of changing social meanings' (Adelkhah, 2009, p. 42). Both private and public Shiia rituals are important sites for female assertion in public life.

The religious city of Mashhad

Since the 1970s, religiously motivated travels have constantly increased in Iran and one of the main destination is the city of Mashhad. Mashhad is located in the north-east of Iran. It is the third largest city of pilgrimage in the Muslim world after Mecca and Medina and has approximately 3 million inhabitants. For Shia Muslims, Mashhad is held as the most sacred city because it hosts the shrine of Imam Reza. Travellers visiting Mashhad amount to more than 20 million people a year, and that number is continuing to increase. According to the head of the security department, there are no specific plans or promotion from Astan Quds Razavi to encourage the shrine to increase the number of pilgrims. There are only side programmes such as initiating young people residing in Mashhad. Women represent approximately half of the travellers, estimated at 48% (Municipality of Mashhad, 2015). Precise data about the number of pilgrims are difficult to obtain. As noted by Russell (1999), the problem of differentiating between pilgrims and other tourists can be seen in the official statistics, where existing figures tend to combine travellers with religious, business and cultural motivations. This is, again, due to the pilgrimage–tourism hybridisation.

In the twentieth century, the increased number of journeys undertaken to visit Imam Reza Shrine were guided by diverse kinds of incentives and varied due to a series of infrastructural improvements. The building in itself has historically been the object of different interpretations from governments in terms of its main purpose. With the 'secularisation' programme of the Pahlavi regime (1925–1979), a series of renovations and transformations was initiated to the shrine with a process of 'museumising' the shrine to shrink the spiritual meaning of the shrine (Gurkas, 2012, p. 133). Indeed, Iran's modern institutionalised tourism occurred after the Pahlavi took power in 1925 at a period when *ziyarat* was gradually replaced by the modern secular practice of *siyahat* (explorations as a tourist) (Karimi, 2017). After the 1979 revolution, the newly established Islamic republic supported further development of the shrine (Gurkas, 2012, p. 133) to welcome the increased number of travellers. Iran experienced a rapid population growth accompanied by government measures to increase the country's communication and transportation sectors internally and with its neighbours, leading to an increase in both domestic and outbound tourism, as well as new leisure activities (Alipour, Kilic, & Zamani, 2013; Sheykhi, 2004).

The shrine is a total of 225,223 m^2 and in the last ten years, gradually, more space has been allocated to women pilgrims in the shrine. In addition to the mausoleums, the shrine hosts multiple halls for seminaries and ceremonies, libraries, Islamic research centres and a university. Out of the 30 porticos inside the shrine, eight of them are exclusively for women (all located on the northern side of the shrine), eight others are exclusively for men and the remaining 14 are mixed (family suites). The main and most sacred part of the shrine – the Holy Burial

Chamber – was divided in 2016 along gender lines to offer more space to women. A hall has also been turned into a dormitory for women with the capacity of hosting over 800 people – such halls have existed for men for decades. According to the head of the security department, who is a female cleric, women need more facilities than men, but they are often assigned to spaces where the access is more challenging (i.e. narrower entrance or difficult access through staircase) yet more women would need accessible facilities because they perform pilgrimage while being pregnant, when they are elderly or are accompanied by their toddlers.

Jahangardi and women in Mashhad

Performing *Jahangardi* in Mashhad aside from the main pilgrimage is an ancient practice, which the municipality has encouraged with the construction of new infrastructures in the last 20 years. The main touristic activity while on pilgrimage is to go shopping at the Bazaars surrounding the shrine to buy *soghatis* (souvenirs). Pilgrims perceive Mashhad as famous for the parks and the nearby outdoor space of Torghabeh-Shandiz and for its nearby poets' tombs, mainly Ferdowsi's tomb in Tus. These places are advertised by Astan Quds publications as 'touristic attractions'. The *Guide Map of Mashhad City and the Holy Shrine Complex of Imam Reza (PBUH)* (Astan Quds Razavi Department of Propagation and Islamic Relations, 2013) is an official document of the shrine including a list of 'Some Touristic Attractions of Mashhad and Its Surroundings'. In addition, in the last two decades, a number of facilities for the development of tourist attractions in Mashhad have emerged, which resulted in the construction of more sites such as the 'Western' shopping malls, fast food restaurants such as *Proma*, and the water park *Sarzamine Mojhaye Aabi* ('Water Waves Land'), one of the largest water parks of the country. Luxurious restaurants and hotels have been built in the whole city. As Niloufar, a school teacher who came from Yazd with her family explained:

> I come to visit Imam Reza at least once a year with my three children and we always go to the aquatic park after the pilgrimage. It is in part why my children are looking forward to coming to Mashhad every time.

This vision of Mashhad is shared among other informants who travel with their young children. Even though for many pilgrims, pilgrimage is itself an activity associated with leisure, the growth of recreational centres in the city has been one of the prerequisites for the development of 'secular' planned tourism.

These new infrastructures are considered as opportunities for women's employment, especially for female university students, but the harsh economic situation does not allow to draw any conclusions as to whether it is economically empowering. As one of the informants who studies French literature at Ferdowsi University of Mashhad reported:

> I have chosen to study French and many students chose to study foreign languages like English and Arabic, with the perspective to work in one of the

international hotels as a translator or receptionist. Tourism is a fascinating sector to work in, but these academic and professional skills will be helpful if we decide to move to another sector or to study abroad, too.

Indeed, opportunities brought with tourism in Mashhad affect women and men alike, especially in times of recession. It brought a range of limited entrepreneurship initiatives for women, with agencies organising women-only tours. In contrast, the shrine, with its strict gender division, offers a more fertile ground specifically for women, to be more present in the public sphere.

Ziarat and women in Imam Reza Shrine

As of July 2017, according to the shrine's official statistics, there are 16,000 women and 42,000 men working in the shrine. Women are involved in a variety of sections, but around 70%, approximately 1,000 a year, are active in the security apparatus. The bomb attack in 1994 during Ashura (a mourning ritual) in the heart of the shrine of Imam Reza increased radically the authorities' awareness of the need for a greater security apparatus. Enhanced security measures were taken by the shrine as well as the city. One of the first changes was to employ more women at the entrance for body inspection to perform controls on women entering the shrine. Instead of banning women from the shrine, another strategy has been used to adapt to the growing number of visitors.

Other positions include women working in the lost properties office (*peidashodegan*) and, since 2011, in carpet service (preparing women's prayer rooms) and female doctors are based in the emergency department. Female drivers also drive women-only buses and finally, since 2016, a new employment has been the 'shoes' keeper' (*Kafshdari*), which enables avoidance of contact with male pilgrims. According to the manager of women's security, more than four thousand women are working in the religious teaching section. They are more or less equally divided between different offices, which include religious enquiries and answers (established in 1988), prayer recital (*namaz*), Quranique readings and classes, and dispute resolution (established in 1994). The Kindergarten (*Kabotarane*) section was newly established in 2016. Women employed in these sectors gain a higher status as they occupy skilled jobs and, to some extent, positions of authority. However, a woman cannot be a candidate to become a *mujtahid* (a jurist who exercises *ijtihad*, independent reasoning, to interpret Islamic law) and give legal decisions. However, in this case again, women occupy positions that enable them to take roles in public spaces.

Women play a key role in using these services but also in financing them. The religious foundation of Astan Quds Razavi was established with the aim to administer the property and revenue of the Shrine of Imam Reza, which mainly comes from *warf*. These are endowments whereby people finance social services, charitable or family purposes. Muslim women play a major role in contributing to *warfs* of Astan Quds and it is of common knowledge in Iran that the phenomenon of pilgrim women's endowments in Mashhad has deep-rooted historical ties.

For example, the Goharshad Mosque, which is a former independent mosque built on what is the actual Imam Reza Shrine complex, was built by the order of Empress Goharshad, the wife of Sultan Shahrokh of the Timurid Dynasty in the fifteenth century. Today, Goharshad Mosque is one of the prayer halls incorporated within the Imam Reza shrine complex. Today, this institution is the largest economic, religious and cultural non-state power in Iran. The 'multi-functional' shrine as a charitable institution taking care of the poor and the needy illustrates the secular–religious nature of the institution.

Pilgrimage tourism and women's social and physical mobility

A variety of profane and spiritual motivations explain a journey to Imam Reza's Shrine. The range of motivations greatly varies with the age, social class and perception of what constitutes women's role in the Iranian society.

In the 1990s, the tourism industry responded to women's special needs by creating tours for women. It became a way to help the pilgrims who were travelling alone to overcome the limitations on their physical mobility and make the journey more enjoyable. The first women-only tours were organised for female students from the University of Mashhad and then expanded to all Iranian women tourists. As one woman who created one of the first women-only tour operators explains:

> When I created my tour operator in Mashhad, it was very well received by the city's and the shrine's authorities. This service was answering to a logistical problem that many women and their families were facing and that could easily be solved.

Indeed, a main challenge for Iranian women travelling in their country, as well as in other parts of the word, is the danger of being harassed, and in addition, to be travelling alone without a 'mahram' (Toodeh Roostah, 2016). A woman's mahram is a male relative with whom marriage is not permitted. Based on this traditionalist approach, a woman travelling alone is negatively perceived and raises suspicion. However, this concerns only a margin of pilgrims, who are mainly from older generations or young unmarried girls perceived as in need of being protected. Pilgrims in this situation can turn to the touristic industry which helps women whose main declared purpose of travelling is the pilgrimage, by enabling them to embark on one of their many tours exclusively for women, organised by agencies for pilgrimage. These tours specially serve women who, whether voluntarily or involuntarily, are travelling alone. The pattern of women pilgrims' visits to Mashhad depends on the time of year. The main religious celebrations at the shrine include Ashura, which takes place on the tenth day of Muharram (the first month of the Islamic calendar) to mourn Hussein ibn Ali, and the day of Imam Reza's martyrdom, celebrated on 23 August every year. During these periods, pilgrims tend to stay for an average of four days. During the rest of the year, the majority of pilgrims stay for one or two days. On the local level, Imam Reza is also celebrated every Wednesday, when Mashhad's residents who have *Nazr* (to make a spiritual vow) come to pay homage and pray.

It is common that individuals – men and women alike – refer to the travel motivation of pilgrimage as a cover to perform other, more 'secular' activities (Adelkhah, 2016). In practice, the status of pilgrim, perceived as embedded in high moral reputation and ethical values, enables individuals to avoid administrative procedures such as customs checks, and to be under less social scrutiny to perform leisure activities (Adelkhah, 2016). In this vein, resorting to pilgrimage for annual or weekly ceremonies enables some young female students to travel under less social constraints and visit relatives or friends in the city.

Social mobility initiated for the visit to Mashhad comes hand-in-hand with pilgrim women asserting themselves in a variety of different public circles. In the 1990s, scholars such as Betteridge (1992) established that local pilgrimage offered mainly three practices to women: religiously, they play a crucial role in rituals; socially, it offers an arena where they can meet with one another in an approved setting; and personally, it provides women a place in which to experience contact with divinity. However, over 20 years later, a new aspect needs to be added to this list. More women are working in the shrine; the 'professional' level can be added – even if it is volunteering. Their work inside the shrine provides a platform to climb up to other positions entailing more responsibilities, even if they are minor, such as becoming head of as sub-section. For example, Masoumeh used to work in giving directions to pilgrims in different sites and after a few years she became the head of a sub-section of women in these sectors and gained supervisory skills.

Entrepreneurial opportunities for women increase with women's visits to sites around the shrine. The first and main activity after having visited the shrine, is the visit to other religious sites, such as visits to *imamzadehs*. In the city and in the neighbourhood of Mashhad, the most-visited imamzadehs are those of the two brothers Naser and Yaser in Toqabe, a centre of national and international pilgrimage, Yahya in Miami, Ghiasodin Mohamad, Seid Mohamad Alavi and the Ghadamgah (literally, 'the walked place') in Neishabur (where it is said the Imam Reza walked). A female ritual consists of 'walking towards the *imamzadeh*' over two kilometres, which is a ritual only performed by women. This practice gives rise to a variety of small-scale entrepreneurial opportunities by women, such as paid assistance to elderly women who cannot walk alone or the sale of beverages and clothes.

The *Khoddam-e Eftekhary*, the honoured worker

In recent years, there has been an expansion of female presence in the shrine; as of July 2016, women count as almost half of the work force within it, which represents approximately a tenfold increase since the 1980s. Before the 1979 revolution, a person working in the shrine was called *Khoddam* (service provider) and they were paid for their services, but after the revolution, they were called *Eftekhary*; which means 'volunteer', and literally, 'honoured'. They work without financial compensation on a part-time basis. *Eftekhary* women from a range of different socio-economic backgrounds share the idea that it would seem offensive to get paid for their labour, since employment inside the shrine is seen as an honour. In this regard, one of the informants stated that:

> When I come to the *Haram*, I feel closer to Imam Reza. I can discuss with him about my thoughts and I know he listens to me. He was a deeply good person and I respect him for what he did during his life. I enjoy working in this peaceful atmosphere. I don't want to be paid to perform this. I also enjoy the companionship of my co-workers and the social life it creates.

This view is shared by other informants who also believe that they will be rewarded in the hereafter. They say they are not willing to exchange this reward with a monetary reward.

Eftekhary put into sharper focus the interconnectedness between the religious and the secular elements, and also problematise the division between work and personal leisure (as also noted by Kinnaird & Hall, 1996). The contribution of the *Eftekhary* is 'holy', and the retribution is given in a currency within the spiritual realm as well, which consists of a personal journey and transformation. In addition, it is socially rewarding and expands one's network. In some cases, this contribution is later praised and *Eftekhary* workers tend to be associated with ethical attributes and virtuous moral reputations from their extended family. As one of the informants explains:

> It is not easy to be selected to work in the *Haram*. We have to be successful at a series of oral and written examinations and our educational and professional backgrounds are put under scrutiny. At least two referees are also contacted to verify the candidate's social record.

The selective process also highlights that only a particular profile of *Eftekhary* is deemed to conform to the requirements of the shrine. Working as an *Eftekhary* is a valuable position and it is seen by our informants as enhancing the chances of being employed at a higher level within the shrine or in another organisation of Astan Quds at a later stage.

Conclusion

This chapter has highlighted the mutual relationship between women and the religious city by showing, on one hand, some of the impacts of the increase in the number of visitors in Mashhad due to higher mobility and, on the other, the opportunities it created for women who are involved in the religious city, as workers or volunteers. Mashhad is perceived as a destination for pilgrimage to visit the Shrine of Imam Reza, as well as an occasion for social gatherings and activities undertaken under the theme of *Jahangardi* (tourism). This interconnection creates a wide range of opportunities for women in the tourism industry in the new infrastructures built for leisure activities such as the hotels, restaurants and aquatic parks.

The chapter analysed the different ways women are involved in the pilgrimage–tourism nexus and the motivations of women visiting and working in the shrine. Putting women under sharper focus in this context enabled us to shed a new light on the interplay between pilgrimage and tourism in a particular historical and cultural context. For example, some women visiting Mashhad as pilgrims and tourists can use the hybridity of pilgrimage and tourism to travel for leisure as well as for the pilgrimage. For some women of the older generations or younger women, these trips can overcome the challenge previously faced by women wishing to travel on their own. The development of pilgrimage tourism tours offers now greater avenues for their physical mobility.

Can it be then concluded that pilgrimage tourism is economically empowering women? The answer should be nuanced since two sectors (the one inside and the one outside the shrine) respond to different dynamics. On one hand, the tourism industry linked to pilgrimage practices in Mashhad brings a number of new employment opportunities for women, including women's entrepreneurship initiatives in organising women-only tours. On the other hand, these opportunities are limited and they affect a low number of women, especially in difficult economic times.

In aspects linked to women working in the shrine, they can actively be engaged in organising the pilgrimage. Employment in the security, religious teaching and educational sector within the shrine redefines individual women's agency because they can edict opinions and educate and they are placed in skilled jobs and positions of authority, to some extent. Even if their positions are unpaid, they find the motivation to work. Problematising the dichotomy between what is considered work and leisure in a secular sense enables a better grasp of the link between pilgrimage and tourism on individuals working as volunteers within holy sites. The particular 'benefits' that Muslim women gain from performing *ziyarat* and working in the *Haram* cannot fully be understood through secular glasses. Such an approach may consider *Eftekhary* workers as exploited since they are unpaid. As this chapter indicated, faith's adherents working in the *Haram* can find social, personal and professional rewards. The outcome of the interviews shows that women are celebrated by their entourage and add to the high moral standing of their families. Since pilgrimage is positively perceived socially, it can enhance chances of social mobility, even in other paid employments, participating to an empowerment. For example, pilgrim women using their language skills as workers in the shrine can use this experience to work in other industries in the tourism sector. However, few women are leading decision-makers, and at 'management' levels, which remain male-dominated. In addition, a woman cannot be a candidate to become a *mujtahid* and give legal decisions. On this matter, an interviewee pointed out that even women working in giving religious advice only provide what has been previously thought. They do not formulate their personal opinions.

Limitations to this research were linked to the access to precise data and the suspicion raised by officials when they were approached for interviews. This is disturbing because a better understanding of these practices helps the implementation of more adequate infrastructures. It is commonly agreed that women's pilgrimage has economic spinoff effects.

Further examination such as the interaction between pilgrims and the hospitality, restoration and transportation sectors, is needed. Linking pilgrimage and tourism to issues of gender brings many questions as to how to manage tourism sustainably with a gender perspective, especially in the context of a gradual economic transition and expansion. This analysis, if replicated with more attention to social class and differences among generations in the Muslim context, can bring a range of new interesting areas for further research and provide new insights in tourism studies. Travels based on religious and leisure incentives remain to be explored in other modern phenomena such as the practise of *sigheh* (temporary marriage) or the 'martyr pilgrimage' (visits to war torn sites), tackling notions of nationalism. Journeys for leisure or spiritual travels in Iran are steadily rising, bringing new practical implications as well as ways to conceive social change.

Acknowledgements

The authors would like to thank Shadi Ahmadi for her assistance and her precious contribution to this research as well as Bernard Schéou and Shahnaz Nadjmabadi for their comments and suggestions on an earlier draft of this chapter.

References

Adelkhah, F. (1999). *Being modern in Iran*. London: C. Hurst & Co. Publishers.
Adelkhah, F. (2009). Moral economy of pilgrimage and civil society in Iran: Religious, commercial and tourist trips to Damascus. *South African Historical Journal, 61*(1), 38–53.
Adelkhah, F. (2016). *The thousand and one borders of Iran: Travel and identity*. London: Routledge.
Afshar, H. (1985). *Women, work, and ideology in the third world*. London: Tavistock Publications.
Afshar, H. (1997). Women and work. *Political Studies, 45*(4), 755–767.
Alamolhoda. (2016). *There should be no nefast currents on the pilgrimage culture in Mashhad*. Retrieved from http://alamolhoda.com/post/2423
Alipour, H., Kilic, H., & Zamani, N. (2013). The untapped potential of sustainable domestic tourism in Iran. *Anatolia, 24*(3), 468–483.
Apostolopoulos, Y., Sönmez, S. F., & Timothy, D. J. (Eds.). (2001). *Women as producers and consumers of tourism in developing regions*. Westport, CT: Greenwood Publishing Group.
Asad, T. (2003). *Formations of the secular: Christianity, Islam, modernity*. Stanford, CA: Stanford University Press.
Astan Quds Razavi Department of Propagation and Islamic Relations. (2013). *Guide map of Mashhad City and the Holy Shrine complex of Imam Reza (PBUH)*. Mashhad: Astan Quds Razavi Publication.
Aziz, H. (2001). The journey: An overview of tourism and travel in the Arab Islamic context. In D. Harrison (Ed.), *Tourism and the less developed world: Issues and case studies* (pp. 151–160). Wallingford: CABI.

Azizpour, F. & Fathizadeh, F. (2016). Barriers to collaboration among tourism industry stakeholders. Case study: Mashhad Metropolis. *Almatourism-Journal of Tourism, Culture and Territorial Development, 7*(13), 48–65.

Bahramitash, R. & Esfahani, H. S. (2011). *Veiled employment: Islamism and the political economy of women's employment in Iran.* Syracuse, NY: Syracuse University Press.

Betteridge, A. (1992). Specialization in miraculous action: Some shrines in Shiraz. In A. Morinis (Ed.), *Sacred journeys: The anthropology of pilgrimage* (pp. 189–210). Westport, CT: Greenwood Publishing Group.

Cohen, E. (1992). Pilgrimage centers: Concentric and excentric. *Annals of Tourism Research, 19*(1), 33–50.

Ebadi, M. (2015). Forms of pilgrimage at the Shrine of Khāled Nabi, Northeastern Iran. *International Journal of Religious Tourism and Pilgrimage, 3*(1), 66–78.

Eickelman, D. F. & Piscatori, J. (1990). *Muslim travellers: Pilgrimage, migration and the religious imagination.* London: Routledge.

Figueroa-Domecq, C., Pritchard, A., Segovia-Pérez, M., Morgan, N., & Villacé-Molinero, T. (2015). Tourism gender research: A critical accounting. *Annals of Tourism Research, 52*, 87–103.

Ghadially, R. (2005). Devotional empowerment: Women pilgrims, saints and shrines in a South Asian Muslim Sect. *Asian Journal of Women's Studies, 11*(4), 79–101.

Gurkas, H. (2012). Innovation in the tradition of saint veneration in Turkey. In P. Khosronejad (Ed.), *Saints and their pilgrims in Iran and neighbouring countries* (pp. 105–142). Wantage: Sean Kingston Publishing.

Harvey, J., Hunt, J., & Harris, C. C. (1995). Gender and community tourism dependence level. *Annals of Tourism Research, 22*(2), 349–366.

Honarpisheh, D. (2013). Women in pilgrimage: Senses, places, embodiment and agency. Experiencing Ziyarat in Shiraz. *Journal of Shi'a Islamic Studies, 6*(4), 383–410.

Hoodfar, H. (1999). *The women's movement in Iran: Women at the crossroads of secularization and Islamization.* Paris: Women Living Under Muslim Laws.

Jafari, J. & Scott, N. (2014). Muslim world and its tourisms. *Annals of Tourism Research, 44*, 1–19.

Kamalkhani, Z. (1993). Women's everyday religious discourse in Iran. In H. Afshar (Ed.), *Women in the Middle East* (pp. 85–95). New York, NY: Springer Publishing.

Karimi, P. (2017). Tourism, voyeurism and the media ecologies of Tehran's mural arts. In J. Skinner & L. Jolliffe (Eds.), *Murals and tourism: Heritage, politics and identity* (pp. 75–92). Abingdon: Routledge.

Khosronejad, P. (2012). *Saints and their pilgrims in Iran and neighbouring countries.* Wantage: Sean Kingston Publishing.

Kian, A. (1997). Women and politics in Post-Islamist Iran: The gender conscious drive to change. *British Journal of Middle Eastern Studies, 24*(1), 75–96.

Kinnaird, V. & Hall, D. (1996). Understanding tourism processes: A gender-aware framework. *Tourism Management, 17*(2), 95–102.

Mahmood, S. (2009). Agency, performativity, and the feminist subject. *Pieties and Gender, 9*, 11–46.

Moghadam, V. M. (1999). Revolution, religion, and gender politics: Iran and Afghanistan compared. *Journal of Women's History, 10*(4), 172–195.

Municipality of Mashhad. (2015). *Statistical report on travellers to the religious city.* Mashhad: MUNI Press.

Poya, M. (1999). *Women, work and Islamism: Ideology and resistance in Iran.* London: Zed Books.

Russell, P. (1999). Religious travel in the new millennium. *Travel & Tourism Analyst 5*, 39–68.

Sheykhi, M. T. (2004). Globalizing influences on leisure: A perspective from Iran. *World Leisure Journal, 46*(4), 59–67.

Smith, V. L. (1992). Introduction. The quest in guest. *Annals of Tourism Research, 19*, 1–17.

Sönmez, S. F. (2001). Tourism behind the veil of Islam: Women and development in the Middle East. In Y. Apostolopoulos, S. F. Sönmez, & D. J. Timothy (Eds.), *Women as producers and consumers of tourism in developing regions* (pp. 113–142). Westport, CT: Praeger.

Stausberg, M. (2014). Religion and spirituality in tourism. In A. A. Lew, C. M. Hall, & A. M. Williams (Eds.), *The Wiley Blackwell companion to tourism* (pp. 349–360). Hoboken, NJ: John Wiley & Sons.

Swain, M. B. (1995). Gender in tourism. *Annals of Tourism Research, 22*(2), 247–266.

Tapper, N. (1990). Ziyarat: Gender, movement, and exchange in a Turkish community. In D. F. Eickelman & J. P. Piscatori (Eds.), *Muslim travellers: Pilgrimage, migration, and the religious imagination* (pp. 236–255). Berkeley, CA: University of California Press.

Tasnim News. (2016). *Pilgrimage tourism should be developed according to religious and temporal requirements.* Retrieved from https://www.tasnimnews.com/fa/news/1395/12/14/1345246

Timothy, D. J. & Olsen, D. H. (Eds.). (2005). *Tourism, religion, and spiritual journeys.* New York, NY: Routledge.

Toodeh Roostah, F. (2016). Limits to women's tourism in Iran. Mahdudiat Zanan Dar Gardeshari-e Iran. *Modiryar.* Retrieved from http://www.modiryar.com/management-topics/woman/4535

Torab, A. (1996). Piety as gendered agency: A study of Jalaseh ritual discourse in an aurban neighbourhood in Iran. *The Journal of the Royal Anthropological Institute, 2*(2), 235–252.

Velayati, M. (2012). The Iranian State's religo-ideological policies and their impact on young migrant women in Tabriz. In H. Afshar (Ed.), *Women and fluid identities: Strategic and practical pathways selected by women* (pp. 127–145). London: Palgrave Macmillan.

6 Mass faith tourism and life satisfaction of residents: evidence from Mashhad, Iran

Hossein G. T. Olya

Introduction

Faith tourism, also referred to as spiritual tourism or religious tourism, is a significant segment of the international tourism industry. Technological development has facilitated mass faith tourism (Tala & Padurean, 2008). Visitors are interested in visiting holy places for different reasons, as a contribution in heritage or culture, for sense of curiosity, or even to enjoy the uniqueness of that holy place (Wong, Ryan, & McIntosh, 2013). According to Olsen and Timothy (2006), faith tourism has been assumed as one of the oldest forms of non-economic journeys. The concept of pilgrimage, for example, is recognized in many religious belief systems. Faith tourism, in relation to Islamic roles and policies at various levels of governance, is one of the most developed forms of tourism in Iran (Dadpour, Mohamed, & Sirat, 2009). However, faith tourism may have a potentially significant influence on the level of resident satisfaction in tourism destinations (Alipour, Olya, & Forouzan, 2017), particularly given its growth in many areas of the country (see Chapter 4, this volume).

A better understanding of residents' perceptions and attitudes toward tourism and tourism expansion can help policy makers and planners to develop better strategies to provide quality services to visitors and residents alike as well as contribute to sustainable tourism growth and development (Hall, 2008). Indeed, by understanding residents' concerns and problems, policy makers achieve a better support for tourism from the host community and can also improve the quality of residents' lives (Kim, Uysal, & Sirgy, 2013).

Mashhad has long been regarded as a politically and economically influential city in Iran, but is mostly famous for its hosting of the shrine of the eighth *Shiite* Imam Reza. The city's substantial growth of population during holidays and religious occasions as a result of increased visitation has led to significant increases in hotel occupancy as well as flow-on effects for other economic sectors (see Chapter 4, this volume). It hosts pilgrims from a wide range of neighboring Muslim countries in addition to the substantial number of domestic faith tourists it receives.

This chapter investigates the effects of socio-cultural, economic, and environmental impacts of faith tourism on the life satisfaction of Mashhad's residents.

This is significant as Mashhad is the most visited faith tourism destination in Iran which is officially promoted by the government (see Chapter 4, this volume for statistical details). The size of mass faith tourism in Mashhad acts as a magnet for investors and to develop facilities and infrastructure for faith tourists in the city, along with other attractions such as shopping centers (see Chapters 4 and 5, this volume). However, while such tourism-related developments may create economic opportunities, they can also lead to social and environmental changes that can affect life satisfaction. Therefore, it is important to investigate how residents perceive different impacts of faith tourism development in Mashhad and how socio-cultural, economic, and environmental impacts of faith tourism contribute to the life satisfaction of residents.

This study will address three research questions:

• What are the sufficient conditions (i.e., economic impacts) of residents' life satisfaction?
• What are sufficient complex configurations (i.e., combination of impacts of faith tourism) indicating life satisfaction?
• What are the necessary conditions for achieving residents' life satisfaction?

Structural equation modeling is used to investigate the net effect of faith tourism impacts on the life satisfaction of Mashhad's residents. Causal configuration leading to residents' life satisfaction is explored using fsQCA (fuzzy set/Qualitative Comparative Analysis).

Background

Faith tourism is one of Iran's most important types of tourism and almost 30% of international tourists visit Iran for religious and pilgrimage purposes. This compares favorably with business tourists (30%) and visiting friends and relatives (VFR) tourists (26%) (Iran Cultural Heritage, Handcraft and Tourism Organization (ICHTO), (2016). Different Iranian cities tend of offer different types of experiences. For example, Isfahan and Shiraz are best known as historical and cultural destinations whereas Mashhad and Qom are considered the most religious cities in Iran by tourists, especially many local people, interested in visiting these destinations for purposes of pilgrimage (Alipour & Heydari, 2005; UNWTO, 2017).

Located 850 km east of the capital Tehran, Mashhad is regarded to be the second largest city of Iran with a population of 3,131,586 according to the 2011 census and covering an area of 27,478 km^2. The city offers religious and cultural places of interest that attract regional and international travelers and is one of the most important pilgrimage destinations in the Muslim world (UNWTO, 2017). Mashhad is regarded as the holiest city in Iran and its name date backs to the historical event of the death of Imam Reza in 818 AD, the eighth imam of Shiite, who is regarded by Shia as a martyr. Originally a small village called Sanabad, it gradually grew into an urban center after the construction of a holy shrine for Imam Reza and the consequent growth in pilgrimage. The city hosts over

20 million domestic and international tourists each year, many of whom are pilgrims (Alipour et al., 2017; see Chapter 5, this volume, for a discussion of the pilgrim–tourist dichotomy in the context of Mashhad). However, Saghaei and Javanbakht (2013) estimated that the annual number of pilgrims to the city would reach over 27.5 million by 2016. Unfortunately, reliable statistical information on tourism in Iran is not readily available to examine the accuracy of such claims (see Chapters 1 and 2, this volume).

Faith tourism is acting as the engine for growth and development of Mashhad. The Islamic government of Iran places great focus on the facilities and infrastructure of Mashhad and their availability to both domestic and international visitors. Government funding, donations, and private investment has meant that substantial tourism development has occurred in the city particularly in the area of the holy shrine (see Chapter 5, this volume, for further discussion). However, tourism can have critical impacts on community welfare and the wellbeing of residents (Hall & Lew, 2009). The impacts of tourism-related changes can be seen in residents' attitudes and perceptions toward tourists (Gu & Ryan, 2008). The socio-cultural, environmental, and economic impacts of tourism influence the quality of life of the residents (Kim et al., 2013). In response, a strong theme in the tourism-planning literature is the belief that the host community and residents should be highly involved in the process of planning and implementation (Hall, 2008). Residents often have substantial information about destinations and how it could adapt to change (Rasoolimanesh, Jaafar, Ahmad, & Barghi, 2017). In addition, the host community is integral to the destination tourism product and, from a destination management and marketing perspective, should be connected to tourism planning (Olya, Shahmirzdi, & Alipour, 2017).

Even though it is grounded in spirituality and religion, the sheer size of faith tourism therefore potentially has positive (job opportunities and desirable brand image) and negative (pollution, waste, noise) impacts (Alipour et al., 2017; Zhong, Deng, Song, & Ding, 2011). In response, residents may oppose resource overconsumption by visitors. Such conflict of interests may also affect the life satisfaction of the residents (Lee & Chang, 2008) as well as cultural exchange and sense of community (Foruzan, 2014). Crowding is often a significant issue for communities that can lead to negative perspectives of tourism development. However, the generation of job opportunities and economic development due to tourism investment and entrepreneurial activities may positively influence levels of personal and community satisfaction, even though negative effects are recognized, such as increased local costs of living (Kim et al., 2013; Olya et al., 2017).

Research model

This study tries to investigate the effects of the environmental, socio-cultural, and economic impacts of faith tourism on the life satisfaction of Mashhad residents. As shown in Figure 6.1 (a), structural modeling suggests the sufficient factors (e.g., environmental impacts) for indicating outcomes (i.e., life satisfaction). This study also attempts to explore combinations of predictors factors (i.e., a causal

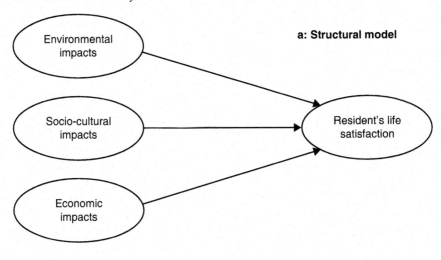

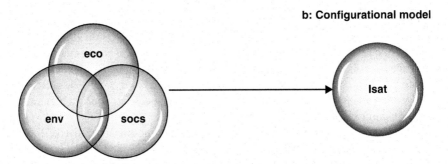

Note: last: life satisfaction of the residents, eco: economic impacts, envi: environmental impacts, soc: socio-cultural impacts of mass faith tourism.

Figure 6.1 Proposed structural (a) and configurational (b) models.

model) leading to high and low levels of life satisfaction. The configurational model depicted in Figure 6.1 (b) illustrates the causal configuration of the environmental, socio-cultural, and economic impacts of faith tourism in indicating residents' life satisfaction.

Method

A structured survey was conducted to measure study variables, the environmental, socio-cultural, economic impacts of faith tourism, and the life satisfaction of residents. The scale items, which were measured using a five-point Likert scale, were adapted from validated scales used in previous research (Gursoy & Rutherford, 2004; Kim et al., 2013; Lee, 2013). Residents of Mashhad who are living around the holy shrine were directly approached to participate in the survey. Using convenience sampling, 103 valid data responses were obtained and used for data analysis. Following Olya and Gavilyan (2016) and Olya and Al-ansi's (2018) studies, measurement, structural, and configurational models were tested. Cronbach's alpha and confirmatory factor analysis model was performed to check reliability and validity of the study measures, respectively. Structural equation modeling (SEM) was used to investigate the net effect of the three categories of impacts of faith tourism on the life satisfaction of Mashhad residents. Causal relationships for indicating life satisfaction were explored using fsQCA. An analysis of necessary conditions was undertaken to identify the necessary faith tourism impacts on Mashhad residents' life satisfaction.

Results

Reliability and validity

The results of measurement model testing are provided in Table 6.1. The values of Cronbach's alpha confirmed reliability of the factors as the alpha coefficient is larger than the recommended level (Cortina, 1993). To check validity of the construct, confirmatory factor analysis was performed. The values of standardized factor loading were larger than the commonly accepted cutoff (> .5) and significantly loaded under assigned factors. The results of fit indices (X^2: 169.669, df = 129, X^2/df = 1.315, IFI = .950, CFI = .948, RMSEA = .057) showed that the proposed measurement model is matched with empirical data (Anderson & Gerbing, 1988; Fornell & Larcker, 1981; Hair, Anderson, Tatham, & Black, 1998).

Results from SEM

The results of SEM are demonstrated in Figure 6.2, which refers to negative aspects of mass faith tourism such as traffic jams and pollution, which reduce the life satisfaction of residents (β = -.29, p < .001). The socio-cultural impacts of life satisfaction improve residents' life satisfaction (β = .32, p < .001). According to the SEM results, economic impacts do not act as a sufficient factor for indicating life satisfaction of the residents (Figure 6.2). The evidence of fit validity of the structural model is provided as fit statistics satisfied the accepted level (X^2: 201.027, df = 132, X^2/df = 1.523, IFI = .915, CFI = .912, RMSEA = .073).

Results from fsQCA

The results of fsQCA are presented in Table 6.2. The results showed that two causal models explain conditions where high levels of residents' satisfaction were obtained (coverage: .618, consistency: .759). The first model indicates that the combination of economic impacts and low socio-cultural impacts of faith tourism leads to high levels of residents' life satisfaction. The second model suggests that low economic impacts and high socio-cultural impacts increase the life satisfaction of Mashhad residents.

Table 6.1 Results from measurement model testing

Scale items	Factor loading	Cronbach's alpha
Environmental impacts		.875
Faith tourism increases traffic congestion	.771***	
Faith tourism results in overcrowding	.783***	
Faith tourism causes noise pollution	.878***	
Faith tourism increases air pollution	.772***	
Faith tourism produces large quintiles of waste products	.734***	
Faith tourism reduces green spaces	.625***	
Faith tourism causes water pollution	.537***	
Socio-cultural impacts		.733
Faith tourism improves our cultural values	.651***	
Faith tourism reduces number of crimes and illegal activities	.655***	
Faith tourism decreases trafficking	.640***	
Faith tourism mitigates socio-cultural tensions	.875***	
Economic impacts		.864
Faith tourism improves income level of residents	.873***	
Faith tourism contributes to development of local economy	.809***	
Faith tourism generates job positions	.695***	
Faith tourism enhances investment and entrepreneurship opportunities	.649***	
Life satisfaction		.921
Your life as a whole	.741***	
The way you spend your life	.889***	
The feeling about life compared to others	.749***	

Note: ***$p < .001$.

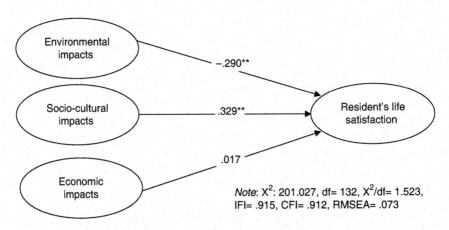

Figure 6.2 Results of structural model.

Table 6.2 Results from fsQCA for predicting high level of life satisfaction

Model: lsat = f(eco, envi, soc)	Raw coverage	Unique coverage	Consistency
Model 1: eco*~soc	.598	.384	.767
Model 2: ~eco*soc	.233	.019	.825
Solution coverage: .618			
Solution consistency: .759			

Note: lsat: life satisfaction of the residents, eco: economic impacts, envi: environmental impacts, soc: socio-cultural impacts of mass faith tourism, ~: negation of a condition.

Table 6.3 Results from fsQCA for predicting low level of life satisfaction

Model: ~lsat = f(eco, envi, soc)	Raw coverage	Unique coverage	Consistency
Model 1: envi*soc	.504	.504	.823
Solution coverage: .504			
Solution consistency: .823			

Note: lsat: life satisfaction of the residents, eco: economic impacts, envi: environmental impacts, soc: socio-cultural impacts of mass faith tourism, ~ indicates negation.

Table 6.4 Results of analysis of necessary conditions for life satisfaction of the residents

Antecedent condition	Consistency	Coverage
Economic impact	**.943**	.604
~ Economic impact	.253	.832
Environmental impact	.756	.686
~ Environmental impact	.543	.711
Socio-cultural impact	.694	.651
~ Socio-cultural impact	.618	.770

Note: Bold number indicates necessary antecedent condition (consistency > .9).

The fsQCA results for predicting low levels of residents' satisfaction are provided in Table 6.3. According to the configurational model testing, negative environmental impacts along with socio-cultural impacts of faith tourism lead to low levels of residents' satisfaction (coverage: .504, consistency: .823). A detailed explanation of the fsQCA approach is available in Olya and Gavilyan (2016).

Results from analysis of necessary conditions

The results of the analysis of necessary conditions are outlined in Table 6.4. According to the results, the economic impacts of faith tourism are necessary for achieving a high level of life satisfaction of the residents (consistency > .9) (Olya & Al-ansi, 2018).

Discussion and conclusion

This empirical study found that mass faith tourism results in environmental challenges in Mashhad which have negatively affected the life satisfaction of residents. Reasons for the negative impacts of faith tourism in Mashhad may result from mismanagement and lack of appropriate planning at a city scale. As Alipour et al. (2017, p. 180) noted,

> institutions, with the real involvement of their stakeholders, need to start designing and implementing strategic planning with a renewed interest in long-term visions and a development framework that can address environmental issues at a comprehensive level and on a metropolitan scale. This can be achieved by strengthening the voice of municipal government and of the institutions in charge of the shrine's affairs.

Policy makers tend to focus on site development and fail to address environmental issues beyond the holy shrine site and the immediate surrounding districts. Decision-makers should prepare a master plan for Mashhad as a city destination given the interests of both permanent residents as well as the more than 20 million visitors to the city and seek to address environmental and other impact issues in the city as a whole. "Under these circumstances, policy makers who are heavily influenced by religious institutions need to adopt a comprehensive environmental policy that encompasses the entirety of the Mashhad metropolitan area" (Alipour et al., 2017, p. 181).

Due to the immense interest of international and local visitors in seeing this holy shrine, pragmatic programs and plans should be determined for improving the level of facilities and accommodations of Mashhad from a sustainable tourism perspective. In order to enhance community wellbeing, residents' attitudes toward the impacts of mass faith tourism should be viewed as the critical factor in terms of tourism expansion and growth and spatial planners need to become much more aware of the significant role of host city management strategies and the needs of residents (see also Chapter 5, this volume).

Residents perceived positively the socio-cultural impacts of faith tourism as a driver of their life satisfaction. These results are not in accordance with Tosun's (2002) study which indicated that many studies found a positive role of economic and negative effects of socio-cultural and environmental impacts of tourism on the satisfaction of residents. One of the justifications for explaining this heterogeneity may be rooted in the type of tourism which residents experience. In other words, the spirituality resulting from living in a destination for faith tourism and residents' interaction with pilgrims is in line with the criteria that residents considered as factors leading to their life satisfaction. According to the SEM results, residents believed that economic impacts of faith tourism is insufficient for achieving life satisfaction. It means that residents consider a combination of the factors as predictors of their life satisfaction.

The findings from the fsQCA results confirmed the complexity of residents' perceptions about faith tourism development in Mashhad (Olya & Gavilyan, 2016;

Olya et al., 2017). The fsQCA results introduced a combination of the predictors, economic and socio-cultural impacts of faith tourism, as complex conditions leading to the life satisfaction of the residents. The results from the fsQCA provide new insights into the modeling of the life satisfaction of residents because, unlike SEM, the results revealed that economic factors served as a sufficient factor for achieving life satisfaction. The fsQCA results showed that economic impacts can contribute to the life satisfaction of the residents while its impact is considered along with socio-cultural impacts of faith tourism. Therefore, decision-makers need to explore the complex combination of the predictors (i.e., configuration) in formulating desired outcomes (i.e., the life satisfaction of residents). Importantly, site managers should be aware that the causal model attaining high level life satisfaction is not simply a mirror opposite of the causal model leading to low level life satisfaction (c.f., Table 6.3 and 6.4).

Sufficient factors and sufficient combinations of the factors are extracted from the results of SEM and fsQCA, respectively. Yet, we need to know what the necessary conditions for obtaining life satisfaction are for Mashhad residents (Olya & Al-ansi, 2018). Interestingly, while the economic impact of faith tourism is insufficient, it is necessary to achieve life satisfaction of Mashhad residents. This study therefore recommends further studies to use three analytical approaches: SEM, fsQCA, and analysis of necessary conditions, for modeling the attitudes and behaviors of residents toward development of faith tourism.

This study is a piece of cross-sectional research that collected data from the vicinity of Imam Reza holy shrine in Mashhad, Iran. However, researchers and managers need to be conservative in generalizing the findings of this study to other religious sites both in Iran and other countries. This study used three major impacts of faith tourism as causal factors; future research may want to employ other contributors (e.g., knowledge and power levels of residents) in formulating the life satisfaction of residents. Nevertheless, the present study found that modeling residents' life satisfaction in religious sites is a complex phenomenon, in which the nature of the tourism affects residents' satisfaction. Modeling of Muslims' attitudes and behaviors is also complex due to the multi-dimensionality of *Sharia* Islamic law. Because Muslims must apply *Sharia* in all aspects of their life it means that a combination of various factors must be understood as ingredients of the complex configuration of asymmetrical modeling of life satisfaction.

Acknowledgments

I would like to cordially appreciate the kind efforts and support of Mr. Iman Forouzan in the completion of this book chapter.

References

Alipour, H. & Heydari, R. (2005). Tourism revival and planning in Islamic Republic of Iran: Challenges and prospects. *Anatolia, 16*(1), 39–61.

Alipour, H., Olya, H. G., & Forouzan, I. (2017). Environmental impacts of mass religious tourism: From residents' perspectives. *Tourism Analysis, 22*(2), 167–183.

Anderson, J. C. & Gerbing, D. W. (1988). Structural equation modeling in practice: A review and recommended two-step approach. *Psychological Bulletin, 103*(3), 411–423.

Cortina, J. M. (1993). What is coefficient alpha? An examination of theory and applications. *Journal of Applied Psychology, 78*(1), 98–104.

Dadpour, R., Mohamed, B., & Sirat, M. (2009, July). *An analysis of the gap between cultural and religious tourism in Iran, a case study on Mashhad.* In Proceedings of 2nd National Symposium on Tourism Research, University Sains Malaysia, Penang, Malaysia. Theories and Applications (pp. 76–82). Social Transformation Platform.

Fornell, C. & Larcker, D. F. (1981). Evaluating structural equation models with unobservable variables and measurement error. *Journal of Marketing Research, 18*(1), 39–50.

Foruzan, I. (2014). *The role of religious tourism in the development and growth of urban metropolis: In the case of Mashhad, Iran.* Unpublished Master's thesis, Eastern Mediterranean University (EMU), Cyprus.

Gu, H. & Ryan, C. (2008). Place attachment, identity and community impacts of tourism—The case of a Beijing hutong. *Tourism Management, 29*(4), 637–647.

Gursoy, D. & Rutherford, D. G. (2004). Host attitudes toward tourism: An improved structural model. *Annals of Tourism Research, 31*(3), 495–516.

Hair, J. F., Anderson, R. E., Tatham, R. L., & Black, W. C. (1998). *Multivariate data analysis* (8th ed.). Upper Saddle River, NJ: Prentice-Hall.

Hall, C. M. (2008). *Tourism planning: Policies, processes and relationships* (2nd ed.). London: Pearson.

Hall, C. M. & Lew, A. A. (2009). *Understanding and managing tourism impacts: An integrated approach.* Abingdon: Routledge.

Iran Cultural Heritage, Handcraft and Tourism Organization (ICHTO). (2016). *Iran highlights of tourism statistics.* Tehran: ICHTO.

Kim, K., Uysal, M., & Sirgy, M. J. (2013). How does tourism in a community impact the quality of life of community residents? *Tourism Management, 36*, 527–540.

Lee, C. C. & Chang, C. P. (2008). Tourism development and economic growth: A closer look at panels. *Tourism Management, 29*(1), 180–192.

Lee, T. H. (2013). Influence analysis of community resident support for sustainable tourism development. *Tourism Management, 34*, 37–46.

Olsen, D. H. & Timothy, D. J. (2006). Tourism and religious journeys. In D. J. Timothy & D. H. Olsen (Eds.), *Tourism, religion and spiritual journeys* (pp. 1–21). London: Routledge.

Olya, H. & Al-ansi, A. (2018). Risk assessment of Halal products and services: Implication for tourism industry. *Tourism Management, 65*, 279–291.

Olya, H. G. & Gavilyan, Y. (2016). Configurational models to predict residents' support for tourism development. *Journal of Travel Research, 56*(7), 893–912.

Olya, H. G., Shahmirzdi, E. K., & Alipour, H. (2017). Pro-tourism and anti-tourism community groups at a World Heritage site in Turkey. *Current Issues in Tourism.* https://doi.org/10.1080/13683500.2017.1329281

Rasoolimanesh, S. M., Jaafar, M., Ahmad, A. G., & Barghi, R. (2017). Community participation in World Heritage site conservation and tourism development. *Tourism Management, 58*, 142–153.

Saghaei, M. & Javanbakht, G. Z. (2013). A statistical analysis of the number of domestic tourists entering the metropolitan of Mashhad on the basis of time series model. *Journal of Geographical Sciences, 13*(28), 71–94.

Tala, M. L. & Padurean, A. M. (2008). Dimensions of religious tourism. *Amfiteatru Economic*, 242–253.

Tosun, C. (2002). Host perceptions of impacts: A comparative tourism study. *Annals of Tourism Research, 29*(1), 231–253.

United Nations World Tourism Organization (UNWTO). (2017). *Contribution of Islamic culture and its impact on the Asian tourism market.* Madrid, Spain: UNWTO.

Wong, C. U. I., Ryan, C., & McIntosh, A. (2013). The monasteries of Putuoshan, China: Sites of secular or religious tourism. *Journal of Travel & Tourism Marketing, 30*(6), 577–594.

Zhong, L., Deng, J., Song, Z., & Ding, P. (2011). Research on environmental impacts of tourism in China: Progress and prospect. *Journal of Environmental Management, 92*(11), 2972–2983.

Part III

Heritage and tourism

7 Cultural heritage management and heritage tourism development in Iran: opportunities and challenges for the future

Fabio Carbone, Anahita Malek and Anahita Lohrasbi

Introduction

The modernization of infrastructure and the aviation fleet, as well as the boost of the whole hospitality's offer, are clearly the key to the agenda of international tourism development in Iran. Within the broad and complex debate related to the latter process (see also Chapters 1 and 2, this volume), this chapter is dedicated to the specific field of cultural heritage management. This is a crucial area for Iran, today, both with respect to socio-cultural and economic development and for the commodification of cultural heritage for tourism (first section). Within this discourse, this chapter analyzes some of the quality issues in cultural attractions, highlighting the concept of quality within the practice of cultural heritage management itself (second section), as well as the importance of the proactive and consistent participation of local communities in the practices of territorial governance (third section). The complex approach adopted for the present analysis will ultimately lead to an outline of further links between cultural heritage management, the process of tourism development and some aspect of the well-being of the country which are not limited to its borders, but which hopefully could go beyond them, for instance in the field of international relations and cultural diplomacy. The moment of extraordinary vitality and new opportunities that Iran is experiencing, is of vast relevance to the content of this chapter, especially in the hope that it will influence stakeholders and inform the future process of decision-making.

Cultural heritage in Iran

The explanation of a given phenomenon can only be the result of an approach that reflects the complexity of the surrounding reality. This section therefore focuses on the different dimensions related to the management of cultural heritage management in Iran, taking into account the historical, social, political and economic aspects as well as the theoretical, technical strategic traits.

Cultural heritage management in Iran: a diachronic overview from the Pahlavi dynasty to the Islamic Republic

The discovery of oil in the country provided immediate economic benefits for the country, but also led to serious and irreversible damage to the cultural, natural and landscape heritage as a result of the improper planning and control of public and private construction activity. What happened is briefly explained by Rouhani (2011, p. 1021):

> Injecting oil money into the economy before establishing the essential infra-structures of development pushed it farther away from sustainable develop-ment, which is meant to respect natural and cultural resources and use them as a driver for further development.

In this context, cities were overwhelmed by urban plans that did not take into account the historic centres or the quality of life of their inhabitants. During the post-war reconstruction after the Iran–Iraq war (1980–1988), many historic build-ings were 'scarified' in the name of building speculation (Rouhani, 2009). Tehran, for instance, lost its historic gates and fortification and, in other cities, new high roads split the integrity of the historic centres (Makki, 1945). For this reason, Tehran, Isfahan, Kashan, Qazvin and many other urban centres were thus defined as 'crucified cities' by De Angelis d'Ossat (1971, p. 6). Today, a different sensitiv-ity characterizes countries that, like Iran, can count on the presence of resources in their subsoil. For instance, the Brazilian Petrobras (Petróleo Brasileiro SA), a national oil company, includes in its action plan the provision of substantial amounts of money for social projects and for the enhancement of cultural and nat-ural resources at national level.

It is also necessary to take into account that the policies of cultural heritage enhancement during the Pahlavi dynasty (1925–1979) were based on particular ideological reasons. Persian architectural elements were systematically included in the construction of new public buildings in order to recall the greatness of the ancient empire. Nevertheless, other assets were destroyed or simply abandoned (Rouhani, 2009). Such an approach was also adopted in other countries in the past. For instance, during the fascist period in Italy (1922–1943) monumental architecture was used for public buildings in order to recall the magnificence of the Roman Empire.

In analysing the current Iranian situation, it is difficult to talk about cultural heritage management without keeping in mind the social and political changes brought by the 'Great Revolution' (1979). As a theocracy, an ideological approach tends to prevail again, over a scientific one, producing 'grey areas' within the cul-tural and cultural heritage management policies. Niknami (2005, p. 346) warns: 'a major problem arises from the uncertainty in decision making by various author-ities that are appointed generally for non-scientific considerations'. Namely, there is an 'inclination to over-interpret an Islamic inheritance, which certainly was always part of the Iranian identity, but never the totality' (Ansari, 2014, p. 92).

In this context, this approach can produce socio-cultural damages, namely in terms of the identity of the Iranian people. In the social sphere, indeed, the propensity, whether it is official or not, to enhance certain cultural aspects to the detriment of others, could feed what Rhode (2015, p. 3) defines the 'unending battle between the Persian and the Islamic identity in Iran'. Now, within the main scope of this book, it is important to note that this socio-cultural situation represents an obstacle also to a sustainable development of tourism. The concept of 'sense of place' of local communities, indeed, is 'usually applied in the context of people who live in a location on a permanent basis and reflects how they feel about the physical and social dimension of their community' (Cooper & Hall, 2016, p. 133). On the one hand, the 'personality' of a destination is strongly dependent on the strength of this sense of place, sense of identity, self-awareness and self-esteem of resident populations and, on the other hand, such personality tends to influence the tourist experience. It is worth keeping in mind the role of cultural heritage managers in this sense, since the presentation of the cultural heritage to the public is, as highlighted by ICOMOS (1990), an essential method to promote understanding of the origins and the development of modern societies. Later in this chapter, today's opportunities to enhance this component in Iran will be explored.

Even if the constructions under the new developmental projects are still seriously threatening large areas of heritage sites (Niknami, 2005), several institutions such as the Iran Cultural Heritage, Handcraft and Tourism Organization (ICHTO) and the Research Institute for Cultural Heritage and Tourism (RICHT), among others, seem to be aware about the importance of a proper protection and cultural heritage management. They are supported by a highly dynamic cooperation with international partners, and it represents one of the most positive aspects that exist in the Iranian scenario in terms of cultural heritage management and tourism development nowadays. It is worth mentioning the presence of the representation of the International Council on Monuments and Sites (ICOMOS) and a UNESCO cluster office in Tehran, which also covers Afghanistan, Pakistan and Turkmenistan. Iran has also been a member of the International Centre for the Study of the Preservation and Restoration of Cultural Property (ICCROM) since 1972. The support of these organizations is not limited to consulting services but often represents a vehicle for seeking new sources of funding, including from the private sector, as it happened in the post-2003 earthquake reconstruction of Bam's cultural heritage. A number of bilateral international agreements are also part of this cooperation in the cultural field. In 2015, for instance, the Iranian minister of culture and Islamic guide subscribed a cultural collaboration protocol with the Italian Ministry of Cultural Heritage and Activities and Tourism, with the objective of performing in areas such as literature, cinema, music, archaeology and figurative arts (MiBACT, 2015).

Cultural resources and tourist attractions

The conviction that a more structured approach to tourism development has so far been neglected because the presence of gas and oil provides a safe income to the country is currently widespread (Khodadadi, 2016a; see also Chapter 1, this volume). If this were true, it would represent a strategic mistake, since tourism can be an integrated and sustainable vehicle for development (Carbone, 2016). In this sense, it is important to keep in consideration the dynamic interaction between tourism and cultural assets (ICOMOS, 1999), since the increasing demand for cultural experiences has made cultural heritage one of the most powerful factors for the competitiveness of tourist destinations (Bowitz & Ibenholt, 2009).

Iran's ancient and modern cultural heritage provide 'the basis for cultural tourism visitation experiences that, potentially, can be set alongside "leading branding" destinations such as Egypt, Greece, India, Italy and Turkey' (Baum & O'Gorman, 2010, p. 176). The path towards this goal, however, requires a process of commodification of the cultural resources, in order to turn them to all intents and purposes into cultural attraction. Literature clearly defines the components of an attraction. One of the classic descriptions of 'tourist attraction' was given by Pearce (1991), and more recently Cooper and Hall (2016, p. 138) outlined the indispensable elements for the natural and cultural resources of a destination to be considered tourist attractions:

1.   Facilities and services, including human resources;
2.   Resource in the form of infrastructure and services; and finally
3.   Information provision.

The access to the international market and international cooperation will surely represent a major boost to Iran's cultural offer, which currently has serious deficiencies, for instance, with respect to communication (see Chapter 1, this volume, for further discussion). However, the main consideration concerns the awareness about the need to undertake a process to turn a cultural (tangible or intangible) resource into a tourist attraction. This process is complex as it includes various aspects, including the adoption of an integrated and sustainable approach, the participation of local communities (see below), communication and, at the same time, preservation. For instance, in Iran the geological heritage varies in its rank from local, national to global importance thus representing an important potential tourist attraction (Lena & Carbone, 2015). Nevertheless, this heritage needs urgent attention from competent authorities for its safeguarding and enhancement (Habibi, Golubova, & Ruban, 2017).

Another important strategic phase within the tourism development process is the definition of the tourist model that is to be developed. Such a decision must reflect a viable and strategic choice, mainly based on the host communities' ambitions and expectations for the future. In this sense, investing in niche tourism could be an innovative strategy for preserving specific tangible and intangible heritage in Iran. Niche tourism, in opposition to mass tourism, represents diversity and ways of marking difference (Robinson & Novelli, 2005). Music tourism, art tourism, literary tourism and architectural tourism constitute good examples and it should be remembered that the intangible cultural heritage in Iran is as wide as the tangible one. For instance, cultural traditions in Iran could represent a superb starting point for implementing practices of valorization for tourists and resident communities.

The different traditional musical genres existing in Iran, for instance, could represent the primary resource for the structuring of tourist products at local or national level, following the example of well-known musical tourism destinations. For example, Vienna, for classical music, *operetta*, waltz; New Orleans, for *Jazz*; Lisbon, for the Portuguese *Fado*; Seville, for *Flamenco* music and dance. Empirical studies have demonstrated that such a promotion and commodification provides not only financial gain but also an increased cultural self-awareness and sense of belonging among communities, beyond being a great vehicle to preserve traditional music (Johnson, 2002). Furthermore, the architecture could also represent the primary resource for other 'special interest tourism' products. In this sense it is worth mentioning the inclusion of Yazd in UNESCO's List in 2017, due to the existence of several well preserved and still operational *badghir*, or 'wind-catching towers', an architectural expedient for the natural cooling of buildings (Russo, 2009).

Finally, the last example of a very specific cultural expression that could represent a resource for the development of 'special interest tourism' is that of traditional festivals. It is important to cite this example because it is very representative of the links between the desired development of tourism and the current cultural policies, including the need for a more inclusive approach to cultural heritage management (see above for the discourse about cultural heritage and *identity* in Iran today). Festivities such as the *Mehregan*, the Zoroastrian festival in honour of Mithra, a divinity associated with interpersonal relationships such as friendship, affection and love, and the *Sadeh*, occurring 50 days before *Nowruz*, the Persian New Year, continue to be nowadays, in a non-Zoroastrian context, dear to the Iranian population's hearts, involving family and friends. However, due to some aversion on the part of the government towards non-Islamic cultural expressions, with the exception of the *Nowruz*, the population is usually forced to celebrate some of these festivities out of public view. Nevertheless, the enhancement of such traditions would not only lead to greater social well-being, but would also offer strategic possibilities within the context of tourism development. Emerging destinations tend to include popular celebrations like these among their core cultural tourism products. In Portugal, for instance, the traditional festival known as *Santos Populares* (13 June) attracts thousands of foreign tourists to Lisbon every year, as well as the celebration in honour of St John (*São João*) in Oporto, on 23 June. Thus, in order to make the most of these opportunities, the Iranian pre-Islamic past and its tangible and intangible heritage should be preserved and promoted beyond any religious political ideology in the future.

Quality issues in heritage attractions

The concept of quality within cultural heritage and cultural attraction management is particularly complex, and many of its key aspects are directly related to international tourism development. It is important to define the concept of quality within cultural heritage management and cultural heritage attractions. From a general point of view, for long-time practitioners, organizations and scholars warned about the necessity of internationally shared standards for the management of cultural heritage sites open to the public. Nevertheless, in theoretical terms the first definition of quality within cultural heritage management only recently appeared in the literature (Carbone, 2017a). On the one hand, such a definition reflects HERITY (from the union of two English words Heritage and Quality, is the non-profit and non-governmental World Organization for the Certification of Quality Management of Cultural Heritage) experience related to its system of quality management of cultural heritage, which adopts four main dimensions to establish the quality of cultural heritage management: perceived value of the site/monument, conservation, communication, available services (Quagliuolo, 2001). On the other hand, Carbone's definition of quality contains, in addition to the dimensions mentioned above, another important aspect to be considered as a quality indicator – that is, the ability of cultural heritage managers to use heritage sites as places for an 'effective intercultural dialogue between hosting communities and tourists' (Carbone, 2017a, p. 71). The implications of Carbone's definition of quality within the management of cultural heritage are considerable and they are closely related to the degree of involvement and participation of local communities in the process of heritage management. An analytical discourse on the quality of heritage management and cultural tourism offer in Iran could be thus developed by going through the above-mentioned dimensions.

In terms of research and conservation, for instance, the numerous archaeological areas, monuments and palaces would require strong investments. New efforts, including new approaches, would be necessary in this sense in order to increase the level of preservation and visitor satisfaction. In this sense, particular attention should be given to the protection of the extremely fragile archaeological heritage, which is *ex natura sua* under constant threat of destruction. In Iran, it appears to have been a problem for years and tends to get worse, which is why archaeologists should formulate and implement systematic regulation in the sphere of protection and management (Niknami, 2005).

Regarding the capacity to communicate to the visitors, it is worth mentioning that ICOMOS (2008) recognizes interpretation and presentation as part of the overall process of cultural heritage management, and a means of enhancing public appreciation and understanding of cultural heritage. In this sense, they established seven principles upon which the interpretation and presentation of cultural heritage should be based:

- Access and Understanding;
- Information Sources;
- Attention to Setting and Context;
- Preservation of Authenticity;
- Planning for Sustainability;
- Concern for Inclusiveness;
- Research, Training, Evaluation.

The Iranian situation is quite stimulating, as the abundance of cultural resources allows thinking about innovative, eventually experimental policies and practices of interpretation and communication based on these supranational principles. Nevertheless, authors observe that, so far, cultural heritage 'is being presented to the Iranian public in a way that is inappropriate to the development and advancement of the society's cultural processes' (Niknami, 2005, p. 345). The ability to communicate is crucial to involve and raise awareness among local people about their past, on the one hand, and on the other hand to meet the needs and expectations of visitors. In this sense it is worth highlighting that the type of tourist that planners should aim to attract in Iran, namely, a high educated, responsible and respectful tourist, is also normally exigent and strongly eager to learn and genuinely engage with the local culture. Opening up to the development of international cultural tourism thus involves a strong investment in human resources by increasing training on new interpretative and communicative techniques, but also within the mere knowledge of different foreign languages. In this respect it is important to note that learning a different language could represent a means of raising awareness about the cultural aspects of the outbound countries, in order to boost not only the operators' (guides, group leaders) language skills but also the 'intercultural competences' defined by UNESCO (2013). This practice would indirectly facilitate and promote intercultural dialogue through tourism, but Yeganeh and Raeesi (2015) show that in Iran teachers still underestimate the cultural component in the teaching of language.

Furthermore, an irreducible value within the context of cultural heritage management and quality in cultural attractions is the preservation of authenticity. On the one hand, the commodification of cultural heritage sites can be viewed from an economic and financial perspective, for instance, as a driver of economic regeneration and/or source of funds for sites' preservation. In this perspective, the commodification of cultural heritage sites may be considered less damaging than alternative uses (or even abandonment). Nevertheless, on the other hand this 'commercial' approach tends to bring visitors into the domain of the consumer market. This situation triggers the temptation for destination managers to attract and satisfy 'consumers' based on mere marketing strategies. In the past, this temptation has led to the loss of authenticity of many destinations such as the Portuguese region of Algarve and, to some extent, several Italian locations, as well as cities like Barcelona. The loss of authenticity represents a form of socio-cultural damage for the local population and can also be considered as a strategic mistake within the tourism development process, since authenticity is one of the main elements of attraction of a destination for cultural tourists. Taking into account, therefore, the great importance that authenticity has in the broadest scope of the quality cultural heritage and cultural attractions management, heritage managers should work closely with tourism operators in Iran, in order to avoid falling into the above described 'trap' of tourism development leading to an irreversible loss of authenticity at heritage sites. Instead, combining authenticity and innovation would be one of Iran's biggest goals in the field of cultural heritage management and tourism development.

Community participation, local development and intercultural dialogue

The participation of local communities in decision making processes and, in particular, their engagement with practices of cultural heritage management represent a modern trend of territorial governance, recommended since the 1990s by supranational bodies and the international academic community (e.g. Rasoolimanesh, Ringle, Jaafar, & Ramayah, 2017; Waligo, Clarke, & Hawkins, 2013; Malek & Costa, 2015; Ansell & Gash, 2008; Hall, 2008; Ostrom, 1993). Local community participation brings a holistic understanding of cultural heritage (Smith, Morgan, & van der Meer, 2003), and socio-cultural development of the local population (Carbone, Oosterbeek, & Costa, 2013), as well as a positive perception towards tourism activities and tourism projects, due to the residents' perception of their greater empowerment within the decision-making process (Dragouni & Fouseki, 2017). At the supranational level, the social value of cultural heritage is recognized by the *Convention on the Value of Cultural Heritage for Society*, known as the Faro Convention (Council of Europe, 2005).

In Iran, the importance of local community engagement in cultural heritage management was officially acknowledged in 1988, with the Iranian Cultural Heritage Organization Charter. Nevertheless, the country is facing many challenges in this respect. Among them, the need for effective participatory policies not only in urban but also rural contexts (see Chapter 8, this volume, for further discussion). In the scope of tourism development, if cultural cities are to be considered Iran's strongest attractions, it is important to remember also that natural resources and landscapes – that is, rural environments and their communities – have a strong touristic potential. While it is advisable to promote the vast natural resources and landscapes as a tourist attraction, territorial governance bodies as well as national strategies should consider the involvement of the populations of these areas, in order to strengthen the social capital of the remote, rural communities. From this perspective,

> strategies must ensure a balance between consumption and reproduction of rural collective resources based on the active participation of various agents at local, national and international level and by emphasizing the role of local communities.
>
> (Malek, Carbone, & Alder, 2016, p. 154)

Iran has instead discouraged tourism development among indigenous communities so far by exercising strong central power and control and putting forward a strong national image (O'Gorman, McLellan, & Baum, 2007). For instance, the research conducted by Donato and Lohrasbi (2017) within Takht-e Soleyman World Heritage site shows the lack of engagement of the local community within the process of tourism development and cultural heritage management of the area. The same research registered, on the other hand, the great desire for participation on the side of resident communities. The latter is evidence of the discrepancy between the policies implemented and the growing sensitivity of the population and their desire to participate in the process of tourism development.

There is a current lack of 'community-based tourism' projects in Iran, which would be recommendable to a destination like this, where the concept of *hospitality* is deeply rooted in the population, in general, and in rural communities in particular. This kind of tourism is characterized by strong involvement of the local population (commonly, rural communities), which has close contact with tourists at different levels, from engaging them in traditional productive works through to providing them with overnight stays in private houses together with local families. From the point of view of the complexity and competitiveness of a tourist destination, it should be noted that the involvement of resident populations in cultural heritage management practices and tourism development also goes hand in hand with the current trends in tourist demands (Carbone, 2011). Nevertheless, the opposite perspective is worth mentioning too, since in promoting rural tourism and rural communities' engagement, it is necessary to consider the many socio-cultural risks for rural populations themselves, especially in developing countries, as is the case with Iran (Malek et al., 2016). Once again, the search for a sustainable balance between tourism development and local communities' 'well-being' (and cultural and natural environment safeguarding) is the first challenge for policymakers in Iran, like in any other developing destinations.

In both rural and urban contexts, finally, the 'Paideia approach for cultural heritage management', defined by Carbone et al. (2013), could be the suitable model for Iran, informing policymaking processes related with cultural heritage management, local communities' participation and tourism. This proposal supports a multi-stage approach to heritage management in which the first step is all about engaging the local population in cultural heritage management in order to raise awareness and self-esteem and boost intercultural capacities. In a second stage, a proactive encounter with visitors, thus the intercultural dialogue is promoted. In Iran, this proposal could be applied by involving the education sector, local authorities and stakeholders at different levels (public and private, local and national organizations, representatives of civil society, universities and parastatal organizations) as already claimed by Niknami (2005). In this sense, it is also worth mentioning the growing role of the web, social networks and participatory technologies (e.g. free and open source wiki software platform) which have potential for a greater political, social and technological democratization of culture. For Iran this will represent a great opportunity to embrace such change.

Future challenges for cultural heritage managers in Iran: going beyond borders

The ability of cultural heritage managers to capture the complexity of the implications of their work can benefit sustainable, integrated development. Cultural heritage management should lay the foundations for the achievement of more complex goals at local, national and international level, through the implementation of 'models of operationalization of complexity' (Carbone, 2017b, p. 103). Social, economic and cultural development of local communities is clearly acknowledged internationally among the benefits of a strategic, integrated and participant-involved process of cultural heritage management. However, less emphasis has been put, for instance, on the relationship between cultural heritage management, international tourism and cultural diplomacy (Carbone, 2017b). In this sense, 'responsible tourism and peace are partners – the one strengthens the other – they belong together' (De Villiers, 2014, p. 79).

Historically, both on the supply and the demand side, tourist activities in Iran have been highly influenced by the external perceptions of the country and mainly related to international political issues (see Chapter 1, this volume). The country's image has been negatively influenced by events such as the Islamic Revolution and its social consequences, the war between Iran and Iraq and sanctions (Alavi & Yasin, 2000). The lack of solidity in destination image has a strong and direct negative effect on the generating areas (Cooper & Hall, 2016). Indeed, Iran's negative image in many Western countries represents an obstacle for international tourism development. In this sense, Khodadadi (2016b, p. 90) points out 'a lack of resources to tackle this negative narrative'. Even if this statement appears to be questionable, Iran has at its disposal several instruments to tackle and reverse this negative perception. The strong international promotion of the great Iranian history, the traditions, the human capital itself, represent the most effective of these instruments. Cultural heritage management and international tourism should be in this sense strictly associated with a national agenda of cultural diplomacy, defined as 'the skills to persuade through culture, values and ideas rather than through military means' (Nye, 2002, pp. 8–9).

In order to reach this purpose, the application of supranational guidelines that integrate multi-level partnerships should be established for the enhancement of cultural heritage and promotion of cultural values at national and international scales (Carbone, 2017a). Domestic promotion would boost cultural self-awareness and self-esteem among the local population while consistent international promotion would create in the medium and long term a positive and stable image essentially based on culture that would positively contribute to international tourism development and Iranian international relations. The great changes and the socio-economic ferment Iran is experiencing represent an opportunity to promote a positive national brand and image, not only from the point of view of international tourism development but also in the broader scope of international relations in a global scenario.

Conclusion

The (sustainable) future of a country must be based on solid roots, which are represented by its values and its cultural heritage. The ability to preserve and enhance such roots, on behalf of both residents and visitors, is thus one of the key aspects within the development process. In Iran, the end of sanctions should not be considered the *panacea* for all the national issues. Neither should tourism be. Rather, a new approach to improving Iranians' socio-cultural conditions could represent a key to sustainability. The policies of cultural heritage management thus play a key role.

An integrated, more democratic and more participation-driven heritage management would bring a renewed socio-cultural prosperity in the country. This, in turn, would lead to numerous opportunities, including in the field of international tourism development. The protection and promotion of Iranian cultural heritage can effectively allow the country to afford the luxury of aiming for the development of niche tourism and 'special interest tourism', rather than mass tourism. Moreover, the degree of involvement and participation of local populations, particularly in rural areas, should be considered as a quality indicator of cultural heritage management and territorial governance. Such participation should also characterize the tourism development process. The personality of the country as a tourist destination is related to the local populations' own self-esteem. The implications of this approach to cultural heritage would go far beyond the mere tourism development. A specific model of cultural heritage management could support the national cultural diplomacy agenda, and the alliance between cultural heritage management, international tourism and cultural diplomacy would be a vehicle for Iran to receive a positive international recognition.

The country is experiencing a new historic phase, full of opportunities for a new impetus towards an integrated and sustainable development and a greater openness towards the international community. In this context, international tourism will represent a powerful instrument to reach these goals. Nevertheless it is imperative to recognize the significance of culture and cultural heritage management within this process, as well as the ability of cultural heritage managers to grasp the complexity of their work and its implication for a bright and promising future for all Iranian people.

Acknowledgements

A particular thank to Narges Shojaie, Mehrnaz Shafieian and Rahman Mehraby for the valuable contribution they gave to this work by sharing ideas, experiences and hopes. Hajar, Sarah, Mehrnoosh, Shirin, Roshanak, Bherang, Dhorsa, Pedram, Mahan, Gholam, Omid, Alí, Solmaz ... These are just some of the names of the people I met in Iran. Each one of them explained to me something about their enchanting country. Each one of them offered me a thousand smiles. Special people, keepers of an ancient and vibrant culture. They must be the first beneficiaries of the upcoming tourism development in their fascinating country, Iran. *Inshallah!* (Fabio 'Karan' Carbone).

References

Alavi, J. & Yasin, M. M. (2000). Iran's tourism potential and market realities: An empirical approach to closing the gap, *Journal of Travel & Tourism Marketing, 9*(3): 1–22.
Ansari, A. M. (2014). *Iran.* Oxford: Oxford University Press.
Ansell, C. & Gash, A. (2008). Collaborative governance in theory and practice. *Journal of Public Administration Research and Theory, 18*(4): 543–571.

Baum, T. G. & O'Gorman, K. D. (2010). Iran or Persia: What's in a name, the decline and fall of a tourism industry? In R. Butler & W. Suntikul (Eds.), *Tourism and political change* (pp. 175–185). Oxford: Goodfellow Publishers.

Bowitz, E. & Ibenholt, K. (2009). Economic impacts of cultural heritage: Research and perspectives. *Journal of Cultural Heritage, 10*(1), 1–8.

Carbone, F. (2011). *A new approach in management of heritage for tourism development: The Paideia approach*, in proceedings of the International Conference on Tourism & Management Studies (pp. 455–463). University of Algarve, Portugal.

Carbone F. (2016). An insight into cultural heritage management of tourism destinations. *European Journal of Tourism Research, 14*, 75–91.

Carbone, F. (2017a). International tourism and cultural diplomacy: A new conceptual approach towards global mutual understanding and peace through tourism. *Tourism: An International Interdisciplinary Journal, 65*(1), 61–74.

Carbone, F. (2017b). Archaeology and sustainability: Model of operationalization of complexity. In L. Oosterbeek, B. Werlen, & L. Caron (Eds.), *Sustainability and sociocultural matrices* (Vol. 1, pp. 103–119). Mação, Portugal: Terra & Memoria Institute.

Carbone, F., Oosterbeek, L., & Costa, C. (2013). Paideia approach for heritage management. The tourist enhancement of archaeological heritage on behalf of local communities. *PASOS – Journal of Tourism and Cultural Heritage, 11*(2), 285–295.

Cooper, C. & Hall, C. M. (2016). *Contemporary tourism. An international approach* (3rd ed.). Oxford: Goodfellow Publishers.

Council of Europe. (2005). *Council of Europe framework convention on the value of cultural heritage for society*. Council of Europe Treaty Series – No. 199, Faro, 27.X.2005.

De Angelis d'Ossat, G. (1971). Le Citta' Crocifisse (Shahr haye beh Salib keshideh Shodeh), *Asar, 22–23*, 6–12.

De Villiers, D. (2014). Cornerstones for a better world: Peace, tourism and sustainable development. In C. Wohlmuther & W. Wintersteiner (Eds.), *International handbook on tourism and peace* (pp. 78–86). Austria: Drava.

Donato, F. & Lohrasbi, A. (2017). When theory and practice clash: Participatory governance and management in Takht-e Soleyman. *Journal of Cultural Heritage Management and Sustainable Development, 7*(2), 129–146.

Dragouni, M. & Fouseki, K. (2017). Drivers of community participation in heritage tourism planning: An empirical investigation. *Journal of Heritage Tourism*. https://doi.org/10.1080/1743873X.2017.1310214

Habibi, T., Golubova, N. V., & Ruban, D. A. (2017). New evidence of highly-complex geological heritage in Iran: Miocene sections in the Zagros Fold-Thrust Belt. *Geological Research Journal, 13*, 96–102.

Hall, C. M. (2008). *Tourism planning: Policies, processes and relationships* (2nd ed.). London: Pearson.

International Council on Monuments and Sites (ICOMOS). (1990). *Charter for the protection and management of the archaeological heritage*. Lausanne: ICOMOS.

International Council on Monuments and Sites (ICOMOS). (1999). *International cultural tourism charter. Managing tourism at places of heritage significance*. Mexico City: ICOMOS.

International Council on Monuments and Sites (ICOMOS). (2008). *Charter for the interpretation and presentation of cultural heritage sites*. Québec, Canada: ICOMOS.

Johnson, H. (2002). Balinese music, tourism and globalisation: Inventing traditions within and across cultures. *New Zealand Journal of Asian Studies, 4*(2), 8–32.

Khodadadi, M. (2016a). A new dawn? The Iran nuclear deal and the future of the Iranian tourism industry. *Tourism Management Perspectives, 18*, 6–9.

Khodadadi, M. (2016b). Challenges and opportunities for tourism development in Iran: Perspectives of Iranian tourism suppliers. *Tourism Management Perspectives, 19*(Part A), 90–92.

Lena, G. & Carbone, F. (2015). Geoarcheologia, turismo e sviluppo sostenibile, Geologia dell'Ambiente. *Italian Magazine of Environmental Geology (Special Issue on Geology and Tourism), XXIV*(1), 17–23.

Makki, H. (1945). *Tarikh bist saleh ye Iran* [Twenty Years of Iranian History], Tehran Bongah Tarjomeh va Nashr-e-Ketab.

Malek, A. & Costa, C. (2015). Integrating communities into tourism planning through social innovation. *Tourism Planning & Development, 12*(3), 281–299.

Malek, A., Carbone, F., & Alder, A. (2016). Community engagement, rural institutions and rural tourism business in developing countries. In A. Oriade & P. Robinson (Eds.), *Rural tourism and enterprise: Management, marketing and sustainability* (pp. 145–157). Oxfordshire: CABI.

MiBACT. (2015). *Italia–Iran: Sottoscritto protocollo di collaborazione culturale* [Italia–Iran signed a protocol for international cultural cooperation]. Retrieved from http://www.beniculturali.it/mibac/export/MiBAC/sitoMiBAC/Contenuti/MibacUnif/Comunicati/visualizza_asset.html_443474203.html

Niknami, K. A. (2005). Iran: Archaeological heritage in crisis. Developing an effective management system for archaeology. *Journal of Cultural Heritage, 6*(4), 345–350.

Nye, J. S. (2002). *The paradox of American power*. New York: Oxford University Press.

O'Gorman, K., McLellan, L. R., & Baum, T. (2007). Tourism in Iran: Central control and indignity. In R. Butler & T. Hinch (Eds.), *Tourism and indigenous peoples. Issues and implications* (pp. 251–264). Oxford: Butterworth-Heinemann.

Ostrom, E. (1993). A communitarian approach to local governance. *National Civic Review, 82*(3), 226–233.

Pearce, P. (1991). Analysing tourist attractions. *Journal of Tourism Studies, 2*(1), 46–55.

Quagliuolo, M. (2001). *Qualitá nella gestione di un bene culturale: Il riconoscimento HERITY* [Quality in the management of a cultural asset: The HERITY recognition]. Paper presented at the 6th International Meeting on Cultural Heritage Management, 'Qualitá e Beni Culturali e Ambientali', Barletta, Italy.

Rasoolimanesh, S. M., Ringle, C. M., Jaafar, M., & Ramayah, T. (2017). Urban vs. rural destinations: Residents' perceptions, community participation and support for tourism development. *Tourism Management, 60*, 147–158.

Rhode, H. (2015). The unending battle between the Persian and Islamic identity in Iran. In A. Cohen (Ed.), *Identities in crisis in Iran: Politics, culture, and religion* (pp. 3–21). London: Lexington Books.

Robinson, M. & Novelli, M. (2005). Niche tourism: An introduction. In M. Novelli (Ed.), *Niche tourism: Contemporary issues, trends and cases* (pp. 1–11). Oxford: Elsevier.

Rouhani, B. (2009). Different concepts of cultural heritage in Iran. In *International Conference on Intangible Heritage-Sharing Culture*, May–June 2009 (pp. 593–602). Pico Island, Azores, Portugal.

Rouhani, B. (2011, November–December). *Development and cultural heritage in Iran: Policies for an ancient country*. In ICOMOS 17th General Assembly, Paris, France.

Russo, S. (2009). *L'altopiano iranico fonte di civiltà e ispirazione: Architettura sostenibile*. [Iranian highland as a source of civilisation and inspiration: Sustainable architecture]. Roma: Gangemi Editore.

Smith, L., Morgan, A., & van der Meer, A. (2003). Community-driven research in cultural heritage management: The Waanyi women's history project. *International Journal of Heritage Studies, 9*(1), 65–80.

United Nations Educational, Scientific and Cultural Organization (UNESCO). (2013). *Intercultural competences. Conceptual and operational framework*. Paris: UNESCO.

Waligo, V. M., Clarke, J., & Hawkins, R. (2013). Implementing sustainable tourism: A multi-stakeholder involvement management framework. *Tourism Management, 36*, 342–353.

Yeganeh, M. T. & Raeesi, H. (2015). Developing cultural awareness in EFL classrooms at secondary school level in an Iranian educational context. *Procedia – Social and Behavioral Sciences, 192*, 534–542.

8   Residents' perceptions towards heritage tourism development: the case of the historical city of Kashan, Iran

S. Mostafa Rasoolimanesh and Hamid Ataeishad

Introduction

Tourism plays a key role in the world economy (World Tourism Organization (UNWTO), 2014) with the number of international tourists forecast to reach 1.8 billion by 2030 (UNWTO, 2016). However, Iran has only played a limited role as an international destination for the past 40 years (see Chapter 1, this volume), despite the country having many natural and cultural tourist attractions. As of 2017, the United Nations Educational, Scientific and Cultural Organization (UNESCO) has inscribed 22 Iranian cultural and natural sites as World Heritage sites (WHS), with 11 elements having been inscribed as intangible cultural heritage (UNESCO, 2017a, 2017b). In addition, there are 68 elements tentatively listed as WHSs or as intangible cultural heritage, including ongoing nominations and backlogged nominations (UNESCO, 2017a, 2017b). Therefore, the potential for tourism growth and for tourism to become a major contributor to the Iranian national economy is significant. In particular, reports following the lifting of international sanctions against Iran indicate significant interest in visiting Iran, and already, the number of international tourists to Iran has increased from 2.93 million in 2010 to 4.92 million in 2016 (UNWTO, 2017) (see also Chapter 1, this volume).

However, tourism cannot be sustained without the support of local community members (Rasoolimanesh & Jaafar, 2017), and this support is largely contingent upon residents' perceptions of how tourism development impacts their community (Andereck, Valentine, Knopf, & Vogt, 2005; Rasoolimanesh, Jaafar, Kock, & Ahmad, 2017a). The development of tourism can potentially exert a number of positive and negative effects on the lives of local community members (Sharpley, 2014; Rasoolimanesh, Roldán, Jaafar, & Ramayah, 2017b). As may be expected, perceptions of the positive impacts of tourism tend to increase residents' support for tourism development, while perceived negative impacts reduce support (Rasoolimanesh, Jaafar, Kock, & Ramayah, 2015). In particular, the inscription of a heritage site as a cultural WHS enhances the visibility of the site and potentially increases the number of tourists drawn to it (Su & Wall, 2014; Adie, Hall, & Prayag, 2018). Therefore, the inscription of a site as a WHS and the subsequent potential influx of tourists could provide a number of benefits to the local community by increasing income and employment opportunities, improving public infrastructure and facilities, and by promoting local culture and preserving cultural identity (Rasoolimanesh & Jaafar, 2017). However, increasing the number of tourists to a heritage site can also negatively affect local residents by increasing the cost of living, contributing to overcrowding and traffic congestion, and increasing the rate of crime (Látková & Vogt, 2012).

Despite a wealth of natural and cultural tourist attractions, few studies have explored residents' perceptions of tourism in Iran, particularly in relation to heritage sites. Therefore, the current study has been conducted in Kashan city, one of Iran's most historic cities. Kashan city is an internationally recognised historical city with unique architecture, historical houses, carpets and handicrafts, and a wealth of natural heritage. Bagh-e Fin of Kashan was inscribed in 2011 along with eight other gardens, collectively referred to as the Persian Gardens WHS by UNESCO (2017a). The Qālišuyān rituals of Mašhad-e Ardehāl and the traditional carpet weaving skills of Kashan were also inscribed as intangible cultural heritage in 2012 and 2010, respectively, by UNESCO (2017b). This chapter therefore investigates the perceptions of Kashan city residents towards the positive and negative impacts of heritage tourism development and the consequent effects on their support for heritage tourism development.

Residents' perceptions towards tourism development

A number of previous studies in different countries have explored the perceptions of residents towards the impacts of tourism development on local communities (Andereck et al., 2005; Gu & Wong, 2006; Zamani-Farahani & Musa, 2008, 2012; Kim, Uysal, & Sirgy, 2013; Vareiro, Remoaldo, & Cadima Ribeiro, 2013; Sharpley, 2014; Rasoolimanesh et al., 2015, 2017b; Rezaei, 2017). Several studies have also been conducted in rural and urban tourism destinations in Iran (Zamani-Farahani & Musa, 2008, 2012; Rastegar, 2010; Ghaderi & Henderson, 2012; Ahadian, 2013; Abdollahzadeh & Sharifzadeh, 2014; Zamani-Farahani & Henderson, 2014; Rezaei, 2017). Tourism development can have a direct influence on the local community (Rasoolimanesh et al., 2015). Tourism development influences the community's values, behaviour patterns, lifestyles and standards of living (Kayat, 2002; Jaafar, Noor, & Rasoolimanesh, 2015; Jaafar, Rasoolimanesh, & Ismail, 2017; Rezaei, 2017) as well as other economical, socio-cultural and environmental aspects of locations (Sharpley, 2014; Rasoolimanesh et al., 2015).

Several studies identified positive economic impacts in relation to tourism development, such as increased family incomes, improved standards of living, job creation and employment opportunities in the host community (Ko & Stewart, 2002; Choi & Sirakaya, 2006; Rasoolimanesh & Jaafar, 2017). Among studies conducted in Iran, Abdollahzadeh and Sharifzadeh (2014) found that residents of the historical village of Ziyarat perceived a number of positive economic impacts in relation to tourism development. Ziyarat village residents believed that tourism increased their household income, increased the demand for local products, created more jobs for local residents, contributed to long-term business profitability, diversified the local economy and created new markets for their agricultural products (Abdollahzadeh & Sharifzadeh, 2014). In a study conducted by Ghaderi and Henderson (2012) in Hawraman Village, Kurdistan, residents perceived several tourism-related economic impacts on their community, such as increased income and job opportunities, and diversification of the local economy by creating a market for agriculture products and handicrafts. Residents in the vicinity of Ali Sadr cave in Hamedan cite tourism as being integral to the improvement in their quality of life (Ahadian, 2013). Many of these residents believe that the development of tourism has increased their individual and household income. Moreover, tourism has reduced emigration from their community and increased their welfare with many residents expressing an interest in becoming involved in the tourism planning process (Ahadian, 2013).

A number of negative economic impacts of tourism, from the perspective of residents, have been identified in previous studies, including an increase in the cost of living (especially property, goods and other products), relative poverty through low paying jobs in the tourism industry and increasing property taxes (Ghaderi & Henderson, 2012; Látková & Vogt, 2012; Rasoolimanesh et al., 2015). For instance, Ghaderi and Henderson (2012) found that Hawraman residents complained about seasonal and low payment jobs from tourism. This finding was consistent with those of Rastegar (2010), who reported similar negative economic impacts from tourism in Yazd.

The positive and negative socio-cultural impacts of tourism development on local communities have been identified by several studies (Ghaderi & Henderson, 2012; Zamani-Farahani & Musa, 2012; Jaafar et al., 2017; Rezaei, 2017). Tourism can potentially motivate the private and governmental sectors to improve recreational and entertainment facilities; facilitate an understanding of cultural identity; promote the preservation and revival of traditional arts, culture and crafts; and encourage the local community to take pride in their culture (Jaafar et al., 2017; Rasoolimanesh et al., 2017b; Rezaei, 2017). Increasing tourist arrivals to heritage sites can also improve local residents' awareness of the value and importance of their heritage assets (Rezaei, 2017). For example, residents of the historical city of Yazd indicated that tourism played a significant role in improving their cultural awareness and did not consider it a threat to their community (Rezaei, 2017). In addition, increasing tourist arrivals improved residents' awareness of their heritage and made them proud of their cultural and heritage assets (Rezaei, 2017). Moreover, rural residents of Ziyarat village believed that their interactions with tourists contributed to their sense of belonging and community attachment, and gave them a newfound respect for their culture and customs by increasing their awareness of their culture and heritage (Abdollahzadeh & Sharifzadeh, 2014).

The residents of Hawraman village, Kurdistan, noted that tourism created a growing market for local art and crafts, and increased local residents' awareness of their heritage and culture, thus motivating them to preserve that heritage (Ghaderi & Henderson, 2012). However, residents also identified a number of negative socio-cultural impacts associated with tourism development, including changes in their lifestyle, tourists violating local and religious values and beliefs, and a reduction in the quality of local handicrafts to minimise costs (Ghaderi & Henderson, 2012). Residents of Yazd city cited the commodification of local culture and decrease in the originality of traditional beliefs among the negative socio-cultural impacts of tourism development (Rezaei, 2017). Similarly, residents of Sare'in and Masooleh also reported vandalism, an increased rate of crime and drug addiction, and violations of their traditional of lifestyle as negative impacts associated with tourism development in their communities (Zamani-Farahani & Musa, 2012).

From an environmental perspective, tourism can have a positive influence on the physical condition and appearance of neighbourhoods frequented by tourists, especially in areas with historical attractions (Rezaei, 2017). It has been argued that the development of tourism in historical areas can promote the protection of these historical sites (Rasoolimanesh et al., 2017a; Rezaei, 2017). In some instances, increases in the number of visiting tourists to heritage areas can motivate governments and local authorities to view these heritage sites as sources of destination competitiveness, thus leading to the rehabilitation and conservation of historic sites (Rezaei, 2017). For example, residents of Sare'in and Masooleh cited historical site maintenance and conservation among the positive impacts of tourism development (Zamani-Farahani & Musa, 2012; Zamani-Farahani & Henderson, 2014). Similarly, the residents of Ziyarat village attributed tourism as the key factor in the creation of public environmentally protected areas, and an increase in the availability of public infrastructure and other facilities in rural destinations (Abdollahzadeh & Sharifzadeh, 2014). Despite an increase in traffic congestion and over-crowding Ziyarat village residents perceived few negative environmental impacts associated with tourism development (Abdollahzadeh & Sharifzadeh, 2014). The residents of Hawraman village, on the other hand, indicated that they were mindful of a number of negative environmental impacts of tourism, such as uncontrolled construction that had damaged the character of the village. They further argued that the high number of tourists had led to an increase in water consumption and had contributed to the dehydration of local orchards due to the lack of water, as well as littering and leaving rubbish in nature areas by tourists, traffic congestion and over-crowding in the village (Ghaderi & Henderson, 2012).

In summary, previous studies in Iran and elsewhere have shown that residents are capable of perceiving both positive and negative impacts as a consequence of tourism development in their communities, and that they perceive these impacts from economic, socio-cultural and environmental perspectives. Therefore, community members face a critical dilemma in supporting tourism development in their community. While the perceived positive impacts of tourism development might encourage residents to support tourism development, the perceived negative impacts can potentially result in the loss of that support.

Support for tourism development and community participation

Much of the resident perception literature relies on social exchange theory (SET) to explain the effects of residents' perceptions on their support for tourism development (Gursoy, Jurowski, & Uysal, 2002; Ko & Stewart, 2002; Wang & Pfister, 2008; Látková & Vogt, 2012; Haobin Ye, Qiu Zhang, Huawen Shen, & Goh, 2014; Sharpley, 2014; Rasoolimanesh et al., 2015). According to SET, if residents perceive the benefits of tourism development to outweigh the costs and disadvantages of tourism development in their community, they will want to become involved in a process of exchange and interaction with tourists and will support tourism development in their community (Gursoy et al., 2002; Haobin Ye et al., 2014; Rasoolimanesh et al., 2015). Conversely, if residents perceive more negative impacts, they will not be willing to support tourism development in their community (Nunkoo & Ramkissoon, 2011; Rasoolimanesh et al., 2015). There-fore, the following hypotheses are explored in this study:

H1: The perception of positive economic impacts of tourism development by residents of Kashan will have a positive effect on their support for tourism development.

H2: The perception of positive socio-cultural impacts of tourism develop-ment by residents of Kashan will have a positive effect on their support for tourism development.

H3: The perception of positive environmental impacts of tourism develop-ment by residents of Kashan will have a positive effect on their support for tourism development.

H4: The perception of negative economic impacts of tourism development by residents of Kashan will have a positive effect on their support for tourism development.

H5: The perception of negative socio-cultural impacts of tourism develop-ment by residents of Kashan will have a positive effect on their support for tourism development.

H6: The perception of negative environmental impacts of tourism develop-ment by residents of Kashan will have a positive effect on their support for tourism development.

Research method

Study area, historical city of Kashan

The historic city of Kashan is located in the north of Isfahan province, between Tehran and Isfahan. Based on the remains of settlements found in Tape Sialk, the ancient city of Kashan may date back to 6000 BCE (de Planhol, 2012). Archaeo-logical discoveries made in Tape Sialk reveal that Kashan was once a major pre-historic civilisation centre (de Planhol, 2012). Moreover, Kashan remains home to a wealth of tangible and intangible cultural heritage from throughout the centu-ries and spanning different dynasties, including historical houses (e.g. Broujerdi,

Tabatabaei, Ameri, Abbasi), Bazar-e-Kashan, mosques (e.g. Agha Bozorg, Jameh mosque, Miremad), carpets and handicrafts. So far, 323 elements have been inscribed as national cultural heritage and nine elements inscribed as intangible national cultural heritage (Iran Cultural Heritage, Handcraft and Tourism Organization (ICHTO), 2017). Bagh-e Fin was inscribed as tangible heritage along with eight other gardens, collectively recognised as the Persian Gardens WHS. Similarly, the Qālišuyān rituals of Mašhad-e Ardehāl and Kashan traditional carpet weaving skills have been inscribed as intangible cultural heritage (UNESCO, 2017a, 2017b).

Data collection and analysis

This study employed a quantitative design, using a questionnaire to collect data from residents of Kashan city. The questionnaire, based on the resident perception literature, was developed to measure residents' perceptions of the economic, social, cultural and environmental impacts of tourism development in Kashan (Nicholas, Thapa, & Ko, 2009; Rasoolimanesh et al., 2015; Rasoolimanesh, Noor, & Jaafar, forthcoming; Nunkoo & So, 2016; Jaafar et al., 2017). Four question items measure economic positive perceptions (ECO_PP), four items measure socio-cultural positive perceptions (SOCUL_PP), three items environmental positive perceptions (ENV_PP), three items economic negative perceptions (ECO_NP), five items socio-cultural negative perceptions (SOCUL_NP) and four items environmental negative perceptions (ENV_NP). Moreover, five items were adopted from previous studies to measure residents support for tourism development (SUP) in their community (Nicholas et al., 2009; Nunkoo & So, 2016). Questions items were answered on a five-point Likert scale, with 1 referring to *strongly disagree* and 5 referring to *strongly agree*. The questionnaire was translated from English into Persian by the native Persian-speaking researchers. The instrument was then pre-tested ahead of data collection with 35 samples, and interviews were conducted with five expert citizens of Kashan who were working in the heritage tourism industry. This initial pilot test was performed to check the preliminary validity and reliability of the translated questionnaire. Based on the interviews, items that residents found confusing were removed, while others were simply reworded to facilitate participant comprehension.

To collect data from Kashan city residents, two methods were employed: a field survey using systematic cluster sampling and online data collection. In the field survey, data were collected both from different clusters within the vicinity of historical areas, and at a distance deemed fairly remote from these historical areas. Moreover, the online questionnaire survey was posted to different Telegram channels and groups (a messaging app since banned in Iran (Al Jazeera, 2018; Dehghan & Roth, 2018)), asking residents of Kashan to complete the online questionnaire. Therefore, the sample was representative of Kashan city residents living in different parts of the city. The findings of this study are informed by 404 survey responses (250 from the field survey and 154 from the online survey). Data collection was performed in October and November 2017.

Descriptive data analysis was performed using SPSS 24.0 and SmartPLS 3.2.7 (Ringle, Wende, & Becker, 2015) was used to perform partial least squares structural equation modelling (PLS-SEM) to assess this study's measurement and structural models. PLS-SEM is a comprehensive multi-variate analysis approach that can simultaneously assess the reliability and validity of constructs (measurement models) and the relationships between constructs (Hair, Hult, Ringle, & Sarstedt, 2017). A sample of 404 is generally adequate for PLS-SEM, according to Reinartz, Haenlein and Henseler (2009), who suggest a threshold of 100 samples. In addition, G*Power was used to calculate the minimum sample size based on power analysis as a more conservative method (Faul, Erdfelder, Buchner, & Lang, 2009; Hair et al., 2017). For the proposed framework to gain a power of 0.95, a minimum sample size of 146 is needed; therefore, a sample of 404 is acceptable.

Results and findings

Descriptive analysis

Table 8.1 summarises the demographics of respondents in this study. The results show that 62.1% of respondents were male. The respondents were categorised into five age groups: 15–25 years (12.1%), 26–35 years (38.6%), 36–45 years (30.2%), 46–55 years (12.6%) and 56 years and above (6.4%). Most of the respondents had completed diploma or degree (65.1%), followed by post-graduate (17.1%), secondary school (8.9%), and primary school or no formal education (8.9%). Most respondents' household income was IRR 10,000,000–30,000,000. Only 80 respondents (19.8%) had a household income in excess of IRR 30,000,000 and 76 respondents (18.8%) had a household income below IRR 10,000,000. Most respondents (61.1%) earned less than 20% of their income from tourism-related industries, 107 respondents (26.5%) earned 20–39.99% of their income and only 50 respondents (12.4%) earned greater than 40% of their income from tourism.

Table 8.2 shows the results of the descriptive analysis. The results indicate that the residents of Kashan city perceived more positive tourism impacts and were supportive of tourism development. Residents believed that 'Tourism development promotes cultural exchange', 'Tourism development facilitates meeting visitors and educational experiences' and 'Tourism development can preserve the cultural identity of host residents'. In addition, the residents of Kashan believed that 'Tourism development attracts more investment', 'Tourism development creates more jobs', 'Tourism development provides more infrastructure and public facilities, like roads' and 'Tourism development increases recreation facilities and opportunities'. Therefore, residents agreed that tourism development had a positive economic and socio-cultural impact on their community. Moreover, residents acknowledged that 'Tourism development helps to preserve historical buildings' and 'Tourism development improves the area's appearance'. Therefore, the results highlight residents' positive perceptions towards the environmental impact of tourism development on their community. However, residents also perceived various negative economic, socio-cultural and environmental impacts on their

Table 8.1 Profile of respondents

Characteristics	Frequency	Percentage
Gender		
Male	251	62.1
Female	153	37.9
Age (years)		
15–25	49	12.1
26–35	156	38.6
36–45	122	30.2
46–55	51	12.6
56 and above	26	6.4
Level of education		
Primary school or no formal education	36	8.9
Secondary school	36	8.9
Certificate/diploma	130	32.2
Degree	133	32.9
Post-graduate	69	17.1
Level of income		
IRR 10,000,000 and below	76	18.8
IRR 10,000,001–20,000,000	149	36.9
IRR 20,000,001–30,000,000	99	24.5
Above IRR 30,000,000	80	19.8
Percentage of income from tourism		
< 20%	247	61.1
20%–39.99%	107	26.5
40%–59.99%	25	6.2
60%–79.99%	10	2.5
≥ 80%	15	3.7

Note: IRR41000 = USD 1.00 at the time of writing.

community, albeit to a lesser extent. The highest negative impacts cited by residents were traffic congestion, increased land and property prices, inflation in the price of goods and services, over-crowding and noise pollution, changes to their traditional lifestyle and culture, and an increase in the rate of crime. However, the results showed that residents were generally more positive and less negative with respect to the impacts of tourism development in Kashan. Therefore, residents were very supportive, indicating that: 'It is important to develop plans to manage the conservation of historical site and growth of tourism', 'The local authorities and state government should support the promotion of tourism' and 'I support tourism and would like to see it become an important part of my community'.

Assessment of model using PLS-SEM

The framework of this study includes seven reflective constructs, identified earlier: ECO_PP, SOCUL_PP, ENV_PP, ECO_NP, SOCUL_NP, ENV_NP and SUP. The analysis of the reflective constructs begins by checking their reliability and

Table 8.2 Results of the descriptive analysis

Construct/associated items	Mean	Standard deviation
Economic perceptions		
Economic positive perceptions (ECO_PP)		
1. Tourism development would create more jobs for my community.	4.141	0.927
2. Tourism development would attract more investment to my community.	4.196	0.900
3. Our standard of living would increase considerably because of tourism.	3.847	0.976
4. Tourism development provides more infrastructures and public facilities like roads, shopping malls, etc.	4.099	0.853
Economic negative perceptions (ECO_NP)		
1. Tourism development would increase the price of goods and services.	3.763	1.101
2. Tourism development would increase the price of land and housing.	3.782	1.029
3. Tourism development would increase the cost of living/property taxes.	3.681	1.121
Environmental perceptions		
Environmental positive perceptions (ENV_PP)		
1. Tourism development helps to preserve the natural environment.	3.851	1.014
2. Tourism development helps to preserve the historical buildings.	4.082	1.005
3. Tourism development improves the area's appearance.	4.040	1.052
Environmental negative perceptions (ENV_NP)		
1. Construction of hotels and other tourist facilities would destroy the environment.	3.540	1.201
2. Tourism development would result in traffic congestion.	3.834	1.266
3. Tourism development would cause over-crowding.	3.530	1.219
4. Tourism development would increase noise pollution.	3.426	1.203
Sociocultural perceptions		
Sociocultural positive perceptions (SOCUL_PP)		
1. Tourism development preserves the cultural identity of host residents.	4.084	0.872
2. Tourism development promotes cultural exchange.	4.213	0.777
3. Tourism development facilitates meeting visitors and educational experiences.	4.114	0.900
4. Tourism development increases recreation facilities and opportunities.	4.020	0.957

(Continued)

Table 8.2 (Continued)

Construct/associated items	Mean	Standard deviation
Sociocultural negative perceptions (SOCUL_NP)		
1. Tourism development increases the rate of crime.	3.270	1.291
2. Tourism development changes the lifestyle of the local community.	3.538	1.147
3. Tourism development changes the traditional culture and my culture may disappear slowly.	3.218	1.235
4. Tourism development disturbs the local community routine.	2.908	1.293
5. Tourism development creates a phony folk culture.	2.886	1.306
Support for tourism development (SUP)		
1. The residents should participate in conservation programmes of heritage sites.	4.156	0.959
2. I believe that tourism should be actively encouraged in my community.	4.194	0.970
3. I support tourism and would like to see it become an important part of my community.	4.235	0.891
4. The local authorities and state government should support the promotion of tourism.	4.367	0.821
5. It is important to develop plans to manage the conservation of historical sites and growth of tourism.	4.441	0.783

validity (Hair et al., 2017). To establish indicator reliability, the outer loading of each item on its associated construct should be higher than 0.7 (Hair et al., 2017). Table 8.3 indicates that the loading for most of the reflective construct items was higher than 0.7. However, items loading 0.5–0.7 should have their composite reliability (CR) and average variance extracted (AVE) checked, and if CR and AVE meet the thresholds then the items can be retained. The CR should be checked to establish internal consistency and AVE to establish convergent validity. The value of CR and AVE for each construct should be higher than 0.7 and 0.5 to establish internal consistency and convergent validity, respectively (Hair, Sarstedt, Ringle, & Mena, 2012; Hair et al., 2017). Table 8.3 shows that the CR and AVE values exceeded the threshold for all constructs. Therefore, the internal consistency and convergent validity was established for each of the reflective constructs in the framework. Given the high values in excess of the CR and AVE thresholds for each construct, many of the items loading 0.5–0.7 can be retained in the framework.

Discriminant validity should also be assessed in addition to reliability and convergent validity. Discriminant validity describes the distinction between the constructs in the framework. This study relies on two of the more conservative methods for assessing discriminant validity: the Fornell-Larcker criterion and the

Table 8.3 Assessment results of the measurement model

Construct/items	Outer loading	CR	AVE
ECO_PP		0.829	0.553
ECO_PP1	0.809		
ECO_PP2	0.865		
ECO_PP3	0.569		
ECO_PP4	0.697		
SOCUL_PP		0.807	0.511
SOCUL_PP1	0.724		
SOCUL_PP2	0.705		
SOCUL_PP3	0.693		
SOCUL_PP4	0.738		
ENV_PP		0.856	0.666
ENV_PP1	0.764		
ENV_PP2	0.846		
ENV_PP3	0.835		
ECO_NP		0.808	0.591
ECO_NP1	0.896		
ECO_NP2	0.790		
ECO_NP3	0.587		
SOCUL_NP		0.842	0.532
SOCUL_NP1	0.761		
SOCUL_NP2	0.899		
SOCUL_NP3	0.870		
SOCUL_NP4	0.579		
SOCUL_NP5	0.426		
ENV_NP		0.868	0.625
ENV_NP1	0.883		
ENV_NP2	0.810		
ENV_NP3	0.677		
ENV_PP4	0.778		
Support for tourism development (SUP)		0.839	0.514
SUP1	0.550		
SUP2	0.734		
SUP3	0.792		
SUP4	0.770		
SUP5	0.711		

Note: See Table 8.2 for the names of items.

heterotrait-monotrait (HTMT) ratio (Henseler, Ringle, & Sarstedt, 2015; Voorhees, Brady, Calantone, & Ramirez, 2016). Using the Fornell-Larcker criterion, the square root of the AVE for each construct should be higher than the construct's highest correlation with other constructs in the model (Hair et al., 2017). To establish discriminant validity using the HTMT ratio, the HTMT value of each construct should be lower than 0.85 (Henseler et al., 2015). Tables 8.4 and 8.5 show the outcomes of using both criteria and indicate that discriminant validity can be established for each of the constructs involved in the framework.

Table 8.4 Discriminant validity (Fornell-Larcker criterion)

Construct	ECO_PP	SOCUL_PP	ENV_PP	ECO_NP	SOCUL_NP	ENV_NP	SUP
ECO_PP	0.744						
SOCUL_PP	0.483	0.715					
ENV_PP	0.467	0.558	0.816				
ECO_NP	0.231	0.293	0.369	0.768			
SOCUL_NP	-0.248	-0.394	-0.314	0.093	0.730		
ENV_NP	-0.067	-0.109	-0.074	0.426	0.505	0.790	
SUP	0.468	0.461	0.384	0.143	-0.347	-0.202	0.717

Note: The square root of AVEs shown diagonally in bold.

Table 8.5 Discriminant validity (HTMT$_{85}$)

Construct	ECO_PP	SOCUL_PP	ENV_PP	ECO_NP	SOCUL_NP	ENV_NP	SUP
ECO_PP							
SOCUL_PP	0.673						
ENV_PP	0.636	0.779					
ECO_NP	0.302	0.364	0.427				
SOCUL_NP	0.271	0.485	0.342	0.314			
ENV_NP	0.177	0.169	0.118	0.659	0.728		
SUP	0.579	0.623	0.490	0.191	0.365	0.198	

Assessment of structural model

In order to assess the structural model and the hypotheses of this study, two criteria have been reported and discussed. The first criterion for this assessment is the value of R^2. The value of R^2 for SUP was 0.329, which is considered high by behavioural research standards (Hair et al., 2017). This R^2 SUP value indicates that 32.9% of the variance for SUP can be explained by residents' positive and negative economic, socio-cultural and environmental perceptions. The second criterion is the significance of the path coefficients, which in this study concerns *t*-values and bias corrected confidence interval (CI) using 5,000 bootstrap re-samples. The results of this study, shown in Table 8.6, support the positive effects of ECO_PP, SOCUL_PP and ENV_PP (H1–H3) on SUP. The highest effect belongs to that of ECO_PP on SUP, followed by SOCUL_PP on SUP. Whereas the lowest effect belongs to that of ENV_PP on SUP. Moreover, the results support the negative effects of SOCUL_NP and ENV_NP on SUP (H5–H6). However, this study could not support the effect of ECO_NP on SUP (H4).

Discussion and conclusion

The current study attempted to investigate the perceptions of residents of Kashan, a historical city in Iran, towards tourism development, and to identify the effects

Table 8.6 Results of hypothesis testing

	Hypothesis	Path coefficient	t- value	Confidence interval (Bias corrected)	Supported
H1	**ECO_PP → SUP**	0.285	5.949	[0.202, 0.361]	Yes
H2	**SOCUL_PP → SUP**	0.212	3.546	[0.116, 0.311]	Yes
H3	**ENV_PP → SUP**	0.069	1.525	[0.000, 0.147]	Yes
H4	**ECO_NP → SUP**	0.051	0.875	[-0.053. 0.135]	No
H5	**SOCUL_NP → SUP**	-0.117	1.892	[-0.216, -0.019]	Yes
H6	**ENV_NP → SUP**	-0.118	1.919	[-0.197, -0.024]	Yes

of these perceptions on their support for tourism development. The results revealed a propensity towards positive economic, socio-cultural and environmental perceptions among residents. This finding is consistent with many other studies, in particular in historical Iranian cities (Zamani-Farahani & Musa, 2012; Rezaei, 2017). The residents of Kashan, consistent with previous studies of heritage areas, believed that the development of heritage tourism contributed to the creation of more jobs and higher income, improved public facilities, helped to preserve their heritage and cultural identity, and facilitated cultural exchange with tourists (Zamani-Farahani & Musa, 2008, 2012; Abdollahzadeh & Sharifzadeh, 2014; Rezaei, 2017). However, the results also elucidated various resident concerns about the negative impacts of tourism development, such as traffic congestion, increasing property and land price, inflation in the price of goods and services, over-crowding and noise pollution, changes in their traditional lifestyle and culture, and an increase in the rate of crime, consistent with some previous studies (Ghaderi & Henderson, 2012; Zamani-Farahani & Musa, 2012; Rezaei, 2017). Despite Kashan being a very religious city, residents were least concerned over negative socio-cultural impacts; their primary concerns were about negative environmental and economic impacts. This finding is also consistent with a recent study conducted in the historical city of Yazd (Rezaei, 2017). The results indicate that Kashan residents were highly supportive of tourism development, as indicated by the positive bias in their perceptions of positive impacts, as compared to negative impacts, for tourism development on their community. This finding is consistent with SET, with previous studies indicating that residents are more supportive of tourism development when they perceive more benefits than costs for their community (Gursoy et al., 2002; Ko & Stewart, 2002; Wang & Pfister, 2008; Látková & Vogt, 2012; Haobin Ye et al., 2014; Rasoolimanesh et al., 2015).

The findings of this study reveal the positive effects of economic, socio-cultural and environmental positive perceptions on residents' support for tourism development, with these findings being consistent with SET and several previous studies (Gursoy et al., 2002; Ko & Stewart, 2002; Haobin Ye et al., 2014; Rasoolimanesh et al., 2015). The findings identified the highest perceived positive impacts for ECO_PP, followed by SOCUL_PP and ENV_PP, respectively. Several previous studies have identified the importance of positive economic and socio-cultural impacts of tourism development with respect to community members in historical areas (Ghaderi & Henderson, 2012; Zamani-Farahani & Musa, 2012; Rezaei, 2017), these being consistent with the results of the current study. Moreover, the findings of the current study revealed the negative and significant effects of socio-cultural and environmental negative perceptions among residents on their support for tourism development. Residents with more negative socio-cultural and environmental perceptions towards tourism development were less inclined to support tourism development in Kashan. These results are consistent with SET and the findings of several previous studies that reported on the effects of residents' perceptions of negative impacts (Gursoy et al., 2002; Nunkoo & Ramkissoon, 2011; Haobin Ye et al., 2014; Rasoolimanesh et al., 2015).

The focus of the current study has been perceptions of residents living in the historical city of Kashan with respect to heritage tourism development. As such, this study makes a significant contribution to the development of tourism in historical Iranian cities. In addition, the results have a number of practical implications for Kashan local authorities looking to develop tourism sustainably. The results indicate that Kashan residents have a number of positive perceptions regarding the impacts of tourism development; however, these same residents also have some concerns about the negative impacts of tourism development. Local authorities should aim to reduce these negative impacts.

The findings indicate that residents' positive perceptions of the economic and socio-cultural impacts of tourism development positively influence their support for tourism. Local authorities looking to gain the support of residents for tourism development should therefore seek ways to increase the economic and socio-cultural impacts of tourism development if resident support for tourism is regarded as significant. The results also identified residents' negative socio-cultural and environmental perceptions regarding the impacts of tourism development in Kashan. Interventions from local authorities may help to mitigate such impacts. In summary, the results suggest that local Kashan authorities should aim to develop effective plans with the participation of residents in order to manage the process of tourism development and the conservation of heritage sites if they wish to make tourism in Kashan more sustainable.

This study, of course, was not without its share of limitations. Data were collected from different parts of the city and were analysed to identify the perceptions of residents and the effects of these perceptions on residents' support for tourism development. Heterogeneities may exist among the perceptions of residents based on their distance from heritage sites or other criteria, which we did not consider in this study. This can be a major limitation of the current study and one that future studies should look to ameliorate if they wish to better understand the perceptions of residents of historical cities in Iran. Nevertheless, given the significance of heritage tourism and historical urban centres in Iranian tourism, this study points towards the need for further research on heritage tourism and its adoption by management authorities, in order to improve the sustainability of historical cities in Iran.

References

Abdollahzadeh, G. & Sharifzadeh, A. (2014). Rural residents' perceptions toward tourism development: A study from Iran. *International Journal of Tourism Research, 16*(2), 126–136.

Adie, B. A., Hall, C. M., & Prayag, G. (2018). World Heritage as a placebo brand: A comparative analysis of three sites and marketing implications. *Journal of Sustainable Tourism, 26*(3), 399–415.

Ahadian, O. (2013). Residents' perceptions of tourism development–implications for small economies business: The case study of Ali Sadr, Iran. *Current Issues in Tourism, 16*(1), 97–106.

Al Jazeera. (2018). Iran to block Telegram messaging app: Reports. The app, used during last year's protests, will be replaced by a similar app built by the government, officials say. *Al Jazeera*, 1 April. Retrieved from https://www.aljazeera.com/news/2018/04/iran-block-telegram-messaging-app-officials-180401095059178.html

Andereck, K., Valentine, K., Knopf, R., & Vogt, C. (2005). Residents' perceptions of community tourism impacts. *Annals of Tourism Research, 32*(4), 1056–1076.

Choi, H. & Sirakaya, E. (2006). Sustainability indicators for managing community tourism. *Tourism Management, 27*(6), 1274–1289.

de Planhol, X. (2012). Kashan ii. Historical geography. *Encyclopaedia Iranica*. Retrieved from http://www.iranicaonline.org/articles/kashan-ii-historical-geography

Dehghan, S. K. & Roth, A. (2018). Ayatollah leaves Telegram as Iran prepares to block messaging service. *The Guardian*, 18 April. Retrieved from https://www.theguardian.com/world/2018/apr/18/iran-prepares-to-block-messaging-app-telegram

Faul, F., Erdfelder, E., Buchner, A., & Lang, A.-G. (2009). Statistical power analyses using G*Power 3.1: Tests for correlation and regression analyses. *Behavior Research Methods, 41*(4), 1149–1160.

Ghaderi, Z. & Henderson, J. C. (2012). Sustainable rural tourism in Iran: A perspective from Hawraman Village. *Tourism Management Perspectives, 2–3*, 47–54.

Gu, M. & Wong, P. P. (2006). Residents' perception of tourism impacts: A case study of homestay operators in Dachangshan Dao, North-East China. *Tourism Geographies, 8*(3), 253–273.

Gursoy, D., Jurowski, C., & Uysal, M. (2002). Resident attitudes: A structural modeling approach. *Annals of Tourism Research, 29*(1), 79–105.

Hair, J. F., Sarstedt, M., Ringle, C. M., & Mena, J. A. (2012). An assessment of the use of partial least squares structural equation modeling in marketing research. *Journal of the Academy of Marketing Science, 40*(3), 414–433.

Hair, J., Hult, G., Ringle, C., & Sarstedt, M. (2017). *A primer on partial least squares structural equations modeling (PLS-SEM)* (2nd ed.). Los Angeles, CA: Sage.

Haobin Ye, B., Qiu Zhang, H., Huawen Shen, J., & Goh, C. (2014). Does social identity affect residents' attitude toward tourism development? *International Journal of Contemporary Hospitality Management, 26*(6), 907–929.

Henseler, J., Ringle, C. M., & Sarstedt, M. (2015). A new criterion for assessing discriminant validity in variance-based structural equation modeling. *Journal of the Academy of Marketing Science, 43*(1), 115–135.

Iran Cultural Heritage, Handcraft and Tourism Organization (ICHTO). (2017). *The national cultural heritage list of Iran*. Tehran, Iran. Retrieved from http://www.ichto.ir/Portals/0/r.docx

Jaafar, M., Noor, S., & Rasoolimanesh, S. (2015). Perception of young local residents toward sustainable conservation programmes: A case study of the Lenggong World Cultural Heritage Site. *Tourism Management, 48*, 154–163.

Jaafar, M., Rasoolimanesh, S. M., & Ismail, S. (2017). Perceived sociocultural impacts of tourism and community participation: A case study of Langkawi Island. *Tourism and Hospitality Research, 17*(2), 123–134.

Kayat, K. (2002). Power, social exchanges and tourism in Langkawi: Rethinking resident perceptions. *International Journal of Tourism Research, 4*(3), 171–191.

Kim, K., Uysal, M., & Sirgy, M. J. (2013). How does tourism in a community impact the quality of life of community residents? *Tourism Management, 36*, 527–540.

Ko, D. & Stewart, W. (2002). A structural equation model of residents' attitudes for tourism development. *Tourism Management, 23*(5), 521–530.

Látková, P. & Vogt, C. (2012). Residents' attitudes toward existing and future tourism development in rural communities. *Journal of Travel Research, 51*(1), 50–67.

Nicholas, L., Thapa, B., & Ko, Y. (2009). Residents' perspectives of a world heritage site: The Pitons Management Area, St. Lucia. *Annals of Tourism Research, 36*(3), 390–412.

Nunkoo, R. & Ramkissoon, H. (2011). Residents' satisfaction with community attributes and support for tourism. *Journal of Hospitality and Tourism Research, 35*(2), 171–190.

Nunkoo, R. & So, K. K. F. (2016). Residents' support for tourism: Testing alternative structural models. *Journal of Travel Research, 55*(7), 847–861.

Rasoolimanesh, S. M., & Jaafar, M. (2017). Sustainable tourism development and residents' perceptions in World Heritage Site destinations. *Asia Pacific Journal of Tourism Research, 22*(1), 34–48.

Rasoolimanesh, S. M., Jaafar, M., Kock, N., & Ramayah, T. (2015). A revised framework of social exchange theory to investigate the factors influencing residents' perceptions. *Tourism Management Perspectives, 16*, 335–345.

Rasoolimanesh, S. M., Jaafar, M., Kock, N., & Ahmad, A. G. (2017a). The effects of community factors on residents' perceptions toward World Heritage Site inscription and sustainable tourism development. *Journal of Sustainable Tourism, 25*(2), 198–216.

Rasoolimanesh, S. M., Roldán, J. L., Jaafar, M., & Ramayah, T. (2017b). Factors influencing residents' perceptions toward tourism development: Differences across rural and urban world heritage sites. *Journal of Travel Research, 56*(6), 760–775.

Rasoolimanesh, S. M., Noor, S. M., & Jaafar, M. (forthcoming). Positive and negative perceptions of residents toward tourism development: Formative or reflective. In S. Rezaei (Ed.), *Quantitative tourism research in Asia: Current status and future directions*. Singapore: Springer.

Rastegar, H. (2010). Tourism development and residents' attitude: A case study of Yazd, Iran. *Tourismos, 5*(2), 203–211.

Reinartz, W., Haenlein, M., & Henseler, J. (2009). An empirical comparison of the efficacy of covariance-based and variance-based SEM. *International Journal of Research in Marketing, 26*(4), 332–344.

Rezaei, N. (2017). Resident perceptions toward tourism impacts in historic center of Yazd, Iran. *Tourism Geographies*. doi: 10.1080/14616688.2017.1331261

Ringle, C., Wende, S., & Becker, J. (2015). *SmartPLS 3 (version 3.2.3, computer software)*. Boenningstedt, Germany: SmartPLS GmbH.

Sharpley, R. (2014). Host perceptions of tourism: A review of the research. *Tourism Management, 42*, 37–49.

Su, M. & Wall, G. (2014). Community participation in tourism at a World Heritage site: Mutianyu Great Wall, Beijing, China. *International Journal of Tourism Research, 16*(2), 146–156.

United Nations Educational, Scientific and Cultural Organization (UNESCO). (2017a). The state parties: Iran (Islamic Republic f). *UNESCO, World Heritage Center.* Retrieved from http://whc.unesco.org/en/statesparties/ir

United Nations Educational, Scientific and Cultural Organization (UNESCO). (2017b). Iran (Islamic Republic of) and the 2003 convention. *UNESCO, Intangible Cultural Heritage.* Retrieved from https://ich.unesco.org/en/state/iran-islamic-republic-of-IR

Vareiro, L., Remoaldo, P., & Cadima Ribeiro, J. (2013). Residents' perceptions of tourism impacts in Guimarães (Portugal): A cluster analysis. *Current Issues in Tourism, 16*(6), 535–551.

Voorhees, C. M., Brady, M. K., Calantone, R., & Ramirez, E. (2016). Discriminant validity testing in marketing: An analysis, causes for concern, and proposed remedies. *Journal of the Academy of Marketing Science, 44*(1), 119–134.

Wang, Y. & Pfister, R. (2008). Residents' attitudes toward tourism and perceived personal benefits in a rural community. *Journal of Travel Research, 47*(1), 84–93.

World Tourism Organization (UNWTO). (2014). *UNWTO tourism highlights, 2014 edition.* Madrid, Spain: UNWTO.

World Tourism Organization (UNWTO). (2016). *UNWTO tourism highlights, 2016 edition.* Madrid, Spain: UNWTO.

World Tourism Organization (UNWTO). (2017). *UNWTO tourism highlights, 2017 edition.* Madrid, Spain: UNWTO.

Zamani-Farahani, H. & Henderson, J. C. (2014). Community attitudes toward tourists: A study of Iran. *International Journal of Hospitality and Tourism Administration, 15*(4), 354–375.

Zamani-Farahani, H. & Musa, G. (2008). Residents' attitudes and perception towards tourism development: A case study of Masooleh, Iran. *Tourism Management, 29*(6), 1233–1236.

Zamani-Farahani, H. & Musa, G. (2012). The relationship between Islamic religiosity and residents' perceptions of socio-cultural impacts of tourism in Iran: Case studies of Sare'in and Masooleh. *Tourism Management, 33*(4), 802–814.

9 The role of socio-cultural events in rebuilding Iran's image

Bardia Shabani and Hazel Tucker

Introduction

Human rights violations, conflict and other political events can have a significant negative effect on a country's tourism image and tourist arrivals (Neumayer, 2004). Even if tourist areas are secure, tourism may decline precipitously when political conditions appear unsettled, with tourists simply choosing alternative destinations. Countries which have a negative image in this way often attempt to improve their tourism image with advertising campaigns (Sönmez, Apostolopoulos, & Tarlow, 1999), adopting various models, such as a multi-step model for altering place image, adopting certain media policies and using crisis communication techniques (Avraham, 2015). Hosting socio-cultural events is also part of place image strategies and can play a pivotal role in demonstrating that a place is safe, hospitable and friendly, thereby replacing a problematic/negative image with a positive one (Beirman, 2003; Avraham, 2013).

This chapter discusses the role of festivals and other socio-cultural events in the rebuilding of image, or image recovery, of a destination, with specific focus on Iran. While Iran offers numerous historic sites, diverse landscapes and other tourist attractions to visitors, as discussed in other chapters in this book tourism has been heavily affected by the country being subjected to international economic sanctions for over 20 years. Beginning in 1995, these sanctions remained in place until January 2016, when all international sanctions (related to the country's nuclear programme) were officially lifted (see also Chapter 1, this volume). The agreement lifting the sanctions has resulted in turning the situation around so that, in the context of the Middle East region where terrorist attacks have significantly increased in recent years, including in countries such as Turkey which has been one of Iran's main competitors in tourism, Iran can now be considered one of the safe and secure countries of the region.

Benefiting from this new political situation, Iran has attached considerable significance to developing its tourism industry, and it has made a push to increase inbound tourism in recent years. As destination image plays a key role in the tourist perception of the country, which then influences tourist decision-making processes and experience, Iran is currently attempting to rebuild its image. In particular, attempts are being made to promote the country's rich culture and customs in order to attract international tourists. Festivals and other socio-cultural events play a special role in the lives of communities throughout Iran. They affect both locals and visitors as they provide important activities and spending outlets for both 'host' and 'guest' communities, which in turn potentially boost tourism development at both the destination and the regional levels.

This chapter discusses the role that socio-cultural events can play in the redevelopment of Iran's image as an international tourism destination. Firstly, the subject of destination image recovery after conflict will briefly be outlined, before going on to discuss socio-cultural events more specifically as having a potential role in destination image recovery. The discussion will then focus in on a particular festival – the Rose and Rosewater Festival in Isfahan province – in order to provide an empirical case study to illustrate the relationship between socio-cultural events and the rebuilding of Iran's destination image.

Destination image and recovery after conflict

'Image' comprises the mental structures (visual or not) that integrate the elements, the values and the impressions that people have about a specific place, and it is based on a series of knowledge and perceptions of both an emotional and affective nature. Accordingly, a 'place image' is the sum of beliefs, ideas and impressions that people have of a place (Kotler, Haider, & Rein, 1993). In relation to tourism, then, destination image has a great influence, not only regarding the choice of a destination, but also in the ways in which it affects the tourist behaviour at all stages. Accordingly, Matos, Mendes and Valle (2012) posit three different phases of tourists' behaviour and image formation:

- *Before* (Priori image); the first phase, the decision process before travelling to the destination.
- *During* (Image in Loco); the second phase, the evaluation process between the experience at the destination versus the expectations met.
- *After* (Posteriori image); the third phase, after vacation experience, variables regarding the tourists' experiences and the future behaviour, e.g. the decision process of revisiting and/or recommending the destination to others.

The tourism industry in destinations is very sensitive and highly affected by forces and events in its external environment, meaning that even small-scale crises may have a considerable impact on a destination (Ritchie, 2004; Hall, 2010). Both human and natural disasters can cause crises which prove challenging to the tourism industry in destinations. While natural disasters can potentially just reduce the flow of tourism (Sonmez & Graefe, 1998), 'human' crises, such as crime, war, terrorism, political and civil unrest, have the potential to impact tourism more profoundly, causing major negative and long-lasting marks on a destination's tourism image (Hall, 2010).

Diplomatic conflicts that occur between two (or more) countries may influence the attitude and behaviour of its citizens, which can affect the intention to buy and travel to that specific destination. This effect is referred to as 'animosity' in the international marketing literature (e.g. see Heslop, Lu, & Cray, 2008; Bahaee & Pisani, 2009). Animosity is defined by Klein, Ettenson, and Morris (1998, p. 90) as 'the remnants of antipathy related to previous or ongoing military, political, or economic events' that are perceived as 'grievous and difficult to forgive'. Whenever citizens experience animosity towards a particular country, despite the important natural, archaeological and historical resources that country enjoys, they may refuse to travel to or buy that country's products, even if the consumers value the quality of products and attractions of the destination (Alvarez & Camo, 2014; Nes, Yelkur, & Silkoset, 2012). As consumers' image is based on feelings and emotions, their behaviours will be affected by animosity (Nes, Yelkur, & Silkoset, 2012; Leong et al., 2008; Verlegh & Steenkamp, 1999). This phenomenon and its effect on tourists' intention to visit a destination has been studied and analysed by Podoshen and Hunt (2011), who explain how political conflicts negatively affect the image of the country involved, as well as the intention to visit it.

Lowery and DeFleur (1983) argue that 'perception' and 'media' are two key factors that are important to destination image recovery after conflict. More recently, research into media's effects on destination image shows that mass media creates anew, and reflects existing, public opinion, attitudes and perceptions, and additionally, has the power to alter images quickly (Tasci & Gartner, 2007; Newbold, Boyd-Barrett, & Van den Bulck, 2002). It is possible, also, that socio-cultural events can play a role in boosting destination image recovery, since the outcomes of festivals and events are known to be far wider-reaching than merely their economic impact.

Event impacts

Festivals and events play an important role in the lives of communities. They affect both local people and visitors as they provide important activities and spending outlets for locals and visitors (Getz, 2007). Hall (1992) has previously pointed out that all events have impacts, regardless of type, size and the hosting city, region or country. As such, events inevitably affect participants, host communities and other stakeholders; hence the impacts are considered to be positive or beneficial in cases where the events meet the intended and desired economic, social, cultural, political or environmental outcomes. Failure of predicted outcomes are considered negative impacts, such as environmental damage, pollution, increase of crime rate and disturbing the local residents' normal life (Getz, 2007).

Indeed, the potential of positive desired benefits of events is the principal driver underpinning the support for and increasing popularity of festivals and other socio-cultural events at the local, national and international scale. Positive benefits are believed to occur if local residents are enthusiastic about and support the events as their lives will be directly impacted by tourism-related activities (Weaver & Lawton, 2013). Ideally, tourism should maximise benefits and minimise negative consequences, and so a key task for event managers is to identify and predict the impacts of events, in order to manage them in such a way that 'on balance the overall impact of the event is positive' (Bowdin, Allen, O'Toole, Harris, & McDonnell, 2006, p. 37).

However, events are not always promoted for the economic benefits that they might generate, and they may even be staged at an economic 'loss', but the desired benefits of the event might be overtly socio-cultural: for example, increasing local participation in community activities and revitalising local culture and traditions (Ritchie, 1984), strengthening community identity and pride (De Bres & Davis, 2001), developing social capital (Arcodia & Whitford, 2006) and also events may be staged for political purposes (Roche, 2000).

Moreover, the impacts of events are neither hierarchical nor discrete. This explains all positive and negative impacts of events; some being more immediately evident than others, and some being of potentially greater significance than the intended outcomes. This can be seen in Lee and Taylor's (2005) study in which they explained how the South Korean national team's success at the 2002 FIFA World Cup created a sense of national pride which far outweighed the event's economic returns.

Socio-cultural events in Iran

While Iran has long been an international tourism destination because of its four-season climate, nature, heritage and cultural attractions, tourism in Iran has received a new resurgence since the recent uplift of UN sanctions (Pleitgen, 2015; Pemberton & Leach, 2015). As discussed in Chapters 1 and 3 (this volume), Iran has been subjected to international economic sanctions for more than a decade, but in January 2016 all international sanctions were officially lifted. Moreover, in contrast to other previously popular tourist destinations in the Near/Middle East and Northern Africa (such as Syria, Yemen, Afghanistan, Iraq, Libya and Tunisia), many of which have become no-go areas in recent years as a result of war or terrorism, Iran is now considered a relatively stable and safe country to visit. In 2014, Iran hosted nearly 5 million foreign tourists and it is expected that this number will rise to 20 million per annum by 2025 (PressTV, 2015; UNWTO, 2015). The prospects of the Iranian tourism industry are bright. *National Geographic Traveller* put Iran first in its must-see destinations for travel in 2016 (National Geographic Traveller, 2015). In 2016, Asia and Pacific ranked as the fastest-growing region, including Iran, and enjoyed a growth rate of 9% in the number of international tourist arrivals during that year (UNWTO, 2017).

A predominantly Shiite country, Iran is famous for its hospitable culture, which differs greatly from that of many of its neighbours. Hence, the Iranian Tourism Authorities aim to offer international visitors a memorable experience of Iran. One key way they intend to do so is by hosting socio-cultural festivals that will help the country's image in filling a genuine existing gap in the region's market. According to the International Association for Impact Assessment (IAIA) (2003), festivals can have many different impacts on the lives of local communities and in relation to tourism, both positive and negative, and based on knowledge of these impacts, tourism strategies can be designed to achieve the maximum gain.

Hosting socio-cultural events is a strategy the Iranian Tourism Authorities use in order to increase Iran's profile and hence to increase tourism and benefit the tourism industry in various ways. The desired purpose of hosting festivals and other socio-cultural events can thus be summarised as:

1. Sustainable income: It is expected that hosting festivals will provide employment to residents, who receive revenue from lodging, food and sale of traditional handicrafts. Hence the income will change people's way of life, how they work and will encourage interaction and networking within and between communities.
2. Improvement of local services: Iran's augmented income from festivals will improve infrastructure and transport systems. In addition to a general increase in revenue across the community, local communities' budget level will improve; this can fund projects for the community, notably within the health and education sector.
3. Cultural empowerment and exchange: Community participation adds considerable value to the sustainability of these festivals, changes the norms, beliefs, perceptions, morals and the conduct or behaviour that might enhance quality of life of local residents, and at the same time increase self-esteem as a result of interest shown by outsiders.
4. Local awareness of conservation: In Iran, local people are often heard expressing pride in their cultural heritage, of the pre-Islamic era just as much as of more recent times. Tourists coming from afar will give local communities a sense of the global importance of culture and customs. Awareness of the significance of such cultural resources on their doorstep, and the economic benefits from international tourism, can boost local conservation efforts.
5. Decision making and political awareness: Tourism decision makers in Iran are willing to encourage local communities to participate in decision making processes in their own region more actively. Interactions with other nations will increase the level of political awareness of the host community and will encourage them to participate in decisions that could affect their lives, their perceptions about their safety, their fears about the future of their community and their aspirations for their future and the future of their children.
6. Environmental responsibility: Educating local communities and increasing their awareness regarding the environment is part of Iran's sustainability programme. Through socio-cultural events residents and tourists can be prepared and informed about environmental issues, projects and other matters.

By hosting socio-cultural events, the Iranian authorities aim to encourage international tourists to visit the country more than once, so the country can gain its place in a number of different potential markets. These festivals can also be considered as a platform for creating landmarks, which often represent a less costly means of distinguishing places and regions, as well as generating media interest. Iranian tourism authorities thus look to socio-cultural events as a means for enhancing image. Such events can also help to add life to city streets and to demonstrate a sense of hospitality towards outsiders and provide citizens with renewed pride in their home country. This improvement of community pride has previously been referred to as the 'halo effect' (Hall, 1992), the 'showcase effect' (Fredline & Faulkner, 1998) and the 'feel good effect' (Allen, O'Toole, Mcdonnell, & Harris, 2002).

Similar to some major cultural events that have arguably become 'brands', such as the Edinburgh Festival and Cannes Film Festival, Iran is investing in and making an attempt at creating new brands of socio-cultural festivals based on previous successful models. The Rose and Rosewater Festival in Isfahan province is an example of such an event. The findings of empirical research conducted into this festival and its destination image impacts will now be described in order to present an illustrative case example of the role socio-cultural events can play in destination image rebuilding.

Rose and Rosewater Festival

Kashan is a city of Isfahan province with a land area of 4,392 km^2 and a population of 330,000. It is located 240 km south of Tehran and 220 km north of Isfahan (Ministry of Interior of Iran, 2015). The history of this city dates back to the sixth millennium BC (UNESCO, 2007), and Kashan became an important centre for the production of high quality pottery and tiles between the twelfth and fourteenth centuries; hence 'kashi', the word for tile in modern Persian, comes from the name of this town. On 9 August 2007 Iran put the Historical Axis of Fin, Sialk, Kashan on its Tentative List for possible future nominations for UNESCO World Heritage site listing, and in 2011 Fin Garden was chosen as one of the nine gardens listed as 'Persian Gardens' (UNESCO, 2011).

Apart from its great history, Kashan is famous for its natural scenery. From the eastern side, the city opens up to the central desert of Iran which has become a popular tourism destination, in particular, Maranjab Desert and Caravanserai located near the Salt Lake, and from the western side, the city neighbours a mountainous area which is the location of major rose gardens (Ministry of Interior of Iran, 2017). Additionally, there are many reasons why tourists visit the city of Kashan itself, including ancient sites, nature, local culture and folklore, traditions, historical houses and Persian rugs. Another key reason is a particular festival that Kashan has to offer, namely the Rose and Rosewater Festival. This annual festival is one of the most well-known socio-cultural events in Iran (IRIB English Radio, 2013).

The production of rose water in Iran dates back over 2,500 years and Kashan has been the main region for producing rose water for over 800 years. Rose water in Iranian culture and cuisine is very important and Iranians use it in nearly all of their sweets and many of their ceremonies. In Islamic culture it is believed that the Holy Prophet Muhammad always used rose water and had recommended Muslims to do likewise. Accordingly, Iranians named this flower after the Holy Prophet's name, calling it the 'Muhammadi' flower in Persian. Also, the Kaaba (Muslims' holiest site) in Mecca is washed by Kashan rose water two times a year, as the rosewater produced in this area is considered the purest rose water in the world (IRIB English Radio, 2013).

The most well-known national symbol of Kashan is the large Rose and Rosewater Festival, where visitors can learn about rosewater and other herbal drinks, as well as experiencing traditional dress and music. In spring, during mid-May to early June, the Rose and Rosewater Festival begins with rose flower picking (*Golchini*) and extraction of rose water (*Golabgiri*) in all of the rose gardens of Kashan (IRIB English Radio, 2013). This is a public festival that brings together tens of thousands of visitors from all over the country and abroad. The number of participants in the festival can reach up to 1 million people. Tourists are welcome to visit the gardens and observe all of the procedures related to rose water production for free, while they can taste many different herbal drinks with fresh rose water. During the last 15 years of hosting the festival, the increase in tourist arrivals has dramatically changed the economy of the region, as well as influencing the local culture in positive ways. That is, as well as learning the value of being hospitable and respectful towards visitors, there are renewed incentives to keep the city clean and well-presented. The local community has increasingly embraced the notion that the more welcoming they and their city are towards tourists, the more tourists will enjoy their visit and the more likely they are to come back again and recommend others to visit. Furthermore, tourists' interest in the local culture and traditions, particularly during the festival period, has increased the level of local community awareness of their traditions and customs, thus improving community identity and pride (see also Chapter 8, this volume).

According to Iran Review (2016), international visitors attending the festival invariably have their expectations surpassed, especially in relation to the local cuisine enjoyed and the hospitality culture of local residents. It is this suggestion, that the festival might play an influential part in visitors' overall impressions of Iran as a tourism destination, which prompted the authors to undertake an empirical study involving an interview survey with international visitors at the festival.

The survey was undertaken at the 2017 Rose and Rosewater Festival and was administered in a 'semi-structured interview' format in person by one of the authors (Shabani). Convenience sampling occurred whereby any apparently foreign visitors were approached and asked if they were willing to take part in a short interview survey. Of 23 respondents asked, 20 were interviewed overall. There were nine nationalities among the 20 respondents: Belgium (2); China (2); France (6); Germany (2); Japan (1); Malaysia (1); Netherlands (4); Russia (1); Switzerland (1). The interviews lasted for approximately ten minutes each, on average, and in general, the interviewees expressed a willingness and openness to participate in the research. The interviews were conducted in English with the interviewees asked a series of questions on subjects including: their perceptions of Iran before visiting the country; changes to their perceptions/impressions; and how they felt that their experiences of the festival influenced their impressions of Iran. The respondents' answers to the interview questions were later analysed for identifiable patterns which were 'meaningful' regarding the subject of the relationship between festivals/socio-cultural events and destination image. While the survey was limited in size and scope, it produced nonetheless some informative results. These results were organised around the destination image process mentioned earlier in this chapter (before/prior image, during/image in loco, after/posteriori image), and they will now be outlined.

Before (priori image)

While most of the respondents said that they had learnt about Iran from books (guidebooks and other) and other media, approximately half of them said that they had learnt about Iran from friends. Correspondingly, in answer to the question about what their main reasons for choosing to travel to Iran were, more than a third said that friends had recommended Iran to them. This is an important point to highlight because it immediately draws links between the three 'phases' of destination image: before, during and after. The other main reasons respondents gave for choosing to visit Iran were to experience it for themselves and learn more about Iran's Persian history, culture, architecture and also Iran's natural attractions. Many respondents said that they had heard about Iran being a beautiful country, and a few said that they had wanted to visit Iran to experience the friendliness of the Iranian people. The majority of the visitors interviewed were travelling in a tour group, and this fact might correspond with their responses to the question of what their perception of Iran was before they visited the country. Approximately half of the respondents said that they had a negative image of Iran, and more precisely that it was 'unsafe'. Many respondents said that friends who had visited previously had persuaded them that the negative image of Iran as portrayed in the media was erroneous. Example responses to the question of what their perception of Iran was before travelling to the country include:

Somehow scary and not a very safe country.

Not very safe as you need to watch yourself constantly. Mostly bad.

A pretty comprehensive image. I know some media have said that Iran is not a good place but I knew it was not true and my friends told me Iran is a good place.

Mixed. I've heard Iran is not a safe country but some told me it is a safe country. I was also told that the people are very hospitable.

During (image in loco)

As suggested above, this second phase in the destination image formation process comprises the evaluation process between the experience at the destination versus the expectations met. Interestingly, all of the respondents reported having a very positive 'image in loco' of Iran. All of the respondents who reported having any sort of negative image before their visit said that their image had completely changed and that now they had an extremely positive image of the country. Example responses to the question of how, if at all, their perception had changed during their visit include:

> It is changed 180 degrees. Here is very safe and everybody is happy and smiling at you all of the time and I absolutely adore it here.

> My image is better than before, as the people are very kind, cities are well-developed, safe and clean and everything is organized.

> Iran is a very nice place. I can see people are very friendly and this has changed my image. Here is very safe and I feel safer in Iran than in France!

With regards to the respondents' experiences at the Rose and Rosewater Festival, there were two main strands in the way they explained their enjoyment of the festival. One strand concerned the enjoyment of the 'unique' and 'authentic'/'traditional' focus of the festival in relation to the rose gardens and rosewater production and tastings. The other main strand concerned the enjoyment of the friendly atmosphere of the festival and the opportunity to be among 'local people'. Example responses to the question of how respondents were finding the festival include:

> Very authentic festival, it is free to enter the gardens and see all the procedure of producing rosewater and free rosewater drinks.

> Stunning view, the rose gardens are very beautiful. It's amazing that people will welcome everyone to their gardens and will ask them to join their festival and test their drinks.

> I really enjoyed the hospitality of the people and I can see people are very happy here. Different families asked me to take pictures with them and I feel like a celebrity here!

> I enjoy it very much and it is nice to be with local people.

When asked how they thought attending the festival had influenced their overall image of Iran as a tourist destination, all of the respondents expressed the idea that being at the festival primarily had allowed them to have close contact with Iranian people and to experience their friendliness and hospitality:

> I love talking to the local people and learning about their customs and culture. So at this festival, I had the chance to learn more about Iranian culture.

> Engaging with people here provided me great information about their culture and behaviour.

> The people are very warm and I can feel that they are very happy.

> Happiness is something you can see immediately in people's faces here, children are playing around and families are so relaxed and smiling.

The hospitality culture of Iranians profoundly affected my point of view about this country and I can say that they have the best hospitality culture.

I, for myself, experienced the safety here and saw how Iranians are friendly and helpful. Their behaviour affected my previous image.

After (posteriori image)

In relation to the third phase, pertaining to after the vacation experience and the tourists' future behaviour in terms of both of revisiting and/or recommending the destination to others, although the interviews were able only to give future projections, rather than actual 'posteriori image', responses provided some interesting opinions relating to posteriori image. In line with the responses regarding 'image in loco', discussed above, and the point that experiencing the hospitality and friendliness of the Iranian people at the festival is such an important part of the experience for international visitors, it was this experience that respondents said would encourage them both to revisit Iran and to recommend visiting Iran to others. In response to the question of how experiencing Iran's socio-cultural events such as the Rose and Rosewater Festival might affect tourists' tendency to revisit Iran or to recommend visiting Iran to others, almost all of the responses described their seeing a direct link between experiencing such events and revisiting or recommending Iran. Examples of this direct link being drawn include:

It can help a lot, as people will tell many good things about it so friends and family members will trust and I think this will work even better than any advertisement.

It is very effective that people come and have this experience and I think their first-hand experience will help them to recommend it to others.

These festivals are very good examples of Iranian culture and people will learn about it. Also, the way that they are treating tourists will make me sure to come back again and tell my friends to visit too.

By experiencing this event people would have a better understanding of Iran and the people and I think they will say many good things about Iran.

I think tourists want to experience something new and interesting, and if they want to learn about new culture, I say this is it. Engaging with local people in these festivals will affect tourists' image in a good way and I think they will come back again.

This festival is a good way for tourists to get familiar with traditions, culture and customs (of Iran), so I think this will help the image. Tourists like to talk to the local people and buy the local products. If they like it, they will come back and will persuade other family members to go with them.

Overall, the image components identified most strongly by respondents were the designative aspects of Iranian culture, such as 'hospitality', 'friendliness' and 'cuisine'. The appraisal-evaluative image components associated with the 'character' of Iran, such as 'hospitality', 'security', 'beautiful destination' and 'friendliness', scored very highly. 'Happiness', 'authentic culture' and 'country with a great history' also were prominent aspects of the country's image.

To summarise, it is clear from looking at international visitors' responses to questions regarding their before, during and after visit destination image of Iran, and more particularly how they saw their experiences at the Rose and Rosewater Festival as influencing the three phases of destination image, that the opportunity such festivals provide to experience, first-hand, the hospitality and friendliness, as well as the culture and traditions, of Iranian people, is key. In other words, the role of this socio-cultural event, and one might assume other similar events, in influencing visitors' image of Iran is not so much in the focus, or 'theme', of the event itself (in this case rose gardens and rosewater), but in the vibrant atmosphere created by the event, the opportunities for visitors to be among and to talk to local people, and the ability for Iranian people to show their hospitality to visitors within the 'safe' environment of the festival. Consequently, when asked whether they would recommend Iran to others and how they would describe it in their recommendation, all of the respondents included descriptions of Iran and Iranian people being 'friendly', 'hospitable' and 'safe'.

Conclusion

While it cannot be determined as to how the respondents participating in this interview survey would have responded to questions regarding their destination image of Iran if they had not attended the Rose and Rosewater Festival, the findings of this empirical research demonstrate a positive link between such socio-cultural events and destination image. As was learned from the interviews, the respondents' image of Iran prior to visiting the country was mixed and included significant negative imagery regarding the 'safety' of Iran as a tourism destination. Those who had dismissed the negative imagery put forward through mass media had largely done so on the basis of first-hand accounts from friends and family who had visited Iran previously. In turn, our study's respondents reported that, based on their own first-hand experiences, they were highly likely to recommend visiting Iran to others. Moreover, their time at the Rose and Rosewater Festival during which they were able to have first-hand experiences of the friendliness and hospitality of Iranian people appears to have strengthened their positive image of the country, as well as strengthening their resolve to recommend visiting Iran to others.

In this way, the study conducted at the Rose and Rosewater Festival illustrates the ways in which festivals and other socio-cultural events can play a significant role in the rebuilding of Iran's destination image for international tourism. Indeed, not only can such events boost spending by both 'host' and 'guest' communities, and increase tourism development at both the destination and regional levels, but they can also play an important role in boosting destination image. By contributing to the recovery or rebuilding of Iran's destination image, the outcomes of festivals and events are far broader than merely their economic impact. Indeed, socio-cultural events play the role of a promoter when it comes to destination and tourism development. Since the majority of events are related to local culture and entertainment they attract the interests of tourists, especially those who are already culture-oriented in their destination choice.

Nonetheless, the research presented here illustrates different aspects of the complex process of rebuilding a country's image through socio-cultural events. While the data indicate a marked positive change in the image of Iran among international tourists who were visiting the country, and particularly when they attended socio-cultural events, the image impacts observed in Iran also underlined their complexity. The image of Iran seems to be strongly differentiated in terms of its components and in terms of the image held by different groups of visitors, and thus it is clear that we need to start talking about 'images' rather than 'image'. Accordingly, Iran's tourism policy-makers need to plan various international marketing strategies in order to attract culture and tradition lovers from different countries, as well as considering the prominent role that festivals and other socio-cultural events can play in developing the tourism industry of the country and improving Iran's image internationally.

References

Allen, J., O'Toole, W., Mcdonnell, I., & Harris, R. (2002). *Festival and special event management*. London: Wiley.

Alvarez, M, D. & Camo, S. (2014). The influence of political conflicts on country image and intention to visit: A study of Israel's image. *Tourism Management, 40*, 70–78.

Arcodia, C. & Whitford, M. (2006). Festival attendance and the development of social capital. *Journal of Convention and Event Tourism, 8*(2), 1–18.

Avraham, E. (2013). Crisis communication, image restoration, and battling stereotypes of terror and wars: Media strategies for marketing tourism to Middle Eastern countries. *American Behavioural Scientist, 57*(9), 1350–1367.

Avraham, E. (2015). Destination image repair during crisis: Attracting tourism during the Arab Spring uprisings. *Tourism Management, 47*, 224–232.

Bahaee, M. & Pisani, M. J. (2009). Iranian consumer animosity and US products: A witch's brew or elixir? *International Business Review, 18*(2), 199–210.

Beirman, D. (2003). *Restoring tourism destinations in crisis*. Wallingford: CABI.

Bowdin, G., Allen, J., O'Toole, W., Harris, R., & McDonnell, I. (2006). *Events management* (2nd ed.). Oxford: Butterworth-Heinemann.

De Bres, K. & Davis, J. (2001). Celebrating group and place identity: A case study of a new regional festival. *Tourism Geographies, 3*(3), 326–337.

Fredline, E. & Faulkner, B. (1998). Resident reactions to a major tourist event: The Gold Coast Indy car race. *Festival Management and Event Tourism, 5*(4), 185–205.

Getz, D. (2007). *Event studies: Theory, research and policy for planned events*. Oxford: Butterworth-Heinemann.

Hall, C. M. (1992). *Hallmark tourist events*. London: Belhaven Press.

Hall, C. M. (2010). Crisis events in tourism: Subjects of crisis in tourism. *Current Issues in Tourism, 13*(5), 401–417.

Heslop, L. A., Lu, I. R. R., & Cray, D. (2008). Modeling country image effects through an international crisis. *International Marketing Review, 25*(4), 354–378.

International Association for Impact Assessment (IAIA). (2003). *Social impact assessment – International principles*. IAIA, Special Publication Series No. 2.

Iran Review. (2016). *Festival of Rose and Rose Water*. Retrieved from http://www.iranreview.org/content/Documents/Festival_of_Rose_and_Rose_Water.htm

IRIB English Radio. (2013). *Rose festival in Kashan*. Retrieved from http://english.irib.ir/radioculture/art/cultural-traditions/item/149882-rose-festival-in-kashan

Klein, J. G., Ettenson, R., & Morris, M. D. (1998). The animosity model of foreign product purchase: An empirical test in the People's Republic of China. *Journal of Marketing, 62*(1), 89–100.

Kotler, P., Haider, D., & Rein, I. (1993). *Marketing places: Attracting investment, industry, and tourism to cities, states, and nations*. New York, NY: The Free Press.

Lee, C. & Taylor, T. (2005). Critical reflections on the economic impact assessment of a mega-event: The case of the 2002 FIFA World Cup. *Tourism Management, 26*(4), 595–603.

Leong, S. M., Cote, J. A., Ang, S. H., Tan, S. J., Jung, K., Kau, A. K., & Pornpitakpan, C. (2008). Understanding consumer animosity in an international crisis: Nature, antecedents, and consequences. *Journal of International Business Studies, 39*(6), 996–1009.

Lowery, S. & DeFleur, M. L. (1983). *Milestone in mass communications*. New York, NY: Longman.

Matos, N., Mendes, J., & Valle, P. O. d. (2012). Revisiting the destination image construct through a conceptual model. *Do Algarves, 21*, 101–117.

Ministry of Interior of Iran. (2015). *Kashan*. Retrieved from http://kashan.gov.ir/

Ministry of Interior of Iran. (2017). *Kashan*. Retrieved from http://kashan.gov.ir/Index.aspx?page_=form&lang=1&sub=1&tempname=mainkashan&PageID=2824&isPopUp=False

National Geographic Traveller. (2015). *The cool list: 16 for 2016*. Retrieved from http://www.natgeotraveller.co.uk/smart-travel/features/the-2016-cool-list/

Nes, E. B., Yelkur, R., & Silkoset, R. (2012). Exploring the animosity domain and the role of affect in a cross-national context. *International Business Review, 21*(5), 751–765.

Neumayer, E. (2004). The impact of political violence on tourism dynamic cross-national estimation. *Journal of Conflict Resolution, 48*(2), 259–281.

Newbold, C., Boyd-Barrett, O., & Van den Bulck, H. (2002). *The media book*. New York, NY: Bloomsbury, USA.

Pemberton, R. & Leach, N. (2015). Could IRAN be the top tourism destination of 2016? Country braced for 'tsunami' of visitors after nuclear deal. *Daily Mail Australia*. Retrieved from http://www.dailymail.co.uk/travel/travel_news/article-3279262/Could-Iran-tourism-destination-2016-Country-braced-tsunami-visitors-nuclear-deal.html

Pleitgen, F. (2015). Why your next vacation could be in Iran. *CNN*. Retrieved from http://www.cnn.com/2015/07/09/travel/iran-tourism-persepolis/

Podoshen, J. S. & Hunt, J. M. (2011). Equity restoration, the holocaust and tourism of sacred sites. *Tourism Management, 32*(6), 1332–1342.

PressTV. (2015). *Iran picked destination of choice for tourists*. Retrieved from http://www.presstv.com/Detail/2015/12/22/442788/Iran-top-tourist-destinations

Ritchie, B. (1984). Assessing impacts of hallmark events: Conceptual and research issues. *Journal of Travel Research, 23*(1), 2–11.

Ritchie, B. W. (2004). Chaos, crises and disasters: A strategic approach to crisis management in the tourism industry. *Tourism Management, 25*(6), 669–683.

Roche, M. (2000). *Mega-events and modernity: Olympics and expos in the growth of global culture.* London: Routledge.

Sonmez, S. & Graefe, A. (1998). Determining future travel behavior from past travel experience and perceptions of risk and safety. *Journal of Travel Research, 37*(4), 171–177.

Sönmez, S. F., Apostolopoulos, Y., & Tarlow, P. (1999). Tourism in crisis: Managing the effects of terrorism. *Journal of Travel Research, 38*(1), 13–18.

Tasci, A. D. & Gartner, W. C. (2007). Destination image and its functional relationships. *Journal of Travel Research, 45*(4), 413–425.

United Nations Educational, Scientific and Cultural Organization (UNESCO). (2007). *The historical–cultural axis of Fin, Sialk, Kashan.* Retrieved from http://whc.unesco.org/en/tentativelists/5187/

United Nations Educational, Scientific and Cultural Organization (UNESCO). (2011). *The Persian garden.* Retrieved from http://whc.unesco.org/en/list/1372/

Verlegh, P. W. & Steenkamp, J. B. E. M. (1999). A review and meta-analysis of country of origin research. *Journal of Economic Psychology, 20*(5), 521–546.

Weaver, D. B. & Lawton, L. J. (2013). Resident perceptions of a contentious tourism event. *Tourism Management, 37*, 165–175.

World Tourism Organization (UNWTO). (2015). *UNWTO tourism highlights 2015.* Retrieved from http://www.e-unwto.org/doi/pdf/10.18111/9789284416899

World Tourism Organization (UNWTO). (2017). *UNWTO tourism highlights 2017.* Retrieved from http://www.e-unwto.org/doi/pdf/10.18111/9789284419029

10 Food and tourism in Iran

Amir Sayadabdi and Saman Hassibi

Introduction

Although tourism in Iran has been studied for some time and some aspects of it have been well-researched, food-related tourism of any sort has been largely neglected. This chapter discusses a number of opportunities and challenges related to food and its intersection with tourism in Iran, while highlighting some issues that have already been raised by tourists yet not addressed by scholars nor the liable people or organizations in the Iranian context. The chapter also lays some grounds for future research that helps to reconcile at least some of the issues with regard to food in Iranian tourism.

Until recently, the obvious connection between food and travel and the role of food in the travellers' experience has been overlooked; however, since the 1980s, food and food-related topics and subtopics have received considerable scholarly attention, as a result of which, a variety of new niches such as 'food tourism' (Hall, 2006), 'culinary tourism' (Long, 1998), 'tasting tourism' (Boniface, 2003), 'gastronomic tourism' (Zelinski, 1985) and 'food pilgrimages' (Long, 2006) have emerged in the field of tourism studies, all of which focus on food and the concept of eating and otherness in tourism, though each representing a slightly different approach to the topic. Yet in Iran, this relationship is perhaps best described as just another incidental part of the tourist experience. There has been almost no significant research from either social or marketing perspectives on the role of food in tourism in Iran, although the field presents a great many opportunities for research.

Therefore, this chapter aims to explore different ways that food can be and is being offered to tourists in Iran. The reason for this broad focus is that the existing food and tourism relationships in Iran are so underdeveloped and broad in themselves that they cannot truly fit into any of the known and named niches of food-related avenues of tourism. So this chapter aims to paint a picture by briefly reviewing the main opportunities and challenges related to food and its intersection with tourism in Iran. What were considered as main topics in this chapter reflect the subjective views and priorities of the authors on the matter. Surely, there are other important areas to consider and more detailed research to be done on the topics other than the ones that appear in this limited chapter.

Diverse cuisine, monotonous menus

Iran has a rich culinary diversity with more than 2,500 types of food and over 100 drinks recognized (Iran Cultural Heritage, Handcraft and Tourism Organization (ICHTO), 2016). The geographical diversity that has divided the country into four distinctive climatic regions, ranging from subtropical to subpolar between the mountainous and the plain areas (Gervers & Schlepp, 2002), has led to the growth of different produce in each region which consequently formed a culinary repertoire that is regionally distinctive and features diverse styles specific to those particular regions. It is not only the cuisine, but also the food traditions that are considerably different from one region to another. This is mainly because of the great diversity of ethnic groups in different regions of Iran including, among others, Turks and Azeris (in the north-west), Kurds (in the west), Armenians (in the north-west and central Iran), Baluchis (in the east) and Arabs (in the south), each of which display a different set of food traditions. Moreover, as traditional foods are closely linked to religion (e.g. Briones Alonso, 2015; Ebaugh & Chafetz, 2000), the impacts of different religions that have been practised in the country throughout history are embedded within the cuisine and reflect the diversity available in contemporary Iranian cuisine.

Yet, such culinary diversity is not likely to be offered to tourists in Iran. Most restaurants and eating establishments offer a monotonous menu to travellers consisting mainly of 'national' dishes such as *Chelo Khoresh-e Gheymeh* or *Ghormeh Sabzi* – meat-based stews with legumes that are served on the side of plain white or saffron rice – and, above all, different kinds of *Chelo Kabab*s. These dishes, although potentially appealing and delicious during the first days of travels, will leave the travellers' taste buds wanting for more. This is apparent in the comments of many foreign visitors to Iran, not only present-day but also in the memoirs or travelogues from decades ago, suggesting that the monotony of what foreign visitors see as 'local food' has been an issue for some time. For instance, having tasted too many 'similar dishes', Harnack notes in his 1965 (p. 20) memoir that 'most Persian food, I was to discover, was delicious but amazingly monotonous, just a few favourite items, repeated again and again'. This is similar to Sir Pritchett (1964, p. 201) who finds Persian cuisine 'excellent, though a little monotonous' to his taste. Fast forward to the last two decades, the issue seems to have persisted. Williams (2016, p. 103), while acknowledging the quality and taste of Persian food in general, notes that 'the endless diet of kebabs can become quite dull', and Brosnahan (1994, p. 73) reminds his readers that 'although the [Persian] food is generally quite healthy and tasty, […] you will also find it quite monotonous'. The issue extends beyond travel guidebooks, travelogues and memoirs and is evident also in the reviews left on travel websites (e.g. 'After 2 weeks of Iranian food, which is overall delicious, it can get monotonous' (scorpioshanghai, Australian traveller, TripAdvisor, 2017b), observed in comments made by interviewees in academic research (e.g. 'All the way through Iran it was just, everything was just kebabs' (Rosemary, British traveller, cited in Hampton, 2013, p. 14) and mentioned frequently in travel blogs (e.g. 'In restaurants, kebabs reign supreme … That's pretty much it – delicious indeed, but gets old' (Ragg, 2015).

Anything but kebab, please!

The excessive appearance of *Chelo Kabab* (one or two skewers of one of the varieties of grilled kebab, steamed white rice that is usually garnished with saffron rice, and is served with a couple of grilled tomatoes, some butter and ground sumac) on the menu of many local restaurants all over Iran is quite understandable. Being an 'occasional' dish which is difficult to emulate at home (Ham et al., 2015), there is naturally a local demand for *Chelo Kabab* to be present on the menu of many restaurants. Quite understandably, with only about 2 million international tourists annually (Vafadari & Cooper, 2010) in relation to the size of the population, the restaurants have to offer what the local market demands in order to survive. However, the carried-to-excess presence of *Chelo Kabab* on the menus of restaurants that are quite often frequented by *foreign tourists* rather than *local people* cannot easily be fitted into the framework of an ordinary demand–supply scheme; if anything, there is a demand for 'anything but kebab' (Muir, 2000) by foreign tourists to Iran who are in search of more diverse foods.

The reason behind serving kebab in 'touristy' establishments likely stems from a desire to pleasure guests and meet their needs, embedded deeply in the Iranian culture. Not only is *Chelo Kabab* considered to be the Iranian 'national dish', it is also considered to be a dish well-worth the guests; the foreign visitor is thus looked at as a 'guest' who should be honoured and offered the best of foods, that is, in the view of Iranian restaurateurs, *Chelo Kebab*.

As part of a culture with a desire to accommodate guests, many of these establishments, especially in the last decade, have also developed more 'Westernized' menus for Western travellers, to welcome guests with more 'familiar' options and make them feel more at home. Ironically, however, 'feeling at home' is rarely what foreign visitors of Iran seek. As a country relatively untouched by mass tourism (O'Gorman, McLellan, & Baum, 2007), foreign tourists of Iran can often be categorized under what Cohen (1972) calls 'non-institutionalized' tourists, who do not comply with conventional features of mass-tourism such as 'familiarity' (Vogt, 1976); they attempt, instead, to share the lifestyle of those in the culture with which they come into contact (Ateljevic & Hannam, 2008). Simply put, although the intention of Iranians may aim at accommodating guests' needs, there is a misconception of what their guests' needs really are in terms of food and eating.

This is further observed in the experience of vegetarian or vegan travellers to Iran who have often described the food aspect of their travels as 'problematic' or 'difficult' (Hampton, 2013). Evidence of this is the existence of many threads or blog posts enquiring or informing on how to *survive* as a vegetarian in a country with a meat-dominated cuisine such as Iran, or the ones, such as the following, expressing disappointment over the lack of vegetarian choices:

> Being vegetarians we were rather looking forward to Persian food because we know there are a number of great dishes. Unfortunately we figured out that these are home-cooked dishes, and when Iranians go to a restaurant they want to eat meat. Thus, the choice for us as tourists is rather limited and we

have falafel sandwiches most evenings. Iranians tend to chuckle at that notion because a falafel sandwich is not considered a real meal … We got invited to an Iranian home once, though, where our hosts cooked a fantastic vegetarian dinner for us.

(Thoma & Ducke, 2015)

It is important to note here that it is the lack of diversity in *public eating establishments* (and not in *Iranian cuisine*) that is being critiqued by the travellers. The travellers are usually aware of Iranian diverse culinary culture ('we know there are a number of great [vegetarian] dishes'), but will soon discover that finding such diversity is almost impossible in the public sphere and, therefore, will be left no choice but to 'have falafel sandwiches most evenings' which, in the view of Iranians, is not even a 'real meal'. Experiencing diverse foods that can address diverse eating habits would only be possible, as they will further discover, in an Iranian domestic context ('we figured out that these are home-cooked dishes') where a sizable number of 'everyday' dishes are vegetarian. For instance, many types of soups (*ash* or *eshkene*), some of which easily lend themselves well to vegan options such as *ash-e reshte* (noodle soup with beans and herbs) or different kinds of pilaf such as *adas polo* (lentil pilaf served with caramelized onion and raisins), are consumed by the majority of Iranians on a regular basis, even by those who do not follow a vegetarian or vegan diet. However, it is perhaps the very everydayness of these dishes that makes restaurateurs not want to serve them at eating establishments (Shaida, 1991) and fill the menu with extensive varieties of kebabs instead.

Part of this issue arises from an existing difference between what the host (i.e. Iran) *thinks* the tourist demands, and what the tourist *actually* demands. Host cultures, as Zuelow (2011, p. 13) points out, tend to

behave for the benefit of the tourist. They play a role, acting out stereotypical regional or national parts, eventually forgetting that they are acting. They become what hosts *think* the tourist wants … rather than offering visitors the chance to see something *real*.

In Iran, too, a gap exists between the host's perception of tourists' expectations and tourists' actual expectations when it comes to food. To date, this gap has not only remained largely unaddressed, but has been actively ignored. For example, a number of key players in the Iranian hospitality industry have suggested that kebab should be promoted much more widely within the tourism industry so that 'all foreign visitors can become familiar with our national food' (Radio Goftegoo, 2016). Such perceptions held by the host are in conflict with the demands of foreign tourists who seem to be not only already familiar with kebab, but even tired of it, and seek a more varied and unique culinary experience during their travels. Cohen and Avieli (2004) point out how the very same local food can be paradoxically both an attraction and an impediment for the very same tourist, if experienced in different situations. Kebab fits right into this argument; it is at first an attractive food experience, but if repeated numerously it can become an impediment and eventually affect the overall satisfaction of the tourist in a negative way.

Considering all the misunderstandings and misrepresentations, there is no wonder that 'lack of diversity' is the main complaint of the international tourists visiting the country in terms of food, causing them to usually leave Iran with an incomplete or doubting impression on one of the greatest aspects of Iranian culture that could have easily become one of the highlights of their trip. Promoting and investing in the great variety of ethnic and local food as well as the rich *street food* repertoire can be handy in leading the culinary experiences of travellers in the right direction for Iranian cuisine. As numerous studies have shown, the availability of both regional and a dietary diversity in a travel destination, or lack thereof, plays an important role in contributing to tourists' experiences, enjoyment and satisfaction (e.g. Yüksel & Yüksel, 2002; Adeyinka-Ojo & Khoo-Lattimore, 2016) as well as their decision to revisit (Yoon & Uysal, 2005). Having the chance to experience the local and ethnic foods of different regions of a country, the tourist gets to experience not only the diverse culinary traditions of the country's different regions, but also the country's ethnic diversity. Ethnic food can therefore become part of a 'multicultural, cosmopolitan urban tourism product' (Derek, 2017, p. 225), through which tourists are not only eating the other (as something distinct from their own culture), but also eating the differences between various others (Molz, 2007). Similarly, offering a diverse selection of food that can satisfy both different tastes and different dietary practices has been identified as an important factor in the overall satisfaction of tourists when visiting a destination (Yoo, 2015). There is also a growing interest among tourists in purchasing local produce and eating the street food (Everett, 2016). Iran, too, has a long history with regards to street food vendors and their products; from freshly picked walnuts, unripe almonds and sour plums in spring to cooked beetroots and fava beans in winter, and homemade soups and porridges sold from car boots in Ramadan. However, the potentials of such experiences, too, have generally been neglected.

Tourists, especially the niche that travels to Iran, are searching for authentic experiences and attempt to associate with the lives of local people and their culture (Bookman, 2006) and, in this way, they are inclined to try local indigenous food, no matter how unusual, to add to the cultural experience during their travels (Cheung & Luo, 2016). However, being unable to experience the diverse local gastronomic adventures (due to the monotony of the food offered in restaurants), their 'food neophilia' remains only partly satisfied, which can consequently affect their overall travel satisfaction, and change their pre-perception of Iran as a country 'offering a wealth of culinary delights' to a post-perception of 'a kebab and kofte country' (Lonely Planet, 2013).

Hospitality and hospitableness

The relationship between the cultural aspect of hospitality in Iran and its effects on the Iranian hospitality and tourism industry is generally a neglected area. This is despite the fact that such important an element of Iranian culture has largely affected the experience of foreign visitors to Iran. Any simple search on the web can show tons of examples of this experience by casual travellers or travel experts who have visited the country. The examples also show, in many cases, that the hospitableness was shown to or observed by the guest through a culinary gesture such as an invitation to a meal or a treat to a traditional food item.

In examining the concept of hospitality and hospitableness, Lashley (2016, p. 5) explains that the array of motives for hosts offering hospitality to guests can be ranked from the most calculative reasons (where hospitality is offered with the hope of ensuing gain) to the most generous (where hospitality is offered merely for the joy and pleasure of the guest). He calls the latter form 'altruistic hospitality', in which hospitableness is offered 'as an act of generosity and benevolence, and a willingness to give pleasure to others'. This 'ideal type, or pure form, of hospitality' is ultimately about generosity and entirely bereft of any personal gain for the host apart from the emotional satisfaction generated by the practice of hospitableness. In Iran, particularly when it comes to foreign visitors, this form of hospitality can easily be detected. In Iranian culture a proper hospitality, characterized by lavishness and generosity, is considered an important sign of respect and honour towards the guest (Heidtmann, 2011). The form and genuineness of this hospitality can differ depending on various factors which call for an independent study itself.

The altruistic nature of hospitality shown in the behaviour of the Iranians towards the foreign visitor is usually practised by treating the guest to a free meal at the very least. In return, not only is no repayment of any kind expected, but also discouraged. For example, in her blog post *60 Things to Know before Travelling to Iran*, Reynolds (2016) writes under 'hospitality' category:

> Iranians love treating foreigners. People you meet (who are sometimes total strangers) are going to want to take you out and pay for everything. Do offer to pay yourself, but if they refuse, just give in and go with the flow.

Hospitable behaviours such as these resonate also with Telfer's (2000) concept of 'genuine hospitality' in which the genuine hospitable behaviours are merely motivated by a desire to please the guest and are, among other things, stemmed from affection for particular people. Telfer (1996, p. 83) also places emphasis on the role of food as of primary importance to hospitality because 'giving and sharing food is a symbol of the bond of trust set up between host and guest'. The parallels are clear here: in Iranian hospitableness towards 'particular people' (i.e. foreign visitors), 'a desire to please' seems to be the main and only motivation, and it is the act of 'giving and sharing food' that is of central importance to the hospitality displayed. After all, the provision of food in Iranian culture is a key signifier of acceptance, hospitality and friendship (Harbottle, 1997) and Iranians, as people who are, since the 1979 revolution, often portrayed in the Western media as religious fundamentalists and the enemy of the West and Westerners (Dorman, 1979; Kamalipour, 1997; Atai, 2007; Saleem, 2007; Marandi & Tari, 2017), reject such notions by showcasing their hospitableness through the deployment of the provision of food as a way to affirm their acceptance and friendship towards the Western guest, and to bond a trust between themselves and their guest.

This becomes clearer if we turn to 'anecdotes' that are told by foreign visitors about Iranian hospitality, many of which involve culinary elements. For example, the travel writers of *babakoto* recall the Iranians' 'overwhelming, legendary hospitality' through eating 'an immense amount of delicious food and drinking litres of sweet tea'. Calling Iranians 'the friendliest and most hospitable people in the world', Rijntjes (2016) tells the 'tales of Iranian hospitality' through an anecdote in which a perfect stranger treated the travellers to sheep's brain sandwiches followed by Iranian tea and refused to accept any money in return saying 'accepting money for food is not the Iranian way', or another anecdote in which a shopkeeper invited the travellers into his shop and made them a bottle of 'real Iranian doogh' (a yogurt-based drink favoured by Iranians). Ragg (2015) also points out that any chat with locals in Iran 'inevitably will end with an invitation for lunch, dinner or tea'. Huang (2014), too, considers getting invited to total strangers' homes for a festive meal or being treated to an endless flow of tea in a vendor shop as 'completely normal', and notes that such experiences of 'genuine generosity' can become 'the highlight of the trip' for any foreign visitor to Iran. Similarly, Sánchez (2016) finds Iranian hospitality the 'greatest treasure of Iran' and notes that the best way of experience the 'real meaning of hospitality' is when one gets invited to an Iranian home for a meal.

While such genuine hospitality behaviours, especially when combined with culinary elements, can be overwhelming for the foreign visitor, they may occasionally seem odd, particularly to those coming from a Western background whose cultural values are considerably different from that of Iranians (Heidtmann, 2011). This is especially so when the traditional custom of *tarof* is at play, during which the guest is served food continuously and excessively by the host who believes that the guest, who may be in fact full and satisfied, is refusing to have more food just to be polite. Foreign visitors are sometimes even warned about such gestures and are taught 'tactics' to deal with such situations. In his *Survival Guide for the Non-Iranian Traveller*, Taghavi (1998) warns about such 'hospitality attacks' and writes, in a humorous style:

> If you're served food, be careful. As your plate empties, your host will keep serving food onto your dish, sometimes without asking you, sometimes despite your objections. Your best bet is to eat slowly, slower than your host. Try to bore your host with your eating pace. Have some defensive moves ready. Like, the minute they try to fill your plate, grab your plate and move it away behind you and swear on your grandmother's grave you're so full, you're about to explode. If you have to, grab the plate, get up and run around the room yelling 'no thank you no thank you' keeping the plate away from the hosts at all times. Another tactic may be to stage a counterattack. As soon as your host's plate begins to empty, you start serving HIM more food. This way they'll know they're dealing with a professional and may back off. Remember, if you're not really careful, you WILL explode.

Such behaviours may seem rather odd to an 'outsider' visiting Iran, but are usually perceived as interesting and overwhelming to the point that they become the 'highlight of the trip', thus recommended to those who have not yet visited Iran. Such aspects of a visit not only make for a unique perceived attraction of the destination, positively affecting the experience of foreign tourists and encouraging them to revisit (Liu, 2006), but also project images from the destination, affecting potential tourists through the creation of expectations, fantasies and the hypothetical structure of the tourist experience, thus leading to the formation of a desire to visit for image verification (Tussyadiah, 2010).

There are two major issues with regards to experiencing the culture of hospitality in Iran. First, important aspects of Iranian culture, such as hospitality, are often of a 'visitor-generated' nature, rather than a 'destination-promoted' one. The official channels that promote Iran as a destination (e.g. ICHTO) mostly focus on the tangible historic and heritage aspects such as ancient cities and monuments, and are less occupied with promoting the culture of the Iranian people. Currently, the typical Iranian package tour is fully planned for sight-seeing, and does not provide the visitors with the chance to come into contact with the real lives of real people and taste real foods in real homes (Vafadari & Cooper, 2010). Most Iranian tour operators have a pre-organized arrangement with mainstream restaurants and only a few of them offer the foreign guest the chance to experience a homemade meal in an Iranian home. Thus, experiencing hospitality, and in particular food-themed hospitality, has remained a delightful yet uncalculated outcome of the trip to Iran, the promotion of which has only occurred through an unplanned word-of-mouth process, generated by tourists who have, often by chance and quite unexpectedly, experienced such hospitality first-hand.

Second, genuine Iranian hospitality can perhaps only be experienced by tourists in domestic, private settings in local people's homes, and seldom in tourist accommodation facilities and eating establishments (such as hotels and restaurants), in which foreign visitors' prior expectations about Iranian hospitality is often not met. For example, not only do many of these establishments, including many restaurants and local tea-houses, not follow even the basic rules of hospitality (not even rules of 'ulterior motive' hospitality; see Lashley, 2016), they also charge the international tourists more than they would charge the domestic ones. Although this is quite a common practice in Middle Eastern and Asian countries (Reader & Ridout, 2003), it certainly can alter the tourist's perception when it comes to experiencing 'genuine' hospitality. Moreover, there is currently a tendency among the Iranian hotel and restaurant proprietors, especially in large cities, to 'professionalize' their relationship with their international guests, and to make their setting more modern, like a large hotel, restaurant or diner in a formal Western context; a trend that has been encouraged and supported by Iranian hospitality and tourism officials and has resulted in a considerable number of supposedly Western-inspired hotels and restaurants, especially in large Iranian cities. Such attempts, however, are yet again addressing what the officials *think* the international tourists of Iran need instead of what their *real* expectations are. For example, in her travel blog, Napora (2015) describes the supposedly 'modern' Iranian hotels in large cities (such as Tehran and Shiraz) as 'simple', but finds the domestic dwellings in smaller cities as 'fancy and charming' and suggests her readers to stay and eat at the latter establishments, as those are 'part(s) of the Iranian experience'. She also points to the fact that while in 'modern' hotels she was the only foreigner, in domestic dwellings all guests were foreign travellers, which suggests the favourability of the latter over the former among foreign visitors to Iran. Ragg (2015) also finds staying in a 'traditional guesthouse' more rewarding than staying at 'luxury hotels' that, in her view, 'were probably luxury in the 1960s', but not anymore. Hence, although there are some merits that come with the standardization of hotels and restaurants to elevate the satisfaction of tourists, such methods of practice should not overlook the desire of international niche tourists who would like to be able to find the Iranian domestic hospitality in the public sphere, too.

Although there appears to be a demand among international visitors for experiencing domestic hospitality, the appropriate supply is yet to be provided by the tourism officials or the private sector. Therefore, tourist establishments, especially the ones dealing with foreign tourists, can introduce the elements of 'domestic hospitality' to both their food and accommodation services, instead of cutting them out, especially because even in a commercial setting, diners usually evaluate their experience by using the language of domestic hospitality (Warde & Martens, 2000). In this way, Iranian domestic hospitality can be used not only as a source of learning about host and guest relations that is extendable to commercial operations during their communications with guests and staff, but also a source of inspiration for entrepreneurial hospitality activities such as the creation of commercial culinary experiences in domestic dwellings. Iranian hospitableness combined with culinary traditions presents itself as an area in which a proper cultural interaction between hosts and guests can take place, and provides a platform on which the guest 'consumes' the host's culture. Such elements of culture, as Ivanovic (2008) states, can always be 'commodified' as to facilitate tourist consumption.

Food events

Food, as Richards (2012, p. 29) notes, 'provides the basis for a whole series of events, including exhibitions, festivals and celebrations that can help to develop the food experiences and market the tourism product'. Numerous studies have shown how the development of such events have supported the economic growth of local communities and provided valuable income for local people in different countries (e.g. Crispin & Reiser, 2008; Hall & Sharples, 2008). However, Iranian tourism has not yet identified the potentials of such events, except for a small domestic market. Most food events in Iran have been held and promoted in a local and occasionally regional scale. Although these festivals are often declared to be held for the purpose of promoting the local and celebrating the traditional Iranian food, they have mostly taken on a role as a social function for the members of that community or region. For example, the *Festival of Traditional Foods* in Shiraz that had aimed to 'introduce and promote the traditional cuisine of Fars [province] to both local people as well as domestic and international tourists to maintain and retain the culinary traditions as an intangible cultural heritage' (Young

Journalists Club (YJC), 2014), was admittedly only able to attract the people of the city of Shiraz (Tasnim News, 2015); or the *Food Tourism Festival* that had initially aimed to become the 'largest food tourism gathering in the Western Gilan' (Ahmadi, 2016) was only visited, beside the authorities who had promoted the event, by a relatively small number of local people and residents of Sowme'eh Sara, the county in which the event was held (S. Navari, personal communication, 16 July 2017). Therefore, although these events may have attracted local people, they have so far not been very successful mediums for attracting visitors and attendees from outside local or regional communities. Interestingly, as the examples above show, the authorities responsible for such festivals have, at times, mentioned and acknowledged the significance of food and the role of such events in attracting tourists, yet it seems that no action in this direction has been or is being taken.

Apart from a few scattered food fairs, it was only in 2016 that the first national food festival was held simultaneously in eight different regions of the country celebrating the diverse foods and culinary traditions of each region, presenting new products and innovative food-processing methods and bringing together important actors on the food and tourism scene (ICHTO, 2016). Although the festival managed to attract more than 100,000 people in total, it was criticized by a number of government officials as well as spiritual authorities as an 'unnecessary' and 'costly' festival (Sharifi, 2017), casting doubt on its recurrence. Such dispute stemmed from the conflicting views of the two main factions in the government, one viewing such tourism-related events (and generally tourism itself) as a means to achieve economic benefits, and the other considering such events as threatening to the Islamic values that place a high premium on simple living and discourage people from luxuries (O'Gorman et al., 2007).

'Food capitals' as potential food-event destinations

Rural towns and cities sometimes proclaim themselves as the capital of a certain foodstuff and hold food-themed events and festivals based on those food items as a means of attracting visitors. For example, in California, the city of Gilroy that is the self-proclaimed garlic capital of the world, attracts over 100,000 visitors each year by hosting an annual garlic festival (Hall & Sharples, 2008), or the Goychay region of Azerbaijan that identifies itself as the world's best pomegranate-growing region and is self-proclaimed as the pomegranate capital of the world, hosts the annual 'Pomegranate Festival' that is attended by 15,000 visitors each year from all over the country (Bowan, 2017). Many rural regions of Iran, too, proclaim themselves as the capital of particular food items. However, while in countries with more developed tourism such self-proclamation usually takes place 'as a way of celebrating the heritage [of those destinations], while simultaneously using food as a way of differentiating themselves as a place to visit' (Hall & Gössling, 2016, p. 28), in Iran these self-proclamations rarely promote or increase visitor flow to those regions, as promoting the local produce has been mostly limited to the boundaries of the domestic and national market.

There are, however, a few successful examples such as the rosewater distillation ceremonies (*Golabgiri*) in Kashan and its surrounding districts (see Chapter 9, this volume). Taking place annually in spring (mid-May to early June), *Golabgiri* is a traditional and historical Iranian festival during which rosewater, a mainstay in Iranian cuisine, is extracted from rose petals. The festival attracts more than 2 million domestic, as well as 200,000 foreign visitors during the season, which makes Kashan the top-visited destination among all other Iranian cities during the *Golabgiri* period (MagIran, 2008). Besides providing over 1,000 direct and indirect seasonal jobs, *Golabgiri* has also enhanced the overall 'brand image' of Kashan, created a strong sense of place and strengthened community pride among the local people (Arezi & Azkia, 2010). However, in spite of the successful experience of Kashan, no serious attempt has been made to deploy the signature food products of other regions to promote those destinations or create unique food events in them. For instance, Ghaen is the self-proclaimed world's saffron capital; Afin, world's barberry capital; Bandar Torkaman, world's caviar capital; and Rafsanjan, world's pistachio capital, yet none of these places have, so far, taken advantage of their signature product to promote it as a tourist attraction, despite the existence of great potentials in those regions, providing them with unparalleled opportunities to rebrand and redevelop their natural, heritage and cultural resources.

For instance, saffron alone, as an 'ancient foodstuff' cultivated in ancient Persia as early as the tenth century BC (Kafi, Hemmati Khakhki, & Karbasi, 2006), can easily be promoted as a tourist attraction in Khorasan region where 95% of the world's saffron is produced (Shaida, 1990), perhaps by following the successful case of Kashan's *Golabgiri* as well as examining international examples such as, just to name a few, the Pistachio Festival (Bronte, Italy), the Saffron Rose Festival (Consuegra, Spain) and the Date Festival (Indio, California, the United States), all of which are based on ingredients that are cultivated in a much greater quantity in Iran (Food and Agricultural Organization (FAO), 2017) and of comparable quality.

Culinary tours

Although culinary as well as wine tours have grown greatly in the last decades and are now considered a 'usual' venue for tourism in many countries (Long, 2007), in Iran, while the latter form (wine tourism) is non-existent due to the prohibition of alcohol consumption, the former form (culinary tourism) has seen some developments, though only on a limited scale. These culinary tours are a handful in number, mostly operated by private sector travel agencies, and marketed exclusively to foreign visitors. The tours often combine different culinary as well as non-culinary elements and offer itineraries in which, for example, cultural/ historical sightseeing is combined by having the main meals at Iranian homes and eating 'real' Iranian food with them.

The experience of the tourist in these tours is limited to an 'observation-only' basis, with the exception of one tour (Persian Food Tours), in which the tourist assists in shopping for ingredients at a traditional bazaar, learns to use those ingredients to cook several 'authentic' Iranian dishes and tastes them afterwards, while being provided with information on Iranian food habits and food culture in general. A quick look at the reviews of this one-day tour suggests that taking a more experience-centred approach may, in some ways, provide the tourist with a more fulfilling, memorable and meaningful culinary experience, despite the very short duration of the tour. For instance, reviewers commented that 'preparing the food certainly gave us a deeper appreciation of Iranian cuisine' (Heemi27, TripAdvisor, 2016) while providing a 'comprehensive perspective of Iranian culinary culture' (MJSPPortugal, TripAdvisor, 2017d). The experience of visiting and purchasing local food from the traditional bazaar was also frequently mentioned and it was regarded as 'informative' by several participants (e.g. dancav30, TripAdvisor, 2017a; dweinstocksavoy, TripAdvisor, 2017c; Heemi27, TripAdvisor, 2016). In any case, a more in-depth content-analysis (both textual and visual) of the website of these tours as well as gathering data that can reflect the opinions and viewpoints of those who have participated, can reveal much about the perceptions of both culinary tourists and culinary tour operators, and ease the way towards creating better approaches that can benefit both.

Taking these tours may provide the culinary enthusiast an easier access to areas of the Iranian culture that may be ordinarily hard to access for 'outsiders'; however, it should not be neglected that like any other guided tours, there may be an 'aura of superficiality' and a 'staged authenticity' (MacCannell, 1976, p. 98) involved in these tours, too, leading the tourists into believing that they have been shown the back settings of the Iranian food culture when they are really being shown a staged setting made of an imagined cuisine and invented traditions.

Conclusion

Food has generally been viewed in the Iranian tourism industry as an 'incidental' part of travel, and its significance in influencing the experience of the tourist, either positively or negatively, has been ignored to date. There are almost no studies with regard to food and food consumption in the experience of the visitor to Iran or on how such an important element of the Iranian culture can be promoted, particularly to international visitors. In fact, if the global research on the role of food in tourism is in its infancy, it is not even born in Iran. Therefore, this chapter aimed to briefly review some of the major potentials and issues and to identify the areas that need to be explored with regard to the subject of food in Iranian tourism.

The road to promote Iranian food in the Iranian tourism industry is not without serious challenges. Tremendous opportunities also exist. There is currently a gap between what the international tourist needs and what the host (i.e. Iran) *thinks* the international tourist needs in terms of food and eating. Such gaps need to be addressed, first of all, by gathering data and conducting reliable studies and examining the actual perceptions and expectations of international tourists with regard to Iranian food. Understanding foreign visitors' culinary preferences is important for tourism developers and promoters in creating better and more distinctive food experiences by utilizing various food products and foodways in Iran.

While the lack of diversity in restaurant menus seems to be a frequent complaint by international tourists, Iranian hospitality and hospitableness, especially food-themed hospitableness, seems to be the highlight of the trip for many of these visitors. Thus, Iranian tourism can take advantage of the many ethnic and local foods of Iran, many of which can address different dietary practices, while capitalizing on its rich and rather unique hospitality culture and traditions especially in the international market. Arranging specialized and informed culinary tours and promoting regions by holding food-themed events can both contribute to this end. In this way and at this stage, tourism officials seem to have an important role in promoting the different aspects of Iranian culinary culture to both domestic and international visitors. After all, promoting and bringing awareness and knowledge about one or more key features of a destination through the tourism officials, rather than through unofficial channels, can at times be a much stronger tool to increase the visibility of those features or of the destination as a whole. Finally, and perhaps most importantly, the restrictions that are imposed on the tourism industry in general by the authorities have to be addressed. Moreover, the sincerity of cliché claims of aiming 'to use all the capacities' in implementation of food tourism in Iran need to be seriously put to the test. Addressing political ambivalence seems to be one of the first steps towards developing food-based tourism into a respected sector of the economy in general, and the tourism industry in particular.

References

Adeyinka-Ojo, S. F. & Khoo-Lattimore, C. (2016). Role of regional foods and food events in rural destination development: The case of Bario, Sarawak. In C. M. Hall & S. Gössling (Eds.), *Food tourism and regional development: Networks, products and trajectories* (pp. 104–117). Abingdon: Routledge.

Ahmadi, M. (2016). Jashnvare-ye gardeshgari-ye ghaza dar Sowme'eh Sara bargozar shod (The festival of food tourism was held in Sowme'eh Sara). *Gil Negah*, 9 September. Retrieved from http://gilnegah.ir/68548/

Arezi, M. & Azkia, M. (2010). Tasire-e sanat-e golab-giri bar ru-ye zendegi-ye eghtesadi-ye mardom-e Kamo dar shahrestan-e Kashan (The effect of rosewater-making industry on the economic life of the people of Kamo in Kashan county). *Pazhuhesh-ha-ye Tarvij va Amuzesh-e Keshavarzi, 3*(1), 71–82.

Atai, F. (2007) A look to the north: Opportunities and challenges. In H. Katouzian & H. Shahidi (Eds.), *Iran in the 21st century: Politics, economics & conflict* (Vol. 4, pp. 123–135). Abingdon: Routledge.

Ateljevic, I. & Hannam, K. (2008). Conclusion: Towards a critical agenda for backpacker tourism. In I. Ateljevic & K. Hannam (Eds.), *Backpacker tourism: Concepts and profiles (tourism and cultural change)* (pp. 247–256). Bristol: Channel View Publications.

Boniface, P. (2003). *Tasting tourism: Travelling for food and drink*. Abingdon: Routledge.

Bookman, M. Z. (2006). *Tourists, migrants, and refugees: Population movements in third world development*. Boulder, CO: Lynne Rienner Publishers.

Bowan, T. (2017). *The bonsai book: A reference for bonsai plants & aesthetics*. Raleigh, NC: Lulu.com.

Briones Alonso, E. (2015). The impact of culture, religion and traditional knowledge on food and nutrition security in developing countries. *FOODSECURE Working Paper Series, 30*, 1–81.

Brosnahan, T. (1994). *Lonely planet Middle East on a shoestring*. Melbourne: Lonely Planet.

Cheung, S. C. H. & Luo, J. (2016). Modernology: Food heritage and neighbourhood tourism: The example of Sheung Wan, Hong Kong. In C. M. Hall & S. Gössling (Eds.), *Food tourism and regional development: Networks, products and trajectories* (pp. 145–156). Abingdon: Routledge.

Cohen, E. (1972). Toward a sociology of international tourism. *Social Research, 39*(1), 164–182.

Cohen, E. & Avieli, N. (2004). Food in tourism: Attraction and impediment. *Annals of Tourism Research, 31*(4), 755–778.

Crispin, S. & Reiser, D. (2008). Food and wine events in Tasmania, Australia. In C. M. Hall & L. Sharples (Eds.), *Food and wine festivals and events around the world* (pp. 113–129). Abingdon: Routledge.

Derek, M. (2017). Multi-ethnic food in the mono-ethnic city-tourism: Tourism, gastronomy and identity in central Warsaw. In D. R. Hall (Ed.), *Tourism and geopolitics: Issues and concepts from Central and Eastern Europe* (pp. 223–236). Oxfordshire: CABI.

Dorman, W. A. (1979). Iranian people v. US news media: A case of libel. *Race & Class, 21*(1), 57–66.

Ebaugh, H. R. & Chafetz, J. S. (2000). Reproducing ethnicity. In H. R. Ebaugh & J. S. Chafetz (Eds.), *Religion and the new immigrants: Continuities and adaptations in immigrant congregations* (pp. 385–408). Walnut Creek, CA: Altamira Press.

Everett, S. (2016). *Food and drink tourism: Principles and practice*. Thousand Oaks: Sage.

Food and Agricultural Organization of the United Nations (FAO). (2017). *Crops: Statistics Division (FAOSTAT)*. Retrieved from http://www.fao.org/faostat/en/#data/QC/visualize

Gervers, M. & Schlepp, W. (2002). Continuity and change in Central and Inner Asia. In *Central and Inner Asian Seminar*, University of Toronto, 24–25 March 2000 and 4–5 May 2001. Toronto: Asian Institute.

Hall, C. M. (2006). Introduction: Culinary tourism and regional development: From slow food to slow tourism? *Tourism Review International, 9*(4), 303–305.

Hall, C. M. & Gössling, S. (2016). From food tourism and regional development to food, tourism and regional development: Themes and issues in contemporary foodscapes. In C. M. Hall & S. Gössling (Eds.), *Food tourism and regional development: Networks, products and trajectories* (pp. 3–57). Abingdon: Routledge.

Hall, C. M. & Sharples, L. (Eds.). (2008). *Food and wine festivals and events around the world: Development, management and markets*. Abingdon: Routledge.

Ham, A., Barbarani, S., Maxwell, J. L. V., Robinson, D., Sattin, A., Symington, A., & Walker, J. (2015). *Lonely Planet Middle East (Travel Guide)*. Melbourne: Lonely Planet.

Hampton, M. P. (2013). *Backpacker tourism and economic development: Perspectives from the less developed world*. Abingdon: Routledge.

Harbottle, L. (1997). Fast food/spoiled identity: Iranian migrants in the British catering trade. In P. Caplan (Ed.), *Food, health and identity* (pp. 87–110). Abingdon: Routledge.

Harnack, C. (1965). *Persian lions, Persian lambs: An Americans odyssey in Iran*. New York, NY: Holt, Rinehart & Winston.

Heidtmann, D. (2011). *International strategic alliances and cultural diversity. German companies getting involved in Iran, India and China*. Hamburg: Diplomica Verlag.

Huang, N. (2014). 20 photos of Iran that will surprise you [Blog post]. *Wild Junket*. Retrieved from https://www.wildjunket.com/photo-highlights-iran/

Iran Cultural Heritage, Handcraft and Tourism Organization (ICHTO). (2016). 2500 types of food exist in the country! *Islamic Republic News Agency (IRNA)*. Retrieved from http://www.irna.ir/fa/News/82331399/

Ivanovic, M. (2008). *Cultural tourism*. Cape Town: Juta and Company Ltd.

Kafi, M., Hemmati Khakhki, A., & Karbasi, A. (2006). Historical background, economy, acreage, production, yield and use. In M. Kafi, A. Koocheki, M. H. Rashed, & M. Nassiri (Eds.), *Saffron (Crocus Sativus): Production and processing* (pp. 1–12). Boca Raton, FL: CRC Press.

Kamalipour, Y. R. (1997). Introduction. In Y. R. Kamalipour (Ed.), *The US media and the Middle East: Image and perception* (pp. xix–xxi). Westport, CT: Praeger.

Lashley, C. (2016). Research on hospitality: The story so far/ways of knowing hospitality. In C. Lashley (Ed.), *The Routledge handbook of hospitality studies* (pp. 1–11). Abingdon: Routledge.

Liu, T. V. (2006). *Tourism management: New research*. New York, NY: Nova Publishers.

Lonely Planet. (2013). Vegetarian food in Iran. *Lonely Planet, Thorn Tree Forum* [Blog post]. Retrieved from https://www.lonelyplanet.com/thorntree/forums/middle-east/iran/vegetarian-food-in-iran

Long, L. (2007). Culinary tourism. In G. J. Allen & K. Albala (Eds.), *The business of food: Encyclopaedia of the food and drink industries* (pp. 111–114). Santa Barbara, CA: ABC-CLIO.

Long, L. M. (1998). Culinary tourism: A folkloristic perceptive on eating Otherness. *Southern Folklore, 55*(3), 181–204.

Long, L. M. (2006). Food pilgrimages: Seeking the sacred and the authentic in food. *Appetite, 47*(3), 393.

MacCannell, D. (1976). *The tourist: A new theory of the leisure class*. Berkeley, CA: University of California Press.

MagIran. (2008). Mosem-e golab-giri dar shahr-e gol va golab-e Iran nazdik ast [The season of golab-giri is coming to the city of rose and rosewater in Iran]. *Iran Zamin*, 4 April. Retrieved from magiran.com/n1611045

Marandi, S. M. & Tari, Z. G. (2017). Representations of post-revolutionary Iran by Iranian-American memoirists: Patterns of access to the media and communicative events. *ReOrient, 2*(2), 146–159.

Molz, J. G. (2007). Eating difference: The cosmopolitan mobilities of culinary tourism. *Space and Culture, 10*(1), 77–93.

Muir, J. (2000). English cook challenges kebab rule in Iran, *BBC NEWS*, 11 September. Retrieved from http://news.bbc.co.uk/1/hi/world/middle_east/919870.stm

Napora, K. (2015). Visit Iran – Practical information. *My Wander Lust* [Blog post]. Retrieved from http://www.mywanderlust.pl/visit-iran-practical-information/

O'Gorman, K., McLellan L. R., & Baum, T. (2007). Tourism in Iran: Central control and indigeneity. In R. Butler & T. Hinch (Eds.), *Tourism and indigenous peoples: Issues and implications* (pp. 251–264). Oxford: Butterworth-Heinemann.

Pritchett, V. S. (1964). *Foreign faces*. London: Chatto and Windus.

Radio Goftegoo. (2016). *Chelo-Kabab-e irani bayad dar UNESCO sabt shavad (Iranian Chelo-Kabab must be recognized by UNESCO)*. Retrieved from http://radiogoftegoo.ir/NewsDetails/?m=175115&n=61221

Ragg, M. (2015). How to visit Iran independently. *The Crowded Planet* [Blog post]. Retrieved from http://www.thecrowdedplanet.com/how-to-visit-iran-independently/

Reader, L. & Ridout, L. (2003). *First-time Asia* (vol. 14). London: Rough Guides.

Reynolds, A. (2016). 60 things you need to know before traveling to Iran. *Lost with Purpose* [Blog post]. Retrieved from https://www.lostwithpurpose.com/things-know-traveling-iran/

Richards, G. (2012). An overview of food and tourism trends and policies. In Organization for Economic Cooperation and Development (OECD) (Ed.), *OECD Studies on tourism: Food and the tourism experience: The OECD-Korea workshop* (pp. 13–46). Paris: OECD.

Rijntjes, S. (2016). Tales of Iranian hospitality: Part I. *Lost with Purpose* [Blog post]. Retrieved from https://www.lostwithpurpose.com/tales-iranian-hospitality-part-1/

Saleem, N. (2007). U.S. media framing of foreign countries image: An analytical perspective. *Canadian Journal of Media Studies, 2*(1), 130–162.

Sánchez, A. (2016). That time I was invited to an Iranian wedding. *Ani Anywhere* [Blog post]. Retrieved from http://www.anianywhere.com/iranian-wedding/#sthash. DVRklXtL.7dau8YJp.dpbs

Shaida, M. (1990). The golden spice from ancient Persia. In H. Walker (Ed.), *Oxford Symposium on food and cookery 1990: Feasting and fasting: Proceedings. Oxford Symposium* (pp. 194–197). London: Prospect Books.

Shaida, M. (1991). Chellow-Kabab – the national dish of Iran. In H. Walker (Ed.), *Oxford Symposium on food and cookery 1991: Public eating: Proceedings. Oxford Symposium* (pp. 272–275). London: Prospect Books.

Sharifi, K. (2017). *High potentials for boosting culinary tourism.* Retrieved from https://financialtribune.com/articles/people-travel/64575/high-potentials-for-boosting-culinary-tourism

Taghavi, H. (1998). Iranian hospitality attack: A survival guide for the non-Iranian traveler. *The Iranian,* 20 March. Retrieved from https://iranian.com/Travelers/March98/Hospitality/index.html

Tasnim News. (2015). Shiraz mizban-e jashnvare-ye ghaza-haye sonnati-ye ostan-e Fars mishavad (Shiraz hosts the festival of traditional foods of Fars). *Tasnim News,* 28 November. Retrieved from https://www.tasnimnews.com/fa/news/1394/09/07/929125

Telfer, E. (1996). *Food for thought: Philosophy and food.* Abingdon: Routledge.

Telfer, E. (2000). The philosophy of hospitableness. In C. Lashley & A. Morrisson (Eds.), *In search of hospitality: Theoretical perspectives and debates* (pp. 38–55). Abingdon: Routledge.

Thoma, N. & Ducke, I. (2015). As a vegetarian female traveller in Iran. *Westwards* [Blog post]. Retrieved from http://www.westwards.de/westwards/2015/06/iran_female-vegetarian.html

TripAdvisor. (2016). Superb food tour and cooking class. *TripAdvisor, Persian Food Tours* [Posted by Heemi27]. Retrieved from https://www.tripadvisor.co.nz/Attraction_Review-g293999-d11657907-Reviews-or10-Persian_Food_Tours-Tehran_Tehran_Province

TripAdvisor. (2017a). Best cooking class ever! *TripAdvisor, Persian Food Tours* [Posted by dancav30]. Retrieved from https://www.tripadvisor.co.nz/Attraction_Review-g293999-d11657907-Reviews-or10-Persian_Food_Tours-Tehran_Tehran_Province.html

TripAdvisor. (2017b). Delicious but pricey. *TripAdvisor, Fellini* [Posted by scorpioshanghai]. Retrieved from https://www.tripadvisor.co.nz/ShowUserReviews-g293999-d1230 311-r478715182-Fellini-Tehran_Tehran_Province.html

TripAdvisor. (2017c). Informative, enjoyable, and delicious. *TripAdvisor, Persian Food Tours* [Posted by dweinstocksavoy]. Retrieved from https://www.tripadvisor.co.nz/

Attraction_Review-g293999-d11657907-Reviews-or10-Persian_Food_Tours-Tehran_
Tehran_Province.html

TripAdvisor. (2017d). My best experience in Iran. *TripAdvisor, Persian Food Tours* [Posted
by MJSPPortugal]. Retrieved from https://www.tripadvisor.co.nz/Attraction_Review-
g293999-d11657907-Reviews-Persian_Food_Tours-Tehran_Tehran_Province.html

Tussyadiah, I. P. (2010). Destination-promoted and visitor-generated Images – Do they
represent similar stories? In P. Burns, J. A. Lester, & L. Bibbings (Eds.), *Tourism and
visual culture (Volume 2: Methods and cases)* (pp. 156–169). Oxfordshire: CABI.

Vafadari, K. & Cooper, M. (2010). Japanese tourism in Iran. In N. Scott & J. Jafari (Eds.),
Tourism in the Muslim world (Bridging tourism theory and practice) (pp. 159–179).
Bingley: Emerald.

Vogt, J. W. (1976). Wandering: Youth and travel behaviour. *Annals of Tourism Research,
4*(1), 25–41.

Warde, A. & Martens, L. (2000). *Eating out: Social differentiation, consumption and pleasure*. Cambridge: Cambridge University Press.

Williams, S. (2016). *Iran – culture smart!: The essential guide to customs & culture*. London: Kuperard.

Yoo, E. E. (2015). Food in scholarship: Thoughts on trajectories for future research. In I.
Yeoman, U. McMahon, B. K. Fields, J. Albrecht, & K. Meethan (Eds.), *The future of food
tourism: Foodies, experiences, exclusivity, visions and political capital* (pp. 225–236).
Bristol: Channel View.

Yoon, Y. & Uysal, M. (2005). An examination of the effects of motivation and satisfaction
on destination loyalty: A structural model. *Tourism Management, 26*(1), 45–56.

Young Journalists Club. (2014, 14 December). *Fars, mizban-e jashnvare-ye ghaza-ye son-
nati (Fars hosts the festival of traditional food)*. Retrieved from http://www.yjc.ir/fa/
news/5425482/

Yüksel, A. & Yüksel, F. (2002). Market segmentation based on tourists' dining preferences.
Journal of Hospitality & Tourism Research, 26(4), 315–331.

Zelinsky, W. (1985). The roving palate: North America's ethnic restaurant cuisines. *Geoforum, 16*(1), 51–72.

Zuelow, E. G. (2011). The necessity of touring beyond the nation: An introduction. In E.
G. Zuelow (Ed.), *Touring beyond the nation: A transnational approach to European
tourism history* (pp. 1–19). Farnham: Ashgate.

Part IV
Emerging tourisms

11 Tourism and the empowerment of women in Iran

Banafsheh M. Farahani and Hamideh Dabbaghi

Introduction

The post-sanction period provides the right time to redefine Iran's position in the global village and rebuild its relations with other countries. Tourism can be considered as one of the most important areas that can grant such a fresh opportunity to reassess the social and cultural image of the country.

According to the reports of the World Economic Forum (WEF) (2017), Iran was ranked 93 among 136 countries in 2017 in terms of competitiveness. In 2011 it ranked 114 out of 139 countries, which shows a bit of improvement. With an estimated 5.2 million international tourists a year to Iran and about $3.5 billion in expenditure by them, the average Iranian receipts per tourist can be estimated at $665.10 (WEF, 2017). In general, the travel and tourism industry added about $10.1 billion, accounting for 2.5% of Iran's total gross domestic product, with 476,000 jobs, and 1.9% of the total employment in the country. In Emtiaz Newspaper (2016), the head of the Iran Cultural Heritage, Handcraft and Tourism Organization (ICHTO) suggests that average annual growth of foreign tourists is about 12% (see Chapter 1, this volume). Private sector investment in the tourism sector in 2016 was approximately 20–30%.

In addition to contributing to economic development, it should be emphasized that the tourism industry has many cultural and social outcomes. This is because it requires the use of all indigenous capacities of the country (including human resources, infrastructure, location and geography), and the participation of all groups of the population regardless of their gender. Human resources, as the most important part of the tourism industry, can play a role in the field of tourism in the production of products, symbols and intangible cultural heritage (such as the production of artistic works or the implementation of cultural events such as harvesting celebrations) in the field of tourism.

There is a significant connection between empowerment and community development. Stern, Dethier, and Rogers (2005) contend that empowerment is a driver of growth. Sen (1997) also argues that capability expansion generates both economic productivity and social change, citing empirical studies that demonstrate a relationship between expanded female education, reduced gender inequality within the household and reduced fertility rates. However, before it can become powerful in development discourse, particularly at a policy level, the hypothesis that empowerment is a means towards progressive governance and poverty reduction has to be proved empirically (Alsop, Bertelsen, & Holland, 2006).

What about women's role in development?

Women are one of the most important groups of any population. Where women and girls are treated as inferior to men and boys, a vicious circle of limited education, poor employment opportunities, health, forced marriages and all too frequently violence and exploitation can be established and perpetuated. Focusing more support on girls offers an opportunity to replace that vicious cycle with a virtuous one that puts women at the heart of their families and their communities. As a result, women are able to bring in money to their families, get involved with local enterprises and make sure their children are educated. These are vital agents of change (Mitchell, 2013). Therefore, it is vital to consider women's empowerment as a tool for changing communities and enhancing their assets.

Empowerment is an interactive process which occurs between the individual and their environment, in the course of which the sense of the self as worthless changes into an acceptance of the self as an assertive citizen with socio-political ability. The outcome of the process is skills, based on insights and abilities, the essential features of which are a critical political consciousness, an ability to participate with others, a capacity to cope with frustrations and a willingness to struggle for influence over the environment (Kieffer, 1984). Empowerment is an interactive process through which people experience personal and social change (Sadan, 2015), enabling them to take action to achieve influence over the organizations and institutions which affect their lives and the communities in which they live (Lord & Hutchison, 1993). The importance of women's empowerment is also found in their capacity in creating community among poor and weak populations. While men of the same social class tend to accept the definition of success that is accepted in society at large – that a successful man is rich and fulfils a valuable social role – society tends to define a successful woman as married, a mother, mature, responsible and caring. As a result of these differences, women tend not to experience the powerlessness that stems from their social situation with the same intensity that men do (Luttrell, 1988; Sadan, 2015). These interpretations suggest that the community empowerment process of women converts the sources of their powerlessness, which are their traditional roles as housewives and mothers, into a power base. From this starting point, they become stronger and continue to extend their activities to additional domains with a more political character.

In sum, there are two rationales for supporting active policies to promote women. The first is that equity is valuable in and of itself: women are currently worse-off than men, and this inequality between genders is repulsive in its own right. For example, in the United Nation's 2005 report on the Millennium Development Goals (MDG) (as cited in Kharistvalashvili, 2016, p. 51), Kofi Annan, the Secretary General of the United Nations, writes: 'The full participation of women to all levels of decision-making is a basic human right.' The second, a central argument in the discourse of policymakers, is that women play a fundamental role in development. The gender gap in education, political participation and employment opportunities should therefore be reduced not only because it is equitable to do so, but also because it will have beneficial consequences on many other societal outcomes. It should be done, in other words, to increase efficiency. From this a second group of questions is therefore raised:

- What does empowerment for women mean?
- Does the definition that Iranian women have about empowerment match the dominant theoretical definitions and approaches?

In this chapter, an overview of women in tourism and the definitions and theoretical approaches to empowerment are first presented. This is followed by a brief discussion of the women in tourism in Iran concept in its structural context. Then, we will use interviews conducted by women active in the field of tourism to indicate problems in their personal lives and self-employment. Finally, we will present policy recommendations to empower and improve the status of Iranian women in the field of tourism.

Statistical review of women in tourism

The tourism industry can play an important role in empowering women politically, socially and economically. This goal is so important that the World Tourism Organization (UNWTO) is committed to increasing the positive impact of tourism development on women's lives, and with this in mind, seeks to achieve the fifth goal of sustainable development, namely 'Achieving gender equality and empowering all women' (UNWTO & UNDP, 2017). In this regard, the UNWTO launched the World Tourism Day in 2007 with the theme 'Opening Women's Doors to Women' and founded the Women's Tourism Forum in 2008. Since then, the UNWTO has been developing programmes through cooperation with UN women, in order to promote gender equality and empower women in the tourism industry, and encouraging member states to address these issues in tourism policy.

Tourism presents a wide range of income generation opportunities for women in both formal and informal employment. Tourism jobs are often flexible and can be carried out in different locations such as in the workplace, community and the household. Additionally, tourism creates a wide range of opportunities for women through the complex value chains that arise in the visitor economy. Although much information about women's situation in tourism is still missing, the results of an initial survey suggest that tourism is worth investing in and it has the potential to be a vehicle for the empowerment of women in developing regions. Tourism provides better opportunities for women's participation in the workforce, women's entrepreneurship and women's leadership than other sectors of the economy. Women in tourism are still underpaid, under-utilized, under-educated and under-represented; but tourism offers pathways to success. In addition, women make up an average 49.5% of formal hospitality and restaurant industry employees (World Tourism

Organization (UNWTO) and the United Nations Entity for Gender Equality and the Employment of Women (UN Women), 2011). Latin America and the Caribbean have the highest proportion of women in the tourism industry, followed by Africa. In Asia there is a wide disparity between Middle Eastern countries such as Saudi Arabia at 2% female participation in the tourism sector and Thailand at 65%. The higher levels of participation demonstrate tourism's potential contribution to income generation for women. Most women's employment in the tourism industry is concentrated in the service and clerical sector, although these figures vary by region, with a higher proportion of women working in the clerical sector in Latin America and the Caribbean (World Tourism Organization (UNWTO) and the United Nations Entity for Gender Equality and the Employment of Women (UN Women), 2011).

Unfortunately, there are no accurate data on the status of women in different areas of the tourism industry in Iran, although a brief review of women's status according to statistical data is available (Statistical Center of Iran (SCI), 2011). Women in Iran represent 49.6% of the total population (2011), 27.2% of women in Iran are literate and women have an economic participation rate of 13.8%. The overall rate of women's economic participation increased from 9.1% in 1996 to 11.4% in 2011. The female employment rate represents the active working population. It also shows that in 1996, out of the total active female population (employed and unemployed women) of the country 86.7% were employed; while by 2011, according to available census results, this had fallen to 75.8% (SCI, 2011).

But despite the positive changes that have emerged in the status of economic participation and the level of education of Iranian women, the unemployment rate for women in 2011 was 24.2% and with 59.9% classified as housewives, which was 1% higher in 1996 (SCI, 2011). The survey of the unemployment rate by gender from 1997 to 2014 also suggests that women's unemployment rate is twice as high as men's and that the gender gap in the labour market has increased. The increase in women's unemployment rates can be attributed to many factors in terms of the evolution of household livelihoods and the limitation of the agricultural economy, especially for rural women, as well as written and non-written policies that are prevalent in the service, production and labour markets. For example, employers indicate less willingness to hire women if there are men available for similar jobs. Most employers also tend to use male replacement labour when a woman takes maternity leave.

Global reports on the gender gap illustrate the weaker position of women in Iran. According to the Human Development Reports (United Nations Development Programme (UNDP), 2015), Iran ranked 118 in the index of gender inequality. Statistical studies show that women in Iran do not enjoy equal and balanced status. Despite its efforts in the direction of eliminating the educational gap between women and men only 32% of women aged 15 and above are actively engaging in the labour market either by working or looking for work. Among men (aged 15 and above) the corresponding rate is 73%. The global labour force participation rate of women is 52%. Only 25% of Iranian female youth participate in the labour market which is a much lesser extent than male youth. Among young men (15–24 years old) the labour force participation rate is 51%, while among female youth it is only 33%. Although unemployment affects both young men and women, gender disparities are marked (34% of female youth are unemployed, compared to 20% of male youth, according to statistics from 2008). These figures also potentially reflect some of the issues arising from the nature of Iranian society. For example, 'In Iran, a husband has the right to prevent his wife from taking a job that is "incompatible with the family interests or the dignity of himself or his wife" as mentioned in the 2010 Freedom House report' (United Nations Children's Fund (UNICEF), 2010, p. 4).

Empowerment

Empowerment can begin to be understood by examining the concepts of power and powerlessness (Lord & Hutchison, 1993). Power as the main core of empowerment has two central aspects: control over resources (physical, human, intellectual, financial and the self) and control over ideology (beliefs, values and attitudes). If power means control, then empowerment therefore is the process of gaining control. In the latter sense, the concept of power is quite close to the notion of human capability (Sen, 1997; Sadan, 2015). However, there is a distinction between real and surplus powerlessness (Lord & Hutchison, 1993). Real powerlessness results from economic inequities and oppressive control exercised by systems and other people. Surplus powerlessness, on the other hand, is an internalized belief that change cannot occur, a belief which results in apathy and an unwillingness of the person to struggle for more control and influence. Powerlessness has, therefore, come to be viewed as an objective phenomenon, where people with little or no political and economic power lack the means to gain greater control and resources in their lives (Lord & Hutchison, 1993).

Empowerment is defined as a group's or individual's capacity to make effective choices, that is, to make choices and then to transform those choices into desired actions and outcomes (Alsop et al., 2006). As noted above, empowerment can be understood as an interactive process which occurs between the individual and their environment (Sadan, 2015). For the individual – the micro-level – the empowerment process is a process of increasing control and transition from a state of powerlessness. Community empowerment – the macro-level – is a collective social process of creating a community, achieving better control over the environment, and decision making in which groups, organizations or communities participate (Sadan, 2015).

Empowerment can be assessed within different domains of a person's life (the state, the market, society) and at different levels (macro, intermediary and local). Each domain can be further divided into subdomains, which will indicate where and in what areas of their lives actors are empowered. At the intersection of the domains and levels, a person can experience different degrees of empowerment, addressing the issues of whether and to what extent the person is empowered. Two clusters of interdependent factors are associated with the different degrees of empowerment an individual or group experiences: the agency of the actor and the opportunity structure within which the actor operates. Analysis of agency and opportunity structure helps explain why an actor is empowered or not, and to what degree (Alsop et al., 2006). Here, agency is defined as an actor's or group's ability to make purposeful choices, that is – an actor is able to envisage and purposively choose between options (Alsop et al., 2006). An actor may be able to choose options, but the effective realization of those choices will largely depend upon the institutional context, the opportunity structure, within which the actor lives and works and that influence the success or failure of the choices that they make (Alsop et al., 2006).

Other theorists have defined empowerment in terms of psychological constructs. Especially conspicuous is the desire to connect empowerment to two groups of psychological constructs: personality constructs described under the concept of 'locus of control' (Rotter, 1990); and cognitive constructs that focus on self-efficacy (Bandura, 1982). Locus of control is a concept with an internal–external continuum, which in general terms determines that someone whose *locus of control* is inside him is *internal* – they expect reinforcement from themselves and possess inner motivation, and therefore their achievements will be more under their own control as opposed to someone whose locus of control is external. The *external* person perceives reinforcements as being beyond their control and due to chance, fate or powerful others (Rotter, 1990; Sadan, 2015). From this point of view, empowerment is a process of internal and external change. The internal process is the person's sense or belief in her ability to make decisions and to solve her own problems. The external change finds expression in the ability to act and to implement practical knowledge, information, skills, capabilities and other new resources acquired in the course of the process (Parsons, 1989; Sadan, 2015). But what does the concept of empowering women in the tourism industry mean and how can it be used?

Iranian women's roles, limitations and barriers

This study addresses three practical questions that are linked to the meaning of empowerment in the minds of Iranian women working in the field of tourism:

- As an activist in the field of tourism what does 'women's empowerment' mean to you?
- Discuss the dichotomies between your role in the family and your role as an active participant in the field of tourism?
- What are the barriers ahead of you for your success in the tourism industry?

The opportunity structure and barriers in the environment of the tourism industry in Iran provides a context to women's roles, limitations and barriers. As a general classification, the restrictions for women in the tourism industry can be divided into two categories: obstacles facing domestic female tourists and obstacles facing tourism workers.

Obstacles facing domestic female tourists

Except for day-trips outside the tourist's normal place of residence, tourism is a phenomenon that always includes an overnight stay. Therefore, tourist trips require accommodation. However, based on what Iranian law imposes, women travelling by themselves find it difficult to stay in some hotels and their presence is reported to the police (Siamian Gorji, 2013). This suggests that many women, and especially single ones, can experience difficulties in visiting the cities and villages of Iran when they wish to stay as independent travellers in formal tourist accommodation, rather than staying with friends and relations.

One of the other important issues is the psychological security of Iranian women and girls who are familiar with the customs and unwritten culture that creates a series of restrictions for women. Traditionally, a female travelling alone is not regarded as a good thing within Iranian society, and women face a limited number of restrictions, including family opposition, as well as the negative attitude of people from the first moment of travel.

Obstacles facing tourism workers

Tourism is a revenue-generating industry and an incentive to eliminate poverty and unemployment. One of the hallmarks of tourism is its high capacity to create employment for women and young people. However, despite the fact that the tourism industry can provide suitable employment for women, men's employment is significantly higher than that of women. Women make up about 66% of the workforce, but less than 5% of the industry's income (Kazemi Dolabi, 2007). Women in northern cities of the country earn money by renting their homes or rooms. If this is done with appropriate planning and policies, it can provide suitable self-employment opportunities for housewives.

Furthermore, based on gender division (Abbott & Wallace, 1997), the share of Iranian women in tourism management is almost zero, despite being one of the main backbones of this industry. In the eco-tourism sector, women have very restricted opportunities because of difficulties in being able to travel anywhere in a vehicle, so their chances of being chosen as eco-tour guides are reduced.

Analytical findings

Twenty interviews with women active in the field of tourism were conducted and analyzed using MAX QDA qualitative analysis software. In total, 112 concepts were extracted from the text of the interviews, which were categorized into several main themes and sub-themes. Analysis of the responses are discussed thematically below.

Nature and gender of activity in the field of tourism

According to the respondents (Table 11.1), the tourism situation in Iran continues to be based on a traditional approach and it is still not possible to exploit

Table 11.1 The nature of the tourism industry for women

Themes	Responses	Times reported
Nature of activities in the field of tourism in general	Lack of knowledge of the day and specialization in traditional Iranian tourism	3
	Continued traditional approach in tourism activities from the past	1
	The need for long working hours	1
	Full-time employment	1
	Being away from the family	1
In the case of active women in tourism industry	The impossibility of the presence of women in all sectors of tourism industry	1
	The existence of pay discrimination on women's work	1

contemporary knowledge and skills. Therefore, the traditional approach to managing and carrying out tourism activities is still ongoing. The nature of this job requires a long stay at work and is a full-time job because it depends on the presence of tourists and their leisure time. Therefore, at times when leisure is available to those working in other industries, women must stay at work and stay away from family and provide services for tourists. On the other hand, despite diversity and activities in the tourism industry, women do not have access to all sectors, and they are subject to pay discrimination and receive fewer rights than men.

The meaning of empowerment and characteristics of active women in the field of tourism

From the perspective of the interviewed women, tourism has the potential to use their knowledge, experience and capabilities (Table 11.2). The abilities of women in creating and innovating their managerial potential makes them able to play a variety of roles in the tourism industry. Women tend to be more effective, enduring and tolerant than men in their activities and social communication, and they can provide better services. The relationships that active women make with customers in tourism are based on empathy and understanding (Table 11.3). They are more motivated to do their jobs because they want the community to see and believe in their capabilities. They believe they have a lot of discipline and can show self-sacrifice when they encounter problems.

Obstacles and barriers facing women's activity in the tourism industry

Interviewed women believe that the ability of women and men to carry out tourism activities should be evaluated according to their knowledge levels and capabilities

Table 11.2 Definition of empowerment from the perspective of active women in the tourism industry

Theme	Responses	Times reported
Empowerment as	Use of knowledge and experience	1
	Applying capabilities	1

Table 11.3 Individual characteristics in the field of work of active women in the tourism industry

Themes	Responses	Times reported
Values and beliefs	The importance of information and knowledge in making differences between men and women	2
	Equality of ability of both sexes	2
Features at work	High ability of women to create and innovate in comparison with men	1
	Management ability of active women in the field of tourism	2
	Women and their roles in tourism	1
	Rational-based relationships	1
	Better service	1
	More effective social communication	1
	Deeper connections	1
	Endurance and tolerance	1
	Management and planning of women in tourism	1
	Women's empathy and sympathy	1
	Empathy-based relationships	1
	Tasks performance with high motivation	1
	Increasing sense of duty and discipline	2
	Great care in doing things	1
	Self-scarification	1

(Table 11.4), arguing that it is the community, social and cultural context that distinguishes between the genders. Society's and government authority's lack of belief in women's ability, along with religious beliefs that weigh on the work of women in the field of tourism, even affects their personal life. For example, they face cultural resistance at the time of marriage, when they are often forced to leave work. Similarly, there are false religious and cultural beliefs about the nature of women's work in the field of tourism, but the nature of the industry, for example, of often being away from home at particular times of day, has contributed to the traditional resistance to women working in the tourism industry and challenged their capabilities.

Tourism organizations did not have plans to assist the existing potential and the positive effects of women in tourism, so there are still many doubts about the role

Table 11.4 Personal-familial and socio-cultural barriers affecting the reduced presence of active women in the tourism industry

Themes	Responses	Times reported
Personal and family barriers	Marriage as a barrier to activity	2
	The need for women to satisfy their husband	1
	The lack of familiarity with the nature of tourism occupation for women	1
	Family resistance against the independence of single girls	
	Intermittence between celebrations and family gathering with tours	1
	Family distrust of their girls' security in tourism	1
	The contradiction between the status of married women and tourism occupation	1
	Assign a lot of time for the tour	1
	The seasonal and periodical absence of tour leader at home because of the volume of tourism work	1
	Lack of focus on work activities due to family problems	2
Social and cultural barriers	Lack of belief in the capabilities of women in the field of tourism by the community and authorities	1
Contradiction of role and value as a barrier to women's work in the field of tourism		
	Religious beliefs affect women's work in the field of tourism	1
	Cultural resistance for marriage with active women in tourism	2
	The existence of misleading religious and cultural beliefs in women's work in tourism	1
	Cultural contradictions in introduction of culture	1
	The existence of religious resistance to the work of women in tourism due to getting away from home	1
	Traditional look at women and their abilities	1
	There are grounds for gender discrimination	1
	The lack of support from tourism organizations for women in particular	1
	Lack of resources and research	1
	Traditional and patriarchal thinking about the work of women in tourism	2
	Being a woman as an obstacle to work in tourism	1
	Preference of society in hiring men to women	1
	The existence of an unhealthy competitive environment	1
	The contrast between the need to maintain independence in life with a warm environment and solidarity in family	1

(*Continued*)

Table 11.4 (Continued)

Themes	Responses	Times reported
	Confrontation between feelings and emotions with a sense of duty in the workplace	1
	Confronting family values with the workplace	1
	The contrast between the role of modern society and the efforts to gain social credibility by playing a traditional role in the family and trying to maintain and protect family	1
	The need for women to satisfy their spouse	1
	Interference of roles	1

of women in the industry (Table 11.4). Because of traditional thinking and patriarchy in the hidden social and cultural layers of Iran, being a woman is regarded as an obstacle to tourism activity and even employers prefer to employ men in this area. The lack of research resources, as well as the competitive environment and conditions also has an impact on women's activity.

Family can also be a barrier to the development of women's activities in the tourism industry in some cases (Table 11.4). Single girls who work in the field of tourism, usually face resistance from their families due to the form and structure of family in Iran and lack of independence of girls before marriage. Lack of familiarity with the nature of tourism business and a high degree of remoteness from family have led families to be concerned about the safety of girls in this industry. Married women working in the tourism sector are always reminded of marriage as an obstacle to their career and career advancement. This is because, according to traditional interpretations of Islamic law, women in Iran have important duties as spouses and mothers and it is necessary to gain the consent of their spouse for any occupation. The nature of seasonality and the absence of women from their families if working, for example, as a tourist guide, can place the nature of the position in conflict with family interests. Some firms may also regard family interests as reducing women's efficiency and effectiveness in some cases because they have to focus on family problems instead of occupational activities.

The employment of women in the tourism industry provides contradictions and contrasts. For example, Iranian women that work in tourism are constantly forced to go beyond the need for independence in life or to maintain a warm

Table 11.5 Macro-economic conditions affecting the reduced presence of women in the tourism industry

Theme	Responses	Times reported
Conditions and fields of intervention	Economic sanctions	1
	Lack of tourism infrastructure	1
	Management	1

environment and solidarity in the family. Similarly, they are often stuck between practices based on family values and workplace values that are often more international in scope, particularly as a result of conventional hospitality and tourism training that is often embedded within corporate service cultures. Women also have to choose between their willingness to play a modern role in society and gain social credibility or play a traditional role in the family, and try to preserve and protect the family.

Macro-economic conditions are also regarded as influencing the continuation of the current situation of women in the field of tourism and their lack of presence (Table 11.5). For example, economic sanctions and a lack of tourism infrastructure reduce market demands for tourism and therefore potential employment opportunities. This is despite the perceived significance of women's work activities in

Table 11.6 Achievements of women's activities and work in the field of tourism

Themes	Responses	Times reported
Women's achievements in the field of tourism	The positive effect of women's marginalization on work	1
	Effective role of women in academic field	1
	Women's employment as a source of income for family	1
	Promote the status of women in family and promote their sense of value	1
	Variety of roles and responsibilities of women	2
	Women under the guardianship of men in the realm of family through religious teachings	1
	Importance of co-operation in homework due to women's employment	1

Table 11.7 Women's empowerment strategies for tourism

Theme	Responses	Times reported
Women's empowerment strategies in the field of tourism	Provide necessary and specialized training	1
	Improving knowledge and skills of women	1
	Confronting income discrimination	1
	Policies for matching women's potential and career prospects	1
	Contextualization for promotion of women's skills	1

tourism (Table 11.6). However, there are means and policies to increase the position of women working in the tourism industry to increase their capabilities (Table 11.7). Interviewed women believe that providing necessary and specialized training can raise women's awareness and skills in the field of women's capabilities in the tourism industry.

Discussion and conclusion

The concept of women's empowerment is one of the most important goals in developing countries. The reason why empowerment of women and girls is important can be found in most of the documents and reports by the United Nations, the World Bank and literature on this topic, all of which emphasize several points. Women have an important role to play in preserving and managing family and the education of the next generation. Therefore, building their familiarity with individual and social rights and enacting them will boost economic activity, help exiting from the cycle of poverty, increase the level of education in society and help control and access to resources, promote health and encourage community social and economic development. However, it is also important to understand what women themselves mean by their abilities and understand what empowerment means to them, as examined in this chapter with respect to women who are active in the tourism industry.

In defining the concept of empowerment based on the views of women, one should pay attention to their stated needs and demands. Particularly, the needs and desires that are in line with the evolution of the identity and relative success of women in employment and education in the last half-century. In other words, empowerment for women who face economic problems, self-care or responsibility for maintenance of their children is equal to income. But, with the advancement of the equality of discourse and the proper presence of more female employees at the community level, it does not seem that only income means women's empowerment. In emerging conditions, women increasingly talk about social and political spheres and make new demands in these areas such as seeking equal opportunities in areas of employment traditionally divided by gender. For example, women take office jobs in the tourism industry, or they prefer to be tourist guides. Despite the fact that there are stereotypes against tourism work for women based on social and cultural beliefs, the transfer of intangible culture is shaped by women. However, according to our research findings, empowerment, knowledge and experience have changed the current conditions of women in this industry, and although there are still fewer women in management positions than men, there is at least now greater awareness and demands for more women in this field. Nevertheless, there is a need to expand this discourse throughout the wider community. Indeed, it is not possible to realize the social function of women, including in politics, economics, culture and education, without it.

The answer to the second question, namely, 'the duality of the role of women in family and activism in the field of tourism', returns to the contradictions of values that are rooted in religion. The woman in the Iranian family has a legal role that is required to be implemented. For example, a married woman travelling without a man's consent could lead to legal consequences, because she has violated her guardian's orders from the point of view of law and religion. Such value conflicts are likely to be effective in exacerbating these value conflicts in jobs that require a 24-hour timetable of service and long hours away from home, as is common in the tourism and hospitality sector.

Analysis of the third question of the research: 'What are the obstacles facing women in their success in the tourism industry?' showed that barriers can be classified into three broad categories.

Social and cultural resistance as infrastructure

These obstacles are the result of the current beliefs and cultural and traditional approaches to society regarding the role of women in the family and the nature of work in the tourism industry. Similarly, general policies, norms and values, and political structures contribute to the strengthening and reproduction of this type of barrier against women. For example, the family's approach to the way girls are presented in society and society's expectations about the presence of boys in the public environment, as well as lack of individual independence of girls before marriage being under the control of their parents and their families.

The institutional level and role of organizations

The extent to which tourism organizations recognize the social, cultural and religious structures of the community and enact them poses significant challenges for increasing the participation of women in tourism in Iran. If tourism development remains limited and creates only limited employment opportunities, then the self-sustaining male oriented market demand for tourism labour will remain. More overtly, tourist agencies have few plans and policies to increase the use of women in their organizational mission. Nevertheless, for reasons of sustainability and community-oriented tourism development, attention is needed to provide education and incentive policies in this area. Importantly, the capacity to use women in the significant role of developing the skills and knowledge of local residents, can be argued on economic grounds as being beneficial to the growth of the local and national economy.

Individual level

The way women look at their situation and condition is, in many cases, one of the biggest and most important challenges and obstacles in their path to empowerment. Although the women in this study seem to believe in their positive personal qualities and characteristics in their occupational activities, they still talk about the dual contradictions in their role.

Finally, given the nature of the tourism industry, despite technological advances in the world, the industry is still based on the significant role of human resources. This feature is especially important for countries facing unemployment and with the necessary capabilities, such as natural, cultural, historical and social resources, for tourism development. Hence, the tourism industry can be viewed as a solution to the unemployment crisis, inequality and poverty. But in order for tourism development to be successful and sustainable, the local community must benefit equally from the visitor economy and contribute to decision-making and planning. According to the principle of equality in sustainable development, participation of all segments of society, especially those with less effective influence, is indispensable in the development process, and women are among these groups.

References

Abbott, P. & Wallace, C. (1997). The production of feminist knowledges. In P. Abbott & C. Wallace (Eds.), *An introduction to sociology. Feminist perspectives* (2nd ed., pp. 283–302). London: Routledge [Translated into Persian by Manijeh Najm].

Alsop, R., Bertelsen, M. F., & Holland, J. (2006). *Empowerment in practice from analysis to implementation.* Washington, DC: The International Bank for Reconstruction and Development/The World Bank.

Bandura, A. (1982). Self-efficacy mechanism in human agency. *American Psychologist, 37*(2), 122–147.

Emtiaz Newspaper. (2016). *An increase of 12% in foreign tourists.* Retrieved from http://www.emtiazdaily.ir/Newspaper/Page/190/3223

Kazemi Dolabi, A. (2007). Let's build bridges rather than building long walls. *A Thunderstorm Monthly, 10,* Autumn.

Kharistvalashvili, N. (2016). Women's role in developing economies: Case of Georgia. *European Journal of Sustainable Development, 5*(1), 47–52.

Kieffer, C. H. (1984). Citizen empowerment: A developmental perspective. *Prevention in Human Services, 3*(2–3), 9–36.

Lord, J. & Hutchison, P. (1993). The process of empowerment: Implications for theory and practice. *Canadian Journal of Community Mental Health, 12*(1), 5–22.

Luttrell, W. (1988). The Edison School struggle: The reshaping of working-class education and women's consciousness. In A. Bookman & S. Morgen (Eds.), *Women and the politics of empowerment* (pp. 136–158). Philadelphia, PA: Temple University Press.

Mitchell, A. (2013). Women empowerment: Lynchpin of development goals. In *Dialogues at the Economic and Social Council: Achieving gender equality, women's empowerment and strengthening development cooperation* (pp. 21–24). New York, NY: United Nations.

Parsons, R. J. (1989). Empowerment for role alternatives for low income minority girls: A group work approach. *Social Work with Groups, 11*(4), 27–43.

Rotter, J. B. (1990). Internal versus external control of reinforcement: A case history of a variable. *American Psychologist, 45*(4), 489–493.

Sadan, E. (2015). *Empowerment and community planning.* Tel Aviv, Israel: Hakibbutz Hameuchad [Translated from Hebrew by Richard Flantz].

Sen, G. (1997). *Empowerment as an approach to poverty.* Background paper to the Human Development Report. Economics and Social Sciences Indian Institute of Management.

Siamian Gorji, A. (2013). *Introduction to tourism and the arrival of women in this field; bottlenecks and advance constraints.* Retrieved from http://y687.blogfa.com/post-39.acpx

Statistical Center of Iran (SCI). (2011). *Labor force survey.* Retrieved from https://www.amar.org.ir/Portals/0/Files/fulltext/1390/n_niru_s90.pdf

Stern, N., Dethier, J.-J., & Rogers, F. H. (2005). *Growth and empowerment. Making development happen.* The Munich Lectures in Economics. Cambridge: The Massachusetts Institute of Technology Press.

United Nations Children's Fund (UNICEF). (2010). *Iran. MENA gender equality profile. status of girls and women in the Middle East and North Africa.* UNICEF.

United Nations Development Programme (UNDP). (2015). *Human development reports. Table 5: Gender inequality index.* Retrieved from http://hdr.undp.org/en/composite/gii

UNWTO & UNDP. (2017). *Tourism and the Sustainable Development Goals: Journey to 2030.* Madrid: UNWTO.

World Economic Forum (WEF). (2017). *The travel & tourism competitiveness index.* Retrieved from http://reports.weforum.org/travel-and-tourism-competitiveness-report-2017/ranking/

World Tourism Organization (UNWTO) and the United Nations Entity for Gender Equality and the Employment of Women (UN Women). (2011). *Global report on women in tourism 2010. Preliminary findings.* UNWTO and UN Women.

12 Participatory tourism development in Iran: implementing community-based tourism within a migrating nomadic tribe

Fereshteh Fazel Bakhsheshi and Najmeh Hassanli

Introduction

Tourism, as an active agent of change and control among rural communities, has the potential to contribute to the development of rural destinations (Lenao, 2017). However, it can also exacerbate negative economic and social conditions leading to inequality and conflict (Harrison & Schipani, 2007). As an alternative to conventional mass tourism, community-based tourism (CBT) is used to promote more sustainable and equitable tourism practices (Burgos & Mertens, 2017; Kunjuraman & Hussin, 2017; Tolkach & King, 2015). It is argued that "CBT suggests a symbolic or mutual relationship where the tourist is not given central priority but becomes an equal part of the system" (Salazar, 2012, p. 10).

This chapter aims to contribute to the debate on the benefits of CBT by exploring the implementation of a CBT framework in Iran. Once the framework is presented, a case study based on the implementation of the framework within a nomadic community is discussed. The study is based on a two-year project (2012–2014) funded by the United Nations Development Programme (UNDP), Global Environment Facility (GEF), Small Grants Programme (SGP) global initiative on Indigenous Peoples, and Community Conserved Areas (CCAs).

Definition, benefits, barriers and models of CBT

In striving to be "socially equitable, ecologically sound, and economically viable," Dodds, Ali, and Galaskic (2016, p. 2) argue that CBT shares the goals of sustainable development, while differing from other types of tourism, by aiming to maximize benefits for community stakeholders rather than solely for absent investors. There are many definitions of CBT presented in the literature. For the purpose of this study, the following definition by the Responsible Ecological Social Tours Project Foundation (REST) (1997, as cited in Suansri, 2003, p. 14) is used:

> CBT is tourism that takes environmental, social, and cultural sustainability into account. It is managed and owned by the community, for the community, with the purpose of enabling visitors to increase their awareness and learn about the community and local ways of life.

By focusing on ownership and management by the local community, this definition differentiates between CBT and other types of alternative tourism, such as eco-tourism, that are run inside the community and could be argued to be more 'community-oriented' than 'community-based'.

The literature identifies the benefits of CBT to include empowering the community, diversifying livelihoods, enhancing host–guest interactions, protecting cultural and natural resources, providing authentic experiences for the growing market of alternative tourism, and adding value to the tourism product through diversification of tourism (Burgos & Mertens, 2017; Dodds et al., 2016; Ernawati, Sanders, & Dowling, 2017; Tolkach & King, 2015; Salazar, 2012). Sofield (2003, as cited in Salazar 2012, p. 13) notes that "many of the benefits of CBT planning lie in the process, not simply the outcome."

Despite the extensive debate on the benefits of CBT and participatory tourism development in general, Tolkach and King (2015) assert that CBT achievements are modest and successes are rare with many CBT projects generating limited economic benefits for the local communities, thus leading to their dependence on external support. There have also been numerous criticisms of the concept, for instance Blackstock (2005) argued that the literature on CBT diverges from the philosophy of community development in three different ways: (1) the focus in CBT is mainly on sustaining the tourism industry rather than committing to the empowerment of the local community; (2) local communities are often presented as being homogenous without power struggles and conflicting interests; and (3) a lack of understanding of external barriers to local participation and local control. Other scholars have focused on identifying the barriers and challenges for the local community's active participation in CBT projects. Specifically. within the context of developing countries, Tosun (2000) identified three categories of limitations: operational, structural, and cultural. Centralization of power in the public administration for the development of tourism; lack of coordination and cooperation among the different parties involved; and lack of comprehensible information available to the local community are examples of operational obstacles. Structural limitations include attitudes of professionals; lack of expertise and dominance of elites; lack of appropriate legal system; lack of trained human resources; relatively high costs of community participation; and lack of financial resources. Finally, examples within the cultural category include limited capacity of poor people; and apathy and low level of awareness in the local community (Tosun, 2000). In another categorization, Kunjuraman and Hussin (2017) classify challenges for the active involvement of local communities in developing countries into two groups: internal challenges (mental considerations) and external challenges (physical considerations).

Despite all these difficulties, Dodds et al. (2016, p. 4) identified six elements that facilitate the success of CBT. These elements are:

- Participatory planning and capacity building—to strengthen the community's tourism management skills;
- Collaboration and partnerships facilitating links to market—to ensure financial viability;

- Local management/empowerment of community members;
- Establishment of environmental/community goals—to ensure outcomes are in alignment with community's values;
- Assistance from enablers (government, funding institutions, and private sector)—to facilitate access to the formal economy;
- Focus on generating supplemental income for long-term community sustainability.

Three CBT models are presented as the basis of the CBT framework applied in this study. The non-existent role of governments in these CBT initiatives as well as their relevance to a developing country like Iran are the main reasons for their discussion.

The 4D model

The Appreciative Participatory Planning and Action (APPA) approach developed by the Mountain Institute (2000) provides the basic structure for CBT planning. The four steps in the APPA approach are known as the 4Ds of *discovery, dream, design,* and *delivery*; or the 4D model hereafter. In the first stage of *discovery,* participants focus on recognizing those characteristics of the community which would attract tourists as well as identifying the community's strengths and skills that would contribute to CBT. Participatory learning and empowerment of the community through skills development are important components of this stage. In the *dream* stage, participants visualize how they would like their community to benefit from tourism and how, based on the strengths and skills they identified in the previous stage, they could create the best CBT. During the *design* stage, which is perhaps the most challenging of all, participants prioritize and work together to develop plans which help in turning their dreams into reality. The *delivery* stage of the 4D framework focuses on an ongoing implementation of the plans developed in the previous stage. The 4D cycle closes by returning to the *discovery* stage through reflecting upon and evaluating what was learnt (The Mountain Institute, 2000).

The REST model

Responsible Ecological Social Tours (REST), under the Thai Volunteer Service, is a dynamic Thai NGO focusing on the challenges of sustainable community development and environmental protection. The CBT model by REST has so far been implemented in various local communities in Thailand. The model, published as a handbook, is composed of ten steps for implementing CBT within a community (Suansri, 2003):

1. Select a suitable community;
2. Complete a feasibility study in cooperation with the community;
3. Set vision and objectives with the community;
4. Develop a plan to prepare the community to manage tourism;
5. Set direction for organizational management;

6. Design tour programs;
7. Train interpretive guides;
8. Develop a marketing plan;
9. Launch a pilot tour program; and
10. Monitor and evaluate the process.

Pinel's model

In an attempt to initiate and use community assessment as a foundation for community-based tourism planning, Pinel (1998) proposed a CBT planning process model. His model has three feedback loops for evaluating the stakeholders; the facilitating conditions; and the tourism product as well as four phases of community assessment and organization development phase; planning and preparation phase; delivery phase; and monitoring and adjustment phase.

The study setting

Over the years and with the aim of reducing poverty and generating employment, Iran's government has highlighted the development of rural tourism in its national tourism policies and strategies. Accordingly, a Rural Tourism Steering Committee (RTSC) was established in 2004 and 464 target villages with high tourism potential were selected. Subsequently, a three-stage strategic–structural plan including feasibility studies was to be conducted in these villages (Ghaderi & Henderson, 2012). Although this and similar initiatives to diversify the country's rural economy toward cultural/rural tourism are considered favorable for CBT implementation in Iran, the government's central control of the industry has often led to a top-down approach with fewer opportunities for local communities in peripheral areas to participate in tourism development. Similarly, and despite the increasing role of non-governmental organizations (NGOs) in tourism development in Iran, the general top-down approach prevalent in the country and a lack of political will to implement participation has resulted in such organizations getting access to funds without significantly contributing to sustainable community development. In addition, in numerous cases NGOs have merely acted as an economic stakeholder by providing funds to local communities and increasing their dependence on external support.

Therefore, this chapter investigates the implementation of community-based tourism (CBT) in Iran as a participatory and bottom-up approach to tourism development. More specifically, it focuses on applying a CBT framework within a migrating nomadic community: the Heybatlu sub-tribe of the Qashqai tribe. The migrating nomads of Iran, who constitute one of the many diverse ethnic groups, lead a unique pattern of living, distinguishing them from urban and rural communities residing in the country. Their main source of income has principally been from raising livestock. Factors such as their livelihood and the geographical and climatic conditions they live in have been influential in their migration between winter and summer settlements. It should be noted that these migrating nomads lead a different lifestyle to those nomads who have, in the last decades, settled in rural and urban areas of the country. An important characteristic of migrating nomads is their tribal structure with clear patterns of kinship and relationships. Each tribe has an established territory with their owned grazing lands (Iran Chamber Society, 2017). These tribal communities have always been dependent on the conservation of nature within their territories. However, over the years, externally imposed management systems have weakened the traditional and customary governance of natural resources and local knowledge, leading to environmental degradation (United Nations Development Programme (UNDP), Global Environment Facility (GEF), Small Grants Programme (SGP), 2012).

As part of the UNDP, GEF, SGP global initiative on Indigenous Peoples, and Community Conserved Areas (CCAs), the Heybatlu sub-tribe, with the facilitation support of a major NGO in Iran, had prepared a CBT project. Recognizing the importance of sustaining their livelihood and conserving their natural resources, the community believed presenting these as tourism attractions would help in achieving their intentions. This is in line with previous studies demonstrating the tendency of consumers to seek products linked with authenticity, tradition, heritage, and culture (Hassanli, Gross, & Brown, 2016), thus highlighting a potential marketing opportunity for nomadic tourist experiences.

A tourism specialist was invited to work closely with the local community. The project focused on the integrity of the sub-tribe's entire territory including their summer and winter settlements, and their immigration route. Consisting of 60 migrating families and a population of over 300 people, the Heybatlu sub-tribe's territory extends through Fars Province in South Iran with their immigration route toward northern areas of the province in summer and southern areas in winter (UNDP, GEF, SGP, 2012). The project was based on implementing a CBT framework (Fazel Bakhsheshi, 2011) within the Heybatlu community. Thus, in line with the aim of the chapter, the following section will present the framework and discuss its implementation.

The CBT framework and its implementation within the Heybatlu community

To address some of the criticisms made of CBT, three key questions need to be asked and addressed when considering a community's participation in tourism development (Fazel Bakhsheshi, 2011):

What is the community's attitude toward tourism development at the destination?

Residents are a major stakeholder in tourism development since they are directly affected by its negative impacts. As such, Nunkoo, Smith, and Ramkisson (2013) argue that tourism needs to be seen as a 'community industry'. The extent to which the views and desires of the local community are considered in planning and developing tourism at a destination, determines the community's support and

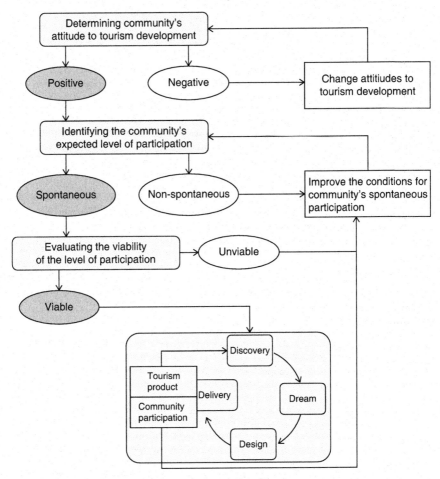

Figure 12.1 The CBT framework.
Source: adapted from Fazel Bakhsheshi, 2011.

receptiveness to tourism and tourists. Therefore, understanding the attitudes and perceptions of residents toward tourism development and its impacts is crucial in gaining their active support (Nunkoo et al., 2013; Choi & Sirkaya, 2005). In their review of literature on tourism attitudes, Andereck and Vogt (2000) concluded that despite residents' concerns about the negative impacts of tourism, communities in general seem to be positively disposed toward tourism.

Many CBT models including the three reviewed previously (the 4D model, the REST model, Pinel's model) assume the answer to the first question to be positive which unfortunately creates challenges in consolidating various stakeholder views and evaluating the community's capacity for participation. The CBT framework used in this study (Fazel Bakhsheshi, 2011) attempts to address this weakness in its first phase (see Figure 12.1). Based on the three key questions detailed below and the 4D model discussed above, the CBT framework employed in this study is comprised of four phases, which are detailed below and presented in Figure 12.1.

What is the level of participation that the community expects to have in tourism development?

Tosun and Timothy (2001) outline a number of arguments in support of community participation in the tourism development process. These include:

- It contributes to a more sustainable tourism through the residents' protection of the area's natural and cultural heritage and their involvement in establishing desirable conditions.
- It contributes to a fair and just distribution of costs and benefits among community members.
- Community participation and its willingness to support tourism increases tourist satisfaction.
- It strengthens the democratization process at the destination.

Community participation in the tourism development process can be viewed in terms of the decision-making process and in the benefits gained from tourism development. However, in many developing countries, rather than creating opportunities for the local community to take part in the decision-making process, community participation is mainly seen as helping the locals gain economic benefits through operating small businesses and being employed as workers (Tosun, 2000).

It is argued that for a successful participation, the community needs to be aware of its role and the role of the tourism industry at the destination (Pinel, 1998). However as argued by Burns and Sancho (2003), a lack of local technical knowledge about tourism along with complicated relationships between various layers of government can lead to misunderstandings about the nature of participation in tourism. The situation is exacerbated in developing countries which often lack enabling socio-economic and cultural environments, thus preventing participatory tourism development (Tosun, 2005).

In response to the absence of a community participation process within the tourism sector, Tosun (1999, 2006) developed a typology of community participation in tourism comprising of three modes of spontaneous, induced, and coercive participation. As an ideal mode, spontaneous participation is voluntary and the community manages to handle their problems without any external help. Induced participation, at the other end of the continuum and the most common mode in developing countries, is top-down, passive, and indirect. Despite the local community having a voice in this mode, their lack of power does not ensure that their views will be considered by other powerful stakeholders such as government bodies. Coercive participation is at the very extreme end and is compulsory, manipulated, and contrived (Tosun 1999, 2006).

In the three CBT models reviewed above (the 4D model, the REST model, Pinel's model) it is incorrectly assumed that the community is aware of its participation level and capable of fulfilling it. As an attempt in addressing the second key question, the CBT framework in the current study has employed Tosun's (1999, 2006) typology to determine the community's expected level of participation in tourism development.

How viable is the community's expected level of participation?

The requirements for this level of participation, including the eligibility of community members as well as their access to required resources need to be assessed to determine whether the expected level of participation is viable or not. For example, as will be explained in more detail in the following sections, to determine the possibility of a community's spontaneous participation in tourism development, the eligibility criteria set by external stakeholders for specific tourism roles and positions need be evaluated.

Phases 1 and 2

Phase 1: determining community attitudes to tourism development

In this initial phase, the local community's attitudes toward tourism development at the destination are assessed using a survey. The second phase is introduced only if there seems to be a positive attitude among the community; otherwise attempts will be made to change the community's attitude through increasing their awareness of the impacts, both non-economic and economic, of sustainable tourism development and/or CBT.

Phase 2: identifying the community's expected level of participation

The second phase incorporates the use of a survey to identify the community's expected level of participation in tourism development based on Tosun's (1999, 2006) categorization.

According to Fazel Bakhsheshi (2008a), the failure of many CBT projects is because they are either based on the community's pseudo participation or that the community's participation is assumed to be appropriate. In both cases projects face many challenges in the implementation phase, thus impeding their success. Fazel Bakhsheshi (2008a) highlights the need for the community's spontaneous participation in order for CBT development projects to succeed.

Therefore, if the community's expected level of participation is spontaneous, the model will go to the third phase. Otherwise, attempts will be made to improve the conditions for the community's spontaneous participation through fostering their self-belief and confidence; highlighting the various roles they could play in tourism development; and allowing them to recognize management of tourism should not be dominated by the elite.

In applying the first two phases of the framework, a survey based on studies by Tosun (2006) and Kibicho (2003), but with certain modifications to fit the Heybatlu community, was distributed among the heads of 60 families. The survey instrument, comprised of 44 items on a five-point Likert scale, was analyzed using SPSS. The results indicated the community's positive attitude to tourism development and an expected level of spontaneous participation.

Phase 3: evaluating the viability of the community's expected level of participation

Once the community's anticipated level of participation is identified as spontaneous, the next phase focuses on evaluating how viable this level of participation is. To do so, initially the criteria and standards set by stakeholders for various tourism roles (e.g. tour operation manager) as well as the required resources for a spontaneous participation are identified. Then, an assessment is undertaken to determine whether community members meet the required criteria and whether they have access to the required resources and facilities. This assessment would determine if a spontaneous level of participation, as the expected level of participation by the community, is viable or not. If viable, the framework enters the next and final phase. If not viable, then consideration needs to be given to factors that facilitate the conditions required for the community's spontaneous participation.

In applying the third phase of the framework within the Heybatlu community, spontaneous participation was found not viable. This was mainly because the community did not possess the required criteria and standards, two examples of which are presented here.

Within the previous phase where the community had identified their desired form of participation to be spontaneous, they had also indicated their interest in having members appointed as tour operation managers with the responsibility of planning, organizing, and handling package tours. Having local tour operation managers also meant that travel agencies and tour operators, as key stakeholders, would have confidence in working with the community. ICHTO, as the government body in charge of all tourism regulations in the country, requires certain qualifications for those wanting to undertake courses in tour operation management. One such requirement is for applicants to hold a bachelor's degree. However, it soon became apparent that no one within the Heybatlu community had a bachelor's degree which is reasonable considering the nature of the nomadic lifestyle (being on the move) and a lack of need for a university degree. With the purpose of easing the aforementioned requirements for nomadic and tribal communities, negotiations were undertaken with representatives from the organization in charge of tourism development at the provincial level. However, all attempts were in vain. It took around two years for one community member, who held a Graduate Certificate (equivalent to two years' full-time university study after high school), to undertake further studies and gain a bachelor's degree. In this period, the tourism specialist working with the community, who was also qualified as a tour operation manager, took on the role.

202 Fereshteh Fazel Bakhsheshi and Najmeh Hassanli

The second example was the need to train community members as tour guides so that there would be less reliance on external tour guides from outside the community. Based on ICHTO requirements, two different tour guide courses exist; while one qualifies a prospective guide to work with domestic tours, the other which is for incoming tours from other countries, requires the applicants to undertake their tests in English. A lack of English language proficiency was a limitation among the Heybatlu nomadic community, and it took a few months for at least one community member to undertake English lessons and successfully complete the tour guide tests in English. In both cases, the necessary costs required for individual community members to become eligible for undertaking tour operation manager and tour guide courses were covered by the project.

Phase 4: implementing the 4D model

The final phase incorporates the implementation of the cyclical 4D model. This model was appropriate due to its use in regions with a similar climate and geography to those in Iran. Within this phase, the four steps of *discovery*, *dream*, *design*, and *delivery*, as outlined in the Mountain Institute's (2000) resource kit are implemented. However, a minor modification is made to the original 4D model to make it more appropriate in the context of the CBT framework in this study. Specifically, the final step of *delivery* considers both the tourism product and the community's level of participation.

In relation to the former, if the tourism product is found to be undesirable or unsatisfactory based on tourists' evaluations, the cycle returns to the *discovery* step for further modification and improvement. Relevant factors such as overpricing, targeting the wrong market, low service quality, and service providers' lack of training could underlie tourists' dissatisfaction. Gaining an understanding of tourists' perspectives would help the community in better meeting their expectations.

The community's level of participation is also reassessed in the *delivery* step. The level of participation might have dropped because at some point the community became content with only benefiting financially from tourism and thus relinquishing their involvement in tourism decision-making. This could be due to reasons such as members losing confidence in their abilities to undertake the required responsibilities or finding their responsibilities too time-consuming and thus delegating tasks to other members in the community. If the assessments indicate that community participation has dropped, then attempts to improve the facilitating conditions for participation need to be undertaken. In case the level of participation remains the same or improves, attempts such as enhancing the tourism product or involving more community members in the process could be considered. For example, once it was verified that the Heybatlu community's level of participation had improved, horse riding tours were introduced by the community to enhance the tourist experience. This also required the community to work with other neighboring communities in hiring horses where there was a shortage. At one point, the community felt empowered enough to negotiate directly with the Organization for Natural Resource Conservation to take responsibility for conserving their Pistachio Forests, which also allowed them to offer a tour of these forests and the harvesting of pistachios to tourists.

Discussion and conclusion

Consistent with the aim of this chapter to explore the implementation of CBT in Iran, a CBT framework was presented and its implementation within the Heybatlu community was discussed. A number of challenges were faced. These, along with how they were addressed, are presented below.

The inappropriate perceptions of key stakeholders

The NGO providing support to the community mainly focused on environmental and general development issues without attention to tourism related issues. This was mainly due to the wrong perception that tourism development did not require specialized knowledge, which impacted the views of other key stakeholders, leading to subsequent tensions between them. In addition, the NGO's inclination for the local community and the CBT project to be fully dependent on them caused many challenges. In other words, while on the surface the NGO claimed the local community's participation to be a main objective of the project; in reality they only considered a limited and passive participation for the locals. All this led to tensions between the NGO and the independent project facilitator who was responsible for conducting workshops and training sessions for community representatives. However, as a result of gaining empowerment through applying the CBT framework, the community was able to assess the project independently from the NGO, present it to the funding body and receive approval (UNDP, GEF, SGP).

Stakeholders' limited understanding of the community's capacity

Both the tourism distribution sector and the tourism academic sector had an unfavorable attitude toward the project. Although the CBT framework had been previously presented as a best paper at a conference and had been applied since the start of the project in 2012, it had not received any feedback or comments from academics, resulting in the project not receiving endorsement from ICHTO or the tourism academic sector. This lack of support meant that the provincial government's tourism development body did not agree to relieve the requirements of having a bachelor's degree for enrolment in the tour operation manager course, thus delaying the use of a local tour operation manager. A perception favoring the dominance of elites and the educated has been identified by Tosun (2000) as a structural limitation to community participation in CBT projects.

In addition, the tourism distribution sector had a very limited understanding of the local community's capacity in tourism. They only expected the locals to be able to operate homestays, rather than plan, operate, and manage the whole tourism product. To overcome this issue as well as increase the community's knowledge of tourism, representatives from the local community were regularly sent to tourism forums and exhibitions, while at the same time they willingly conducted tours free of charge for tour operators to gain their trust. A number of domestic and incoming tour operators have since been working with the local guides and sending tourists to experience the nomadic lifestyle.

The changing role of the NGO, as a key stakeholder, into a shareholder with financial interests

Due to the NGO's lack of awareness about tourism and marketing, the funding from the project was in most cases not spent appropriately. For instance, part of the funding was spent on participating in national tourism exhibitions with the only intention being to showcase the project. This meant that the funds were not spent according to the planned budget and the project fell behind its schedule, resulting in community disappointment. At one stage during the project, the community's level of participation dropped and financial tensions arose among community members. The issue was rectified through a number of meetings between the independent facilitator and community members. During these meetings, the community developed their own practical guidelines for controlling financial and managerial issues which is another example of the community's empowerment.

Based on these challenges, a number of recommendations are provided which could facilitate the success of CBT development initiatives in Iran and other similar contexts. First, forming local NGOs comprising of local people would help in reducing the tensions among internal stakeholders such as community elders, local authorities, and community members. Second, training local facilitators in CBT would not only help in minimizing costs but also empower community representatives to supervise CBT projects and resolve issues as they arise, as well as guarantee appropriate collection of data for the success of such projects. Finally, using simplified and non-specialist language in discussing CBT development initiatives and projects would help the local communities in writing grant applications and applying for community project fundings. Tosun (2000) identified lack of comprehensible information available to the local community as a major operational limitation in the community's active participation in CBT projects. The resources available in Iran on CBT are mainly translated from a source language and are not written in appropriate plain language. Currently, there is only one published book on CBT in Iran with non-specialist language (Fazel Bakhsheshi & Amiri, 2017).

Although the CBT framework has taken into account factors relevant to the context of the county (Fazel Bakhsheshi, 2008b, 2011) and has been successfully implemented and recognized as a successful project (UNDP, GEF, SGP, 2015), a number of limitations are acknowledged. First, the framework has been implemented in one community only and although deemed appropriate within the Heybatlu community, further applications would warrant more reliable findings. In other words, the extent to which the characteristics of a migrating nomadic community has lent itself to a successful application of the framework would need to be examined by applying the framework in other rural communities with different social structures. Second, in line with identifying the need to evaluate community participation projects through the eyes and voices of local people (Park, Phanda-nouvong, & Kim, 2018), the Heybatlu community was engaged in the evaluation of the project upon its completion, where they reflected upon their participation levels and the activities they participated in. However, there is still a need for the project to be re-evaluated after a few years upon its completion to ensure the community is still actively participating in tourism development.

References

Andereck, K. L. & Vogt, C. A. (2000). The relationship between residents' attitudes toward tourism and tourism development options. *Journal of Travel Research, 39*(1), 27–36.

Blackstock, K. (2005). A critical look at community-based tourism. *Community Development Journal, 40*(1), 39–49.

Burgos, A. & Mertens, F. (2017). Participatory management of community-based tourism: A network perspective. *Community Development, 48*(4), 546–565.

Burns, P. M. & Sancho, M. (2003). Local perceptions of tourism planning: The case of Cuellar, Spain. *Tourism Management, 24*(3), 331–339.

Choi, H. & Sirakaya, E. (2005). Measuring residents' attitude toward sustainable tourism: Development of sustainable tourism attitude scale. *Journal of Travel Research, 43*(4), 380–394.

Dodds, R., Ali, A., & Galaskic, K. (2016). Mobilizing knowledge: Determining key elements for success and pitfalls in developing community-based tourism. *Current Issues in Tourism*. doi: 10.1080/13683500.2016.1150257

Ernawati, N. M., Sanders, D., & Dowling, R. (2017). Host–guest orientations of community-based tourism products: A case study in Bali, Indonesia. *International Journal of Tourism Research, 19*(3), 367–382.

Fazel Bakhsheshi, F. (2008a). *Relationship between cultural factors and the expected level of participation in community-based Tourism development: Zaghmarz village*. Unpublished master's thesis. Allameh Tabataba'i University, Tehran, Iran [Original in Farsi].

Fazel Bakhsheshi, F. (2008b). Community-based tourism as a solution for sustainable tourism development in Iran. In *Tourism Development, Environmental Changes and Poverty Reduction Seminar*, Tehran, 2008 (pp. 165–186) [Original in Farsi].

Fazel Bakhsheshi, F. (2011). Iranian community-based tourism development model. In *Tourism Management and Development Seminar: Challenges and Solutions*, Tehran, 2011 [Original in Farsi].

Fazel Bakhsheshi, F. & Amiri, S. (2017). *Community-based tourism*. Mashhad, Iran: Nemati Pazh [Original in Farsi].

Ghaderi, Z. & Henderson, J. C. (2012). Sustainable rural tourism in Iran: A perspective from Hawraman village. *Tourism Management Perspectives, 2–3*, 47–54.

Harrison, D. & Schipani, S. (2007). Lao tourism and poverty alleviation: Community-based tourism and the private sector. *Current issues in Tourism, 10*(2–3), 194–230.

Hassanli, N., Gross, M., & Brown, G. (2016). The emergence of home-based accommodations in Iran: A study of self-organization. *Tourism Management, 54*, 284–295.

Iran Chamber Society. (2017). *Iranian people & tribes: Iranian ethnic groups*. Retrieved from http://www.iranchamber.com/people/articles/iranian_ethnic_groups.php

Kibicho, W. (2003). Community tourism: A lesson from Kenya's coastal region. *Journal of Vacation Marketing, 10*(1), 33–42.

Kunjuraman, V. & Hussin, R. (2017). *Challenges of community-based homestay programme in Sabah*, Malaysia: Hopeful or hopeless? *Tourism Management Perspectives, 21*, 1–9.

Lenao, M. (2017). Community, state and power-relations in community-based tourism on Lekhubu Island, Botswana. *Tourism Geographies, 19*(3), 483–501.

Nunkoo, R., Smith, S. L. J., & Ramkissoon, H. (2013). Residents' attitudes to tourism: A longitudinal study of 140 articles from 1984 to 2010. *Journal of Sustainable Tourism, 21*(1), 5–25.

Park, E., Phandanouvong, T., & Kim, S. (2018). Evaluating participation in community-based tourism: A local perspective in Laos. *Current Issues in Tourism, 21*(2), 128–132.

Pinel, D. P. (1998). *A Community-based tourism planning process model: Kyuquot Sound area, BC*. Unpublished master's thesis. University of Guelph, ON, Canada.

Salazar, N. B. (2012). Community-based cultural tourism: Issues, threats and opportunities. *Journal of Sustainable Tourism, 20*(1), 9–22.

Suansri, P. (2003). Community based tourism handbook. *Responsible Ecological Social Tours Project (REST)*. Retrieved from https://www.mekongtourism.org/wp-content/uploads/REST-CBT-Handbook-2003.pdf

The Mountain Institute. (2000). *Community-based tourism for conservation and development: A resource kit*. Retrieved from http://www.mountain.org

Tolkach, D. & King, B. (2015). Strengthening community-based tourism in a new resource-based island nation: Why and how? *Tourism Management, 48*, 386–398.

Tosun, C. (1999). Towards a typology of community participation in the tourism development process, Anatolia. *An International Journal of Tourism and Hospitality Research, 10*(2), 113–134.

Tosun, C. (2000). Limits to community participation in the tourism development process in developing countries. *Tourism Management, 21*(6), 613–633.

Tosun, C. (2005). Stages in the emergence of a participatory tourism development approach in the developing world. *Geoforum, 36*(3), 333–352.

Tosun, C. (2006). Expected nature of community participation in tourism development. *Tourism Management, 27*(3), 493–504.

Tosun, C. & Timothy, D. J. (2001). Shortcomings in planning approaches to tourism development in developing countries: The case of Turkey. *International Journal of Contemporary Hospitality Management, 13*(7), 352–359.

United Nations Development Programme (UNDP), Global Environment Facility (GEF), Small Grants Programme (SGP). (2012). *Planning and implementing community-based ecotourism by focusing on territorial integrity of Heybatlu sub-tribe of Sish Bayli Tribe of Qashqai tribal confederacy*. Retrieved from https://sgp.undp.org/index.php?option=com_sgpprojects&view=projectdetail&id=17826&Itemid=205

United Nations Development Programme (UNDP), Global Environment Facility (GEF), Small Grants Programme (SGP). (2015). *GEF 5 SGP Iran overview*. Retrieved from http://sgpgef.ir/uploads/docs/GEF%205%20SGP%20Iran%20O-zuudxchkml.pdf

13 Effects of perceived quality and trust on behavioural intentions: an empirical study of health tourists in Mashhad, Iran

Shiva Hashemi, Masoumeh Tavangar,
Azizan Marzuki and Moji Shahvali

Introduction

The fusion of the healthcare industry and tourism has resulted in health tourism, also referred to as medical tourism (Hall, 2012; Cooper, Vafadari, & Hieda, 2015), which for a large number of countries is a significant service industry with substantial economic benefits (Marković, Lončarić, & Lončarić, 2014; Crush & Chikanda, 2015; Hung, 2017). In an increasingly competitive health tourism industry worldwide, to gain a greater market share, health clinics around the world have been improving their amenities and services, resembling those found in high-end hotels (DeMicco, 2017). These clinics commonly offer not only quality medical care but also a superior level of services to their international customers. In such clinics, difficulties frequently faced by overseas patient travellers such as inefficient communication, low quality medical care, uncomfortable atmospherics, low-quality services, unkind staff and luggage handling problems (Snyder, Crooks, Adams, Kingsbury, & Johnston, 2011; Gan & Frederick, 2011; Han & Hwang, 2013) are significantly reduced (Han, 2013).

Iran is a leading health tourism destination in the region and has great potentials with regard to its further development. One reason is the establishment and development of advanced clinics and hospitals. For example, Shahid Sadughi Infertility Treatment Center in Yazd, dental and dialysis centres in Tehran and Mashhad, and hospitals such as Namazi Hospital in Shiraz that has substantial surgery and transplant expertise (Saadatnia & Mehregan, 2014). Moreover, the low costs and high quality of the health services along with the use of the latest available technologies constitute one of the most important factors of the potential success of medical tourism in Iran (Shahijan, Rezaei, Preece, & Ismail, 2015). In order to improve the healthcare services in Iran and attract more foreign patients to the country, there is a need to investigate the strengths and weaknesses of the industry and constantly evaluate the quality of offered services as perceived by incoming medical tourists. Currently, there is limited research on the quality of healthcare in Iran in the eyes of the health tourists, hence forming the motivation behind this study.

The perceived trust of patients towards clinical staff and services, along with quality, is a critical factor in the delivery of medical services (Han & Hyun, 2015). However, to the best of our knowledge, no health tourism research in Iran, and very few international studies have examined the association between healthcare quality and feelings of trust among medical tourists. Quality along with trust can impact travellers' intentions to revisit Iran for their future health needs and/or to suggest this destination to friends and relatives. In addition, while perceived price and its importance have been repeatedly emphasized in the existing marketing literature, to date little research has been conducted on the moderating role of price reasonableness in the hospitality and tourism industry – how much do tourists find the medical prices to be reasonable considering the services that they receive? Thus, the present study was designed to shed light on some of these issues. In particular, the objectives of this study were: (1) to investigate theoretical relationships among perceived quality, trust and intentions to revisit the destination for healthcare; (2) to examine the mediating role of perceived trust in these relationships; and (3) to evaluate the level of perceived quality of health services by tourists in Mashhad, Iran. In the remainder of this chapter, after a short review of the literature, the findings of our study of health tourists in Mashhad will follow, along with a test of the conceptual model.

Health tourism

The terms *health tourism* and *medical tourism* are often used interchangeably to describe health services provided in another country (DeMicco, 2017; Hall, 2011, 2012; Cooper et al., 2015). The concept of health tourism in a broad sense includes all health-seeking activities performed by consumers in another country, usually motivated by seeking cheaper care (Gonzales, Brenzel, & Sancho, 2001). However, what is currently offered takes more than just the preventive and wellness approach of the health resorts and spas and is broadened to include invasive medical treatments, such as hip replacement surgeries or coronary bypasses conducted abroad, particularly for cost considerations. Such a notion has prompted Connell (2006) to delineate medical treatments conducted in another country as *medical tourism* while seeking services such as those offered at spas and health resorts abroad as *health tourism*. However, for the purpose of this study, the general term 'health tourism' will be used to indicate the medical services and treatments specifically received in another country either in conjunction, or not, with tourism activities such as sightseeing. Therefore, this study utilizes the term health tourism and operationalizes it as a phenomenon where international tourists travel to Iran in order to receive treatments to improve their health.

Health tourism in Iran

In relation to the structure of health service providers in Iran, the majority of the clinics and treatment centres are affiliated with the national Ministry of Health. In other words, the Ministry of Health as the representative of the public sector is the main provider of health services in the country (Mosadeghrad, 2014). Nearly half of the modern clinics and hospitals are located in Tehran, the capital. Following Tehran, Shiraz, Mashhad and Tabriz are the main destinations for health tourists (Ayoubian, 2015). International visitors to Iran that are coming for health and medical reasons are mainly from Iraq, Lebanon, Bahrain, Saudi Arabia, Turkey, Tajikistan, Azerbaijan, Armenia and Pakistan, and they mainly seek health services and treatments in the areas of fertility, plastic surgery, heart surgery and dental treatments (Izadi et al., 2012).

Previous studies have found that one of the reasons for the rather high demand for seeking health and medical services in Iran is the high cost of treatments and low quality of health systems in most countries in the region (Ayoubian, 2015). On the other hand, Iran is a relatively low costs and high quality medical services provider. In addition, the geographical location of Iran and the existence of numerous hot and cold mineral springs in various parts of the country make Iran an attractive medical destination for travellers from neighbouring countries and Central Asia (Street, 2010). Other identified competitive advantages and also disadvantages of Iran as a health tourism destination are reviewed in Table 13.1.

In this research, the studied travellers were asked about the main reason why they have chosen Iran as their destination of choice for receiving medical care and the results are reviewed in the next section. Among the four major cities mentioned above, the visitors of the city of Mashhad in the north-east part of the country were chosen as the case for this research. Mashhad is the second most populous city in Iran with a population of almost 2.8 million people and has been recognized by ICHTO as the centre of health tourism among Islamic countries. It is also one of the leading providers of medical care in the country. As one example, the Razavi Hospital is one of the most modern medical care providers in the Middle East. It admits a large number of patients from neighbouring countries every given year. The hospital is planning to develop a health village in Malek Abad, close to the city of Mashhad.

Behavioural intentions

Behavioural intentions of customers can be measured by their repurchase intentions in the future, word of mouth, complaining behaviour and their price sensitivity (Zeithaml, Berry, & Parasuraman, 1996; Chen & Chen, 2010). Thus, behavioural intentions play a key role in marketing because of their importance in the long-term sustainability of the companies (Wu, Li, & Li, 2016). Research in the area of health tourism pays less attention to behavioural intentions (Wang & Wang, 2013; Wang, 2012; Wu et al., 2016), maybe because it is perceived, and often is the case, that health tourists choose a destination for one time and never return. However, their perceived quality and satisfaction with the services that they receive would impact their other behavioural intentions such as positive or negative word of mouth. Thus, studying behavioural intentions is important with regards to health tourists as well.

Table 13.1 Competitive advantages and disadvantages of Iran's health tourism industry

Sources of value	• Well-equipped laboratory and genetic testing facilities • Latest diagnostic and treatment equipment • Knowledgeable experts at an international level • Several specialized clinics with international standards • 51 nursing schools active in the county • Good physical infrastructure in hospitals, research centres and touristic facilities
Capability	• Conducting highly sophisticated operations such as open heart surgery, spinal cord surgery, plastic and retina surgery, implantation, latest fertility treatments
Distinguishing competencies	• International reputation of Iranian physicians, especially among the countries in the region • Leading position of Iran in heart surgery, implantation, plastic and cosmetic surgery, fertility treatment and dentistry • Recent achievements in the medical field (e.g. stem cells) • A suitable cultural environment for Muslims • Lower costs of diagnosis, treatment and accommodation services • Variety of climate in the country, the four seasons • Variety of historical, cultural, natural and tourist attractions throughout
Special features	• Proximity to Central Asia and the Middle East • Quality service with low costs • Cultural and language similarity with neighbouring countries • Significant Iranian diaspora of three million people living aboard
Disadvantages	• Lack of a comprehensive program for health tourism development in Iran • Insignificant role of the private sector in the health tourism industry • Lack of general coordination between relevant organizations working in the industry, e.g. travel agencies, hotels, residential facilities, hospitals, insurance companies and authorities within historical/cultural attractions • No special visa service for health tourists

Source: After Ayoubian, 2015.

Perceived trust

Trust is the belief of patients that they would receive good treatment and medical care from their doctors (Anderson & Dedrick, 1990; Thom & Campbell, 1997), and that the service providers are dependable and could be relied on to deliver their promises (Sirdeshmukh, Singh, & Sabol, 2002). Trust is a complex multi-dimensional construct. Kramer (1999) has argued that trust has cognitive and affective aspects and can promote the relationship between doctors and patients (Thom, 2001). On the other hand, it can be argued that a lack of trust in doctors and health services can be detrimental to health tourists' behavioural intentions. Yet, literature on patient trust in health tourism is very limited (Heung, Kucukusta, & Song, 2011).

Han (2013) emphasized the important role of trust in health tourism contexts. In the few studies conducted in this area, satisfaction of patients with the services that they receive led to higher trust, eventually leading to the formation of positive behavioural intentions such as revisits or positive word of mouth (e.g. Bigne & Blesa, 2003; Choi, Lee, Kim, & Lee, 2005). In line with these findings, trust will be studied in this research as a factor potentially impacting behavioural intentions of the medical tourist population in Mashhad.

Theory of planned behaviour

The theory of planned behaviour (TPB) (Ajzen, 1991) suggests three predictors of behaviour, namely attitude, subjective norm and perceived behaviour control. As an example, TPB suggests that human beings intend to take part in a behaviour such as going to the gym if they have a positive attitude towards it; if their significant other or friends support that behaviour (i.e. subjective norms); and if they have the means to take part in it (e.g. pay for gym membership). The development of TPB was originally based on the theory of reasoned action (TRA), which is designed to explain almost any human behaviour and was proven successful in predicting and explaining human behaviour across various application contexts (Davis, Bagozzi, & Warshaw, 1989).

TPB postulates that *intention* could be the best determinant of an individual's actual behaviour. In other words, an individual with a strong intention is more likely to engage in the behaviour than one with a low intention. In the current study, TPB was used as a guiding framework. High perceived quality in the healthcare industry can positively impact one's attitude towards the services they receive, resulting in the purchasing of those services and other behavioural intentions. The details of this conceptual model along with the hypotheses will be reviewed in the next section.

Proposed conceptual model and hypotheses

The conceptual research model (Figure 13.1) was developed using a multi-dimensional structure based on existing study frameworks noted above (e.g. Loureiro & González, 2008; Han & Hyun, 2015; Wu et al., 2016). Our main interest was to understand the impact of perceived quality and trust on international health tourists' intentions to (re)visit Mashhad as a destination for their healthcare services. A total of ten hypotheses were developed to evaluate the proposed model seen below.

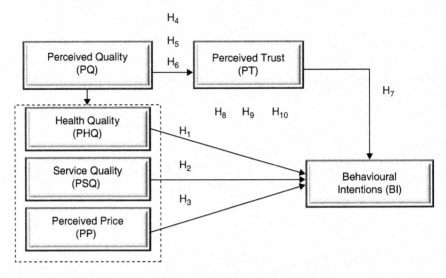

Figure 13.1 Conceptual research framework.

In terms of perceived quality, the multi-level and multi-dimensional model in Figure 13.1 proposes that tourists form their perceptions of quality of the health-care system in Iran through three primary dimensions: perceived health quality at the treatment centre, overall perceived service quality of the destination and perceived price of the services. The perception of quality is then expected to influence perceived trust. In addition, perceived trust is expected to influence future behaviour intention. Altogether, perceived quality and perceived trust are expected to influence health tourists' behavioural intentions.

In this study, perceived health quality (PHQ) was individuals' evaluation of the performances of the health product and services including the hospital amenities, such as cafeteria and Wi-Fi connections and hospital care facilities, such as laboratories, treatments and payment procedures. Perceived service quality (PSQ) at destinations indicates the overall assessment of individuals about the destination's service performances such as visa processes, transportation, hotel facilities, tourist attractions, entertainment centres, location and the friendliness of the host community. Therefore, we propose the first set of hypotheses:

H1: Perceived health quality positively influences behavioural intentions.

H2: Perceived service quality positively influences behavioural intentions.

Reasonableness of prices and the value they bring are also important in the decision-making processes of customers (Ryu & Han, 2010). Literature suggests that to better understand present and future purchase behaviours of customers there is a need to examine the degree to which customers perceive prices to be reasonable (Han & Hyun, 2015). Perceived price (PP) can then build favourable intentions and loyalty of customers (Han & Kim, 2009). Therefore, the following hypothesis is proposed:

H3: Perceived price positively influences behavioural intentions.

Research in health tourism has paid less attention to perceived trust (Wang, 2012; Wu et al., 2016) when studying health service quality, as noted above. Nevertheless, some studies (Kassim & Asiah Abdullah, 2010; Loureiro & González, 2008) have found that when customers have a positive perception of the quality of services and products they receive, they build better trust. Therefore, the next three hypotheses are:

H4: Perceived health quality positively influences perceived trust.

H5: Perceived service quality positively influences perceived trust.

H6: Perceived price positively influences perceived trust.

Trust enables an organization to develop and maintain customers (Harrison, 2003). Zboja and Voorhees (2006) also highlight the decisive role of trust in the buyer–seller relationship in the retailing world. Trust influences behavioural intentions such as positive word of mouth and repurchase and this is well documented in the marketing literature (Luk & Yip, 2008; Zboja & Voorhees, 2006). Therefore, we propose the following hypothesis:

H7: Perceived trust positively influences behavioural intentions.

In marketing research, a general association between perceived quality, perceived trust and intention has been validated (Everard & Galletta, 2005), with trust often having a mediating role (Han & Hyun, 2015). Therefore, the final set of hypotheses for this study is:

H8: Perceived trust mediates the relationship between perceived health quality and behavioural intentions.

H9: Perceived trust mediates the relationship between perceived service quality and behavioural intentions.

H10: Perceived trust mediates the relationship between perceived price and behavioural intentions.

In the next section, the results of testing the abovementioned hypotheses based on the data collected from health tourists in Mashhad, Iran, will be presented. We will first discuss the survey instrument used to collect data and the data collection procedure.

Survey instrument and the data collection procedure

This study employed a self-administered survey to collect data, using a cross-sectional approach, in a quantitative fashion. In June 2017, a total of 140 questionnaires were sent to ten treatments centres in Mashhad that serve international health tourists. A number of designated travel agencies in Mashhad that serve incoming health tourists facilitated the data collection process. The end sample was a convenience sample of 104 valid questionnaires. The survey inquired about: tourists' demographic characteristics, their perception of healthcare quality in Mashhad; their perceived trust in the system; their behavioural intentions; information about the medical treatment(s) received; details about their travel; and ended by openly asking about ways they believe that healthcare services can improve in Mashhad. Other than the open-ended questions, a five-point Likert scale was used, with 1 referring to *strongly disagree* and 5 referring to *strongly agree*. An initial pilot study was conducted to ensure both preliminary reliability and validity of the findings. The language of the survey was in both English and Arabic for the convenience of the participants. Using a comprehensive multi-variate statistical analysis approach – elaborated in the next section – all the relationships between variables in Figure 1 were tested simultaneously. Smart PLS® version 3.0 was used to perform the PLS-SEM analysis described below.

Analyses and results

Data analyses

The software SPSS® was first used for testing the individual hypotheses of this study. Partial least squares structural equation modelling (PLS-SEM) was then conducted for evaluating the measurement and the structural model. SEM is currently a dominant analytic mechanism in tourism empirical research, specifically PLS-SEM path modelling (Sarstedt, 2008; Hair, Ringle, & Sarstedt, 2011a, 2011b, 2013; Hair, Sarstedt, Ringle, & Mena, 2012; Hair et al., 2013). PLS-SEM is widely used for studies with a small sample size, with interval scaled data; where multi-variate normality cannot be entirely contacted. The basic power of such analyses lies in the prediction accuracy and the observations are not truly independent from one another (Sarstedt, 2008). To run a PLS-SEM, the Smart PLS® software was used. One safe assumption in this study is that the data are collected from a single population, a requirement for PLS-SEM (Hair et al., 2012).

Profile of respondents

The descriptive analyses of the demographic variables showed that the number of male and female respondents were fairly even, with slightly more males than females (Table 13.2). Respondents were categorized into four age groups: below 20 years (n = 4), 20–40 years (n = 64), 40–50 years (n = 32) and more than 60 years (n = 4). Most respondents had a high school education or beyond (n = 51). When they were asked about the source of information, most of the respondents stated that they had received their main information about going to Mashhad for treatments from friends and/or relatives (48%). In terms of who they travelled with, over 60% of the respondents had travelled with their friends or relatives. While some had travelled for cosmetic procedures or check-ups, most of them had undergone some form of surgical procedure (40%). In terms of the duration of

Table 13.2 Profile of respondents in this study

Items	Frequency	Percentage (%)
Gender		
Male	61	58.7
Female	43	41.3
Age		
Below 20 years	4	3.9
20–40 years	64	61
40–60	32	31.1
Over 60 years	4	4
Education level		
School	14	13.5
High school	51	49
Certificate/diploma	31	29.8
Graduate degree	8	7.7
Source of information		
Friends/relatives	50	48.1
Internet	19	18.3
Travel agent	17	16.3
Newspaper	4	3.8
Travel guide-books	5	4.8
Business	2	1.9
Travel magazines	4	3.8
Travel partner		
Alone	9	8.7
Family/relative	65	62.5
Partner	4	3.8
Friends	21	20.2
Group	5	4.8
Type of medical treatment	4	
Medical treatment	16	15.4
Cosmetic procedure	30	28.8
Medical check-up	16	15.4
Surgical procedure	42	40.4
Days of travel		
1–3 days	8	7.7
4–7 days	40	38.5
8–11 days	37	35.6
12–15 days	13	12.5
More than 15 days	4	3.8
No idea	2	1.9
Reason for choosing Iran as a health destination		
Low cost of medical	16	15.4
No wait time	4	3.8
High-quality services	29	27.9
Access to latest technology	8	7.7
Greater convenience	4	3.8
Physician or surgeon expertise	41	39.4
Longer hospital stays	2	1.9

their vacation in Mashhad, an estimated 40% of respondents had stayed in Mashhad for four to seven days; and when asked about the main reason why they had chosen Iran and not some other destination for their medical needs, the majority (40%) indicated that they had chosen Iran because of medical or surgical expertise.

Assessment of the measurement model

The first assessment of the measurement model involved an evaluation of reliability and validity of the model and findings. There are two main types of validity: convergent and discriminant. Convergent validity is often assessed by way of two key coefficients (Chin, 2010; Hair et al., 2011a): the Composite Reliability (CR) coefficient and the Average Variance Extracted (AVE) coefficient. Generally, the loadings of each latent variable should be higher than 0.5 for validity to be considered acceptable. A loading lower than 0.4 indicates that an item should be considered for removal and items with a loading of 0.4–0.5 should be considered for removal if their removal increases the CRs and AVEs above the threshold. The CR coefficient is also used for assessing construct reliability; reliability is a property that is different from yet related to validity (Chin, 2010). Other than that, Cronbach's alpha (CA) coefficient is sometimes used for reliability assessments, although CR is usually considered the more suitable of the two for PLS-SEM since it incorporates information about the item loadings into its calculation (Hair et al., 2011a, 2011b; Kock, 2011). Table 13.3 indicates that the CRs for all of the latent variables in the measurement model exceeds 0.8, suggesting an acceptable reliability of the measurement model. In addition to the discussed criteria for convergent validity, the AVEs of the LVs should also be higher than 0.5 for their convergent validity to be considered acceptable (Chin, 2010; Hair et al., 2011a; Kock, 2011). Table 13.3 shows that the AVEs of the constructs were higher than 0.5. Therefore, the measurement model's convergent validity is also acceptable. Furthermore, because the CR and AVE thresholds were exceeded, we can safely conclude that it was not necessary to remove any of the indicators with loadings of 0.4–0.5. Figure 13.2 summarizes the results of internal reliability and convergent validity for our constructs.

On the other hand, discriminant validity as the extent to which each latent variable is distinct from other constructs in the model was achieved. The square root of the AVE for each construct was greater than all of the correlations among the construct and the other constructs in the model (Chin, 2010; Hair et al., 2011a). Assessment of discriminant validity using Henseler, Ringle, and Sarstedt's (2015) heterotrait-monotrait (HTMT) ratio of correlations criterion is also determined as shown in Table 13.4. The correlation matrix given by HTMT is a symmetric matrix and therefore the upper and lower triangular elements are all the same, every value being below 0.90, which is seen as a valid value. Thus, the HTMT ratio criterion is fulfilled in the present study. This is also supported by Gold, Malhotra, and Segars (2001) and thresholds of 0.85 (Kline, 2011) for HTMT 0.90 to confirm discriminant validity. Overall, the measurement model demonstrated adequate convergent validity and discriminant validity.

Table 13.3 Assessment results of the measurement model

Constructs	Loading	AVE	CR	CA
PHQ: Perceived health quality		0.640	0.842	0.726
PHQ3: The hospital has excellent cleanliness and hygiene of installations	0.832			
PHQ4: The hospital has a wide variety of treatments	0.784			
PHQ5: The hospital has quick and simple payment procedures	0.783			
PSQ: Perceived service quality		0.593	0.853	0.770
PSQ 2: Transportation and easy accessibility	0.678			
PSQ 4: Tourist attractions and entertainment centres of the city	0.813			
PSQ5: Peaceful location	0.822			
PSQ6: Friendliness of local people	0.759			
PP: Perceived price		0.576	0.866	0.807
PP1: The treatment cost in hospital is reasonable	0.606			
PP3: This trip offers value for my money	0.831			
PP4: This trip is worth taking for the price paid	0.824			
PP5: Medical expenses are reasonable	0.713			
PP6: Accommodation costs are reasonable	0.769			
PT: Perceived trust		0.567	0.844	0.755
PT1: I trust the doctor so much; I always try to follow his or her advice	0.755			
PT3: I trust that the doctor puts my medical needs first	0.685			
PT4: I trust the hospital to solve my medical problems	0.807			
PT5: Hospitals would be honest and sincere in addressing my concerns	0.784			
BI: Behavioural intentions		0.506	0.876	0.834
BI1: I would consider Mashhad as my first choice for medical treatment	0.617			
BI2: I would say positive things about this medical treatment in Mashhad to my relatives and close friends	0.793			
BI3: I would be willing to recommend this medical treatment in Mashhad to my relatives and close friends	0.762			

(*Continued*)

Table 13.3 (Continued)

Constructs	Loading	AVE	CR	CA
BI4: I will continue to use this hospital's service in Mashhad in the future	0.683			
BI5: I would be willing to do further medical treatments at this hospital	0.694			
BI6: I would continue to use this hospital in Mashhad even if the cost was higher than other destinations	0.801			
BI7: I would be willing to spend more money on the medical treatments in Mashhad even if the price increases in the future	0.598			

Note: PSQ1, PSQ3, PP2 and PP7 were left out due to low loadings; PHQ1, PHQ2 were deleted due to AVE; AVE: average variance extracted, CR: composite reliability, CA: Cronbach's alpha.

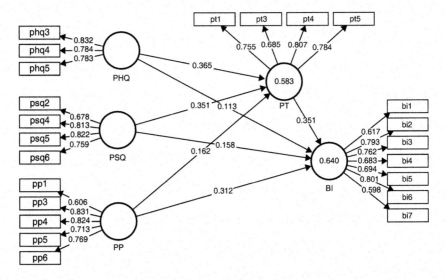

Figure 13.2 Results of the path analysis.

The structural model

The hypothesized relationship between the latent constructs is tested in the structural model once the measurement modelling is validated. This model is assessed based on R^2, beta values and the corresponding t-values, predictive relevance (Q^2) and the effect sizes (f^2). While the actual sample size is only 104, because PLS is performed using a non-parametric technique, bootstrapping is performed with a sample size of 5,000 (Hair et al., 2012). The structural model of PLS was then examined to see whether the hypotheses were supported by the data or not. Table 13.5 and Figure 13.3 represent the results. A one-tailed p-value was used (Kock, 2014).

Table 13.4 Discriminant validity of constructs

Latent variable	BI	PHQ	PP	PSQ	PT
BI					
PHQ	0.780				
PP	0.822	0.765			
PSQ	0.805	0.807	0.749		
PT	0.895	0.900	0.744	0.868	

Note: Criteria discriminant validity is established at HTMT of 0.90, PHQ6, PT 2 were deleted due to HTMT results.

Table 13.5 Results of hypothesis testing

Hypotheses	Description	Path coefficient	SE	t-value	P-values	Decision
H1	**PHQ→BI**	0.113	0.078	1.441	0.075	Not supported
H2	**PSQ→BI**	0.158	0.092	1.721*	0.043	**Supported**
H3	**PP→BI**	0.312	0.114	2.731**	0.003	**Supported**
H4	**PHQ→PT**	0.365	0.088	4.144***	0.000	**Supported**
H5	**PSQ→PT**	0.351	0.100	3.503***	0.000	**Supported**
H6	**PP→PT**	0.162	0.096	1.689*	0.046	**Supported**
H7	**PT→BI**	0.351	0.096	3.651***	0.000	**Supported**

Note: $^*p < 0.05$; $^{**}p < 0.01$; $^{***}p < 0.001$.

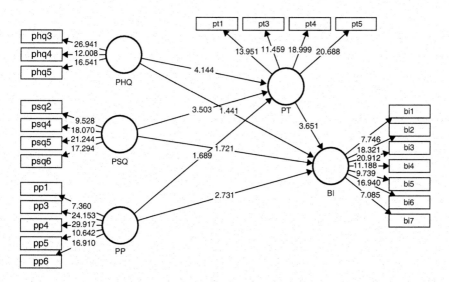

Figure 13.3 Results of bootstrapping.

Table 13.6 Significance of indirect effects: path coefficients (n=104)

Hypotheses	Path	Beta value	SE	t-value	Decision
H8	**PHQ→PT→BI**	0.128	0.052	2.464	**Supported**
H9	**PSQ→PT→BI**	0.123	0.053	2.417	**Supported**
H10	**PP→PT→BI**	0.057	0.037	1.533	Not supported

Note: $^{*}p < 0.05$; $^{**}p < 0.01$; $^{***}p < 0.001$.

Mediating effect of perceived trust

One of the contributions of this study has been the study of the mediating effect of perceived trust in the relationship between perceived quality of the tourists and their behavioural intentions, in Mashhad. The two statistically significant paths were: PHQ→PT→BI ($\beta = 0.128$, $p < 0.05$) and PSQ→PT→BI ($\beta = 0.123$, $p < 0.05$) indicating the mediating role of perceived trust. In other words, H8 and H9 were supported and not H10. Table 13.6 shows the indirect effects and the path coefficients.

Discussion

This research aimed to examine whether there is a relationship between the constructs of perceived quality, perceived trust and behavioural intentions in a health tourism setting. The sample was international health tourists in Mashhad, Iran, who had received some level of health services during the summer of 2017. The results of this study supported the emphasis placed more recently by some researchers (e.g. Loureiro & González, 2008; Wu et al., 2016; Han & Hyun, 2015) on the important role of perceived quality in determining consumers' trust and behavioural intentions. Inconsistent with previous findings however, was the non-significant relationship between perceived health quality and one's behavioural intentions (H1: PHQ→BI). This could have been because of the way PHQ was conceptualized following the input of a panel of experts.

Since health tourists are often dealing with life-changing situations with regards to the services they receive, trust in medical staff and services is an important element. Trust can be formed via different strategies. One would be during the process of service delivery and as a result of quality health services, as suggested by this study. In return, higher trust can lead to more positive behavioural intentions such as suggesting medical services to friends and relatives upon return. Thus, managers should incorporate the element of trust, above and beyond their emphasis on quality health services and pricing. Moreover, positive experiences not only can result in revisit of patients for their future needs, it can also positively impact the expectations and trust of other potential patients who decide to choose Mashhad as the place to receive their health treatments. On the other hand, the majority of the international health tourists travelling to Mashhad indicated that they receive advice and information through family and friends. Thus, investments in offering quality services and building trust in visiting patients would be of even higher value. This will potentially result in more satisfied patients and, in the longer term, a higher market share of health tourists for Iran.

Conclusion

One of the most important opportunities for the development of the health tourism industry in Iran, followed by Mashhad, is the government's attention to this sector in its key policies. Meanwhile, health tourism has seen numerous sources of demand, including: overseas immigrant Iranians, patients from neighbouring and Muslim countries, and patients seeking special treatments due to recent advances in Iran for the development of new therapies. In addition, the presence of hot springs and salt domes, saltwater lakes and sludge facilities are potentially significant complimentary contributions to health tourism development.

One of the most important issues that can lead to a greater attraction of tourists in the long-term is the patient's trust in choosing Mashhad as a health destination. This requires strategic planning both with respect to the external environment and within Iran. In the external environment of planning, factors such as Iran's international relations, the image of Iran globally, and marketing and advertising about the health of Iran's health abilities, strengthening and reform are extremely important. Within the country a number of factors are significant, including the structure of management, planning, policy and legislation in the field of health tourism at the national and regional levels; and the further development of medical capabilities and obtaining international credit validation. Effective communication and improved access to insurance and international banking can be effective in achieving these goals.

This chapter aimed to study the behavioural intentions of health tourists in Mashhad, Iran, inspired by the theory of planned behaviour. However, human behaviour is formed by a variety of factors and is not always rational. According to Mihalič (2000), environmental factors such as season, culture and economics are all important factors that can influence consumers' (i.e. tourists) behaviours. As this study was one of the first attempts to explore health tourists' behaviour regarding health services in Iran, the influence of such environmental factors was not included in the study. Therefore, one limitation of this study is that it falls short in providing a well-rounded explanation of health tourists' behaviour.

A second limitation is that this study was conducted in Mashhad and targeted international tourists only. Recruiting tourists who travel seeking medical benefits is not as easy as compared to pleasure tourists. Therefore, a validation using larger samples gathered at other treatment centres in the country is required to further generalize the findings of this study to the whole country and impact policy and practice. Also, this study focused on perceived quality from the perspective of health tourists only. Some researchers (Wu & Li, 2017; Wu et al., 2016) have suggested that researchers should explore perceived quality in the health tourism industry from the viewpoint of doctors and staff, as well. Therefore, future studies could examine perceived quality by doctors and staff rather than just focusing on the demand side, the tourists. Finally, the limited number of items measuring healthcare quality might have been the reason why one of the hypotheses (PHQ→BI) was not supported. Thus, additional items measuring the concept of healthcare quality is highly suggested for future research.

Such studies can help the healthcare service providers in Iran to stay competitive in the growing market of the health tourism industry worldwide. A recent report by Fars News® indicated that 85,000 international health tourists visited Iran to receive health services and treatments in 2012. This number increased to 300,000 within four years. It is estimated that this number will hit the half-million mark in 2017. Thus, considering this growth, the recent attention of the government agencies to health tourism, the presence and development of specialized clinics in Iran, contemporary facilities, low costs and the high reputation of Iranian physicians, supports the potential of Iran in becoming one of the leading health tourism destinations in the world.

References

Ajzen, I. (1991). The theory of planned behavior. *Organizational Behavior and Human Decision Processes, 50*(2), 179–211.

Anderson, L. A. & Dedrick, R. F. (1990). Development of the trust in physician scale: A measure to assess interpersonal trust in patient–physician relationships. *Psychological Reports, 67*(3 suppl), 1091–1100.

Ayoubian, A. (2015). Health tourism in Iran. In M. Cooper, K. Vafadari, & M. Hieda (Eds.), *Current issues and emerging trends in medical tourism* (pp. 258–280). Hershey, PA: IGI Global.

Bigne, E. & Blesa, A. (2003). Market orientation, trust and satisfaction in dyadic relationships: A manufacturer–retailer analysis. *International Journal of Retail & Distribution Management, 31*(11), 574–590.

Chen, C. F. & Chen, F. S. (2010). Experience quality, perceived value, satisfaction and behavioural intentions for heritage tourists. *Tourism Management, 31*(1), 29–35.

Chin, W. W. (2010). How to write up and report PLS analyses. In V. Esposito Vinzi, W. Chin, J. Henseler, & H. Wang (Eds.), *Handbook of partial least squares. Springer handbooks of computational statistics* (pp. 655–690). Berlin, Heidelberg: Springer.

Chiu, C., Hsu, M., Lai, H., & Chang, C. (2012). Re-examining the influence of trust on online repeat purchase intention: The moderating role of habit and its antecedents. *Decision Support Systems, 53*(4), 835–845.

Choi, K. S., Lee, H., Kim, C., & Lee, S. (2005). The service quality dimensions and patient satisfaction relationships in South Korea: Comparisons across gender, age and types of service. *Journal of Services Marketing, 19*(3), 140–149.

Connell, J. (2006). Medical tourism: Sea, sun, sand and … surgery. *Tourism Management, 27*(6), 1093–1100.

Cooper, M., Vafadari, K., & Hieda, M. (Eds.). (2015). *Current issues and emerging trends in medical tourism.* Hershey, PA: IGI Global.

Crush, J. & Chikanda, A. (2015). South–south medical tourism and the quest for health in Southern Africa. *Social Science & Medicine, 124*, 313–320.

Davis, F. D., Bagozzi, R. P., & Warshaw, P. R. (1989). User acceptance of computer technology: A comparison of two theoretical models. *Management Science, 35*(8), 982–1003.

DeMicco, F. J. (Ed.). (2017). *Medical tourism and wellness: Hospitality bridging healthcare (H2H).* Waretown, NJ: Apple Academic Press and CRC Press.

Everard, A. & Galletta, D. F. (2005). How presentation flaws affect perceived site quality, trust, and intention to purchase from an online store. *Journal of Management Information Systems, 22*(3), 56–95.

Gan, L. L. & Frederick, J. R. (2011). Medical tourism facilitators: Patterns of service differentiation. *Journal of Vacation Marketing, 17*(3), 165–183.

Gold, A. H., Malhotra, A., & Segars, A. H. (2001). Knowledge management: An organizational capabilities perspective. *Journal of Management Information Systems, 18*(1), 185–214.

Gonzales, A., Brenzel, L., & Sancho, J. (2001). *Final report. Health tourism and related services: Caribbean development and international trade.* Submitted to the Regional Negotiating Machinery (RNM). Retrieved from http://www20.iadb.org/intal/catalogo/PE/2009/03451.pdf

Hair, J. F., Ringle, C. M., & Sarstedt, M. (2011a). PLS-SEM: Indeed a silver bullet. *Journal of Marketing Theory and Practice, 19*(2), 139–152.

Hair, J. F., Ringle, C. M., & Sarstedt, M. (2011b). The use of partial least squares (PLS) to address marketing management topics: From the special issue guest editors. *Journal of Marketing Theory and Practice, 18*(2), 135–138.

Hair, J. F., Ringle, C. M., & Sarstedt, M. (2013). Editorial – Partial least squares structural equation modeling: Rigorous applications, better results and higher acceptance. *Long Range Planning, 46*(1–2), 1–12.

Hair, J. F., Sarstedt, M., Ringle, C. M., & Mena, J. A. (2012). An assessment of the use of partial least squares structural equation modeling in marketing research. *Journal of the Academy of Marketing Science, 40*(3), 414–433.

Hall, C. M. (2011). Health and medical tourism: A kill or cure for global public health? *Tourism Review, 66*(1/2), 4–15.

Hall, C. M. (Ed.). (2012). *Medical tourism: The ethics, regulation, and marketing of health mobility.* Abingdon: Routledge.

Han, H. (2013). The healthcare hotel: Distinctive attributes for international medical travellers. *Tourism Management, 36*, 257–268.

Han, H. & Hwang, J. (2013). Multi-dimensions of the perceived benefits in a medical hotel and their roles in international travelers' decision-making process. *International Journal of Hospitality Management, 35*, 100–108.

Han, H. & Hyun, S. S. (2015). Customer retention in the medical tourism industry: Impact of quality, satisfaction, trust, and price reasonableness. *Tourism Management, 46*, 20–29.

Han, H. & Kim, W. (2009). Outcomes of relational benefits: Restaurant customers' perspective. *Journal of Travel and Tourism Marketing, 26*, 820–835.

Harrison, T. (2003). Editorial: Why trust is important in customer relationships and how to achieve it. *Journal of Financial Services Marketing, 7*(3), 206–209.

Henseler, J., Ringle, C. M., & Sarstedt, M. (2015). A new criterion for assessing discriminant validity in variance-based structural equation modeling. *Journal of the Academy of Marketing Science, 43*(1), 115–135.

Heung, V. C., Kucukusta, D., & Song, H. (2011). Medical tourism development in Hong Kong: An assessment of the barriers. *Tourism Management, 32*(5), 995–1005.

Hung, W. T. (2017). *Theorising management accounting practices and service quality: The case of Malaysian health tourism hospital destinations.* Unpublished doctoral thesis. University of Nottingham.

Izadi, M., Ayoobian, A., Nasiri, T., Joneidi, N., Fazel, M., & Hosseinpourfard, M. J. (2012). Situation of health tourism in Iran opportunity or threat. *Journal of Military Medicine, 14*(2), 69–75.

Kassim, N. & Asiah Abdullah, N. (2010). The effect of perceived service quality dimensions on customer satisfaction, trust, and loyalty in e-commerce settings: A cross cultural analysis. *Asia Pacific Journal of Marketing and Logistics, 22*(3), 351–371.

Kline, R. B. (2011). *Principles and practice of structural equation modeling.* New York, NY: Guilford Press.

Kock, N. (2011). Using WarpPLS in e-collaboration studies: An overview of five main analysis steps. In N. Kock (Ed.), *Advancing collaborative knowledge environments: New trends in e-collaboration* (pp. 180–190). Hershey, PA: IGI Global.

Kock, N. (2014). Advanced mediating effects tests, multi-group analyses, and measurement model assessments in PLS-based SEM. *International Journal of e-Collaboration (IJeC), 10* (1), 1–13.

Kramer, R. M. (1999). Trust and distrust in organizations: Emerging perspectives, enduring questions. *Annual Review of Psychology, 50*(1), 569–598.

Loureiro, S. M. C. & González, F. J. M. (2008). The importance of quality, satisfaction, trust, and image in relation to rural tourist loyalty. *Journal of Travel & Tourism Marketing, 25*(2), 117–136.

Luk, S. T. & Yip, L. S. (2008). The moderator effect of monetary sales promotion on the relationship between brand trust and purchase behaviour. *Journal of Brand Management, 15*(6), 452–464.

Marković, S., Lončarić, D., & Lončarić, D. (2014). Service quality and customer satisfaction in the health care industry – towards health tourism market. *Tourism and Hospitality Management, 20*(2), 155–170.

Mihalič, T. (2000). Environmental management of a tourist destination: A factor of tourism competitiveness. *Tourism Management, 21*(1), 65–78.

Mosadeghrad, A. M. (2014). Factors influencing healthcare service quality. *International Journal of Health Policy and Management, 3*(2), 77–89.

Ryu, K. & Han, H. (2010). Influence of the quality of food, service, and physical environment on customer satisfaction and behavioral intention in quick-casual restaurants: Moderating role of perceived price. *Journal of Hospitality & Tourism Research, 34*(3), 310–329.

Saadatnia, F. & Mehregan, M. R. (2014). Determining and prioritizing factors affecting to increase customers attraction of medical tourism from the perspective of Arabic countries. (Case study: Iran-Mashhad Razavi Hospital). *International Journal of Marketing Studies, 6*(3), 155–162.

Sarstedt, M. (2008). A review of recent approaches for capturing heterogeneity in partial least squares path modelling. *Journal of Modelling in Management, 3*(2), 140–161.

Shahijan, M. K., Rezaei, S., Preece, C. N., & Ismail, W. K. W. (2015). International medical travelers' behavioral intention: An empirical study in Iran. *Journal of Travel & Tourism Marketing, 32*(5), 475–502.

Sirdeshmukh, D., Singh, J., & Sabol, B. (2002). Consumer trust, value and loyalty in relational exchanges. *Journal of Marketing, 66*(1), 15–37.

Snyder, J., Crooks, V. A., Adams, K., Kingsbury, P., & Johnston, R. (2011). The patient's physician one-step removed: The evolving roles of medical tourism facilitators. *Journal of Medical Ethics, 37*, 530–534.

Street, M. (2010). Medical tourism in Iran: Analysis of opportunities and challenges with MADM approach. *Research Journal of Biological Sciences, 5*(3), 251–257.

Thom, D. H. (2001). Physician behaviors that predict patient trust. *Journal of Family Practice, 50*(4), 323–328.

Thom, D. H. & Campbell, B. (1997). Patient–physician trust: An exploratory study. *Journal of Family Practice, 44*(2), 169–177.

Wang, H. Y. (2012). Value as a medical tourism driver. *Managing Service Quality: An International Journal, 22*(5), 465–491.

Wang, H. Y. & Wang, S. H. (2013). Mainland Chinese customers' intention toward medical tourism in Taiwan. *International Journal of Social, Management, Economics and Business Engineering, 7*(2), 221–223.

Wu, H. C. & Li, T. (2017). A study of experiential quality, perceived value, heritage image, experiential satisfaction, and behavioral intentions for heritage tourists. *Journal of Hospitality & Tourism Research, 41*(8), 904–944. https://doi.org/10.1177/1096348014525638

Wu, H. C., Li, T., & Li, M. Y. (2016). A study of behavioral intentions, patient satisfaction, perceived value, patient trust and experiential quality for medical tourists. *Journal of Quality Assurance in Hospitality & Tourism, 17*(2), 114–150.

Zboja, J. J. & Voorhees, C. M. (2006). The impact of brand trust and satisfaction on retailer repurchase intentions. *Journal of Services Marketing, 20*(6), 381–390.

Zeithaml, V. A., Berry, L. L., & Parasuraman, A. (1996). The behavioral consequences of service quality. *Journal of Marketing, 60*(2), 31–46.

14 The future(s) of tourism in Iran

C. Michael Hall and Siamak Seyfi

Introduction

Tourism in Iran has, since the 1970s, been plagued by domestic and regional political instability, and security issues. Despite the promise of the nuclear agreement, these issues have remained and appear likely to intensify in the wake of President Trump's hostility to the nuclear agreement. Nevertheless, despite ongoing political pressure from the US Republican Party as well as regional opposition from Israel and Saudi Arabia, Iran's historic nuclear agreement has helped the Iranian tourism industry to grow again. This is evident through the considerable increase in inbound arrivals to the country and the growth in foreign investment in tourism-related infrastructure. A number of international hotel chains, including Accor Hotels, Rotana, and Spain's Meliá, have already invested in the country's hospitality industry (Euromonitor International, 2017; Khodadadi, 2018). It is expected that by the end of 2018, and given an appropriate political environment, at least six different new international hotels will have opened in the country.

Tourism growth since the accords

Tourism was among the main sectors of the Iranian economy that immediately witnessed steady growth after the lifting of international sanctions following the nuclear accord of 2015 which transformed Iran's political and economic climate, and created substantial opportunities for the struggling tourism sector (Khodadadi, 2016a). With the rise in international arrivals, the development and growth of Iran's tourism industry has become one of the focal points of President Rouhani's administration. Iran's declared goal is to increase the country's share of the world's international tourists from 0.9% in 2004 to 1.5% by 2025, the equivalent of attracting 20 million tourists by 2025 and generating $30 billion in annual revenue. For 2017, statistics suggest that around 5 million foreign tourists visited the country, generating some $8 billion in revenue. The 2025 target therefore appears to be very ambitious while, if current trends continue, Iran will likely only attract 7.5 million tourists by 2025 (see Chapter 1, this volume). Nevertheless, there are a number of positives in Iranian tourism.

Although Iran was mainly visited by senior tourists (with the average age of about 60) in recent years, the improvement in the country's image along with affordable prices for foreign visitors due to Iranian currency devaluation has meant that the average age has decreased to between 45 and 50 as increasing numbers of younger travelers visit the country. As a result, cheaper accommodation, like hostels, are now being built in the country and traditional budget accommodation, known as *Mosaferkhaneh* (travelers' house) which has long been used by pilgrims in religious cities such as Mashhad, Qom, and Shiraz are now updating their services and facilities in order to attract foreign tourists. In Tehran, new hostels are being built targeted at young foreign travelers. The growing number of hostels across the country, especially in Tehran, Shiraz, and Yazd, demonstrates the increase in the number of younger foreign tourists who visit Iran.

The development of hostels and the opening of budget accommodation to international tourism also serves to reinforce Iran's positioning as a cheap destination (World Economic Forum, 2017). As a result, Iran has become a new destination for backpackers who prefer to travel at lower cost and do not consume luxury hotels and services. Such a development may also prove advantageous to more rural and peripheral areas where high-end tourism infrastructure may be lacking but which have accommodation acceptable to backpackers. Such price competitiveness is potentially advantageous to Iran, at least in the short-term, as it seeks to overcome negative images, especially in many Western markets (see Chapters 1 and 3, this volume), although the long-term effects of currency devaluation may affect economic performance in the long-term.

The Iranian currency has been steadily losing its value against the US dollar since the 1979 Islamic revolution. Domestic and international political reasons appeared behind the currency and crisis as concerns returned over the reimposition of sanctions as well as that President Rouhani's policies of international engagement and domestic moderation and reform would continue. The significance of President Rouhani's period in office for tourism development in the longer-term cannot be overestimated. As Graham-Harrison (2017) commented

> Iran's reformist president, Hassan Rouhani, staked his government and reputation on opening Iran to the world, sealing a nuclear deal that ended sanctions and courting foreign investment in its wake ... The biggest challenge to Iran's goal of increasing tourist numbers tenfold within the decade may be the pace of change they represent, in a country where Rouhani's conservative rival still managed to garner 16 million votes in the election.

Therefore, challenges such as the currency crisis have an affect both on tourism and the wider political and economic context (see also Chapter 1, this volume). The extent of the currency crisis is substantial in 1979 one US dollar was equivalent to 70 rials. In 2013 when he was first elected one dollar bought 36,000 rials, in April 2017 it was the equivalent to 40,000 rials and 60,000 rials in April 2018, until Vice-President Eshaq Jahangiri said the government would impose a unified rate of 42,000 rials for a dollar, although implementation of this appeared patchy (Dehghan, 2018c). According to Bijan Khajehpour, a Vienna-based Iranian economist, the currency nosedive was not down to the country's economic performance, but could have an impact on it.

> We're in a period of transition both in terms of relationship between the government and the deep state but also space that it has provided for corrupt practices. We're in a very delicate phase in political relationships depending on what the outcome is—Rouhani can either be weakened or strengthened ... If this so-called unification of exchange rate is implemented successfully, if they manage to unify the exchange rate and pull through and provide enough liquidity to the market, then to keep this rate or around this rate, it will be a real achievement.
>
> (Bijan Khajehpour, quoted in Dehghan, 2018c)

The significance of politics

Despite positive developments, the future trajectory of tourism in Iran will undoubtedly be dominated by the country's political relationships which directly affects both the image of the country as a tourist destination, and the flow of inbound and outbound tourism. Iran remains central to immense regional political struggles, including the wars in Syria, Iraq, and Yemen, and there are increasing tensions with its key regional rival, Saudi Arabia. President Trump's aggressive stance toward Iran adds to the difficulties Iran faces for a long-awaited prosperity and has cast serious doubt on the future of the nuclear agreement which could have far-reaching consequences, not only for Iran–US relations but also the wider Middle East region (Wintour, 2018). In the climate of increasing tensions between Iran and President Trump's administration and key regional rivals, such as Israel and Saudi Arabia, the long-term future of the nuclear deal is unknown with its collapse likely while President Trump and the Republican Party remain so opposed to any agreement.

Efforts both by President Trump's government and that of Benjamin Netanyahu's in Israel to undermine the nuclear accords with Iran, however, have not received substantial support elsewhere in the West. European powers led by France, Germany, and the United Kingdom made substantial efforts to push back against both Netanyahu and Trump. Although, as noted by Stephen Walt, a Professor of International Affairs at Harvard, "the Bush administration was better at inventing a phony case for war with Iraq than the Trump team is at conjuring up a phony case for war with Iran. But doesn't mean they won't eventually succeed" (quoted in Dehghan, 2018a). The irony of this situation is that, unlike Israel, Iran does not have a single atomic bomb and has been a party to the Treaty on the Non-Proliferation of Nuclear Weapons since 1970. In contrast, Israel has never signed the Treaty, which means that the International Atomic Energy Agency has no inspection authority in that country, while Israel is estimated to have more than 200 nuclear warheads, mainly "pointed at Iran" (former US Secretary of State, Colin Powell, quoted in Revesz, 2016). Although, as Dehghan observes:

> the fact that Iran is fulfilling its nuclear obligations does not mean it has been a good actor elsewhere. But the agreement was not supposed to address Iran's

regional behaviour or its missile programme, and should not be junked on this basis. In Syria, Iran is arguably making its biggest foreign policy mistake since the revolution. It has long defined its foreign policy as defending the oppressed, but for the first time it is clearly supporting the oppressor.

(Dehghan, 2018a)

Over the past four decades, US–Iranian relations have seen many lows, starting from the CIA-orchestrated overthrow of Iran's democratically elected prime minister, Mohammad Mossadeq in 1953 (as this secular leader had sought to nationalize Iran's oil industry), followed by the US embassy hostage crisis in 1979 and the cutting of the diplomatic ties between the two countries in 1980. In 1984, the United States listed Iran as a state sponsor of terrorism. In 1988 an Iranian passenger plane was shot down over the Gulf, killing all 290 aboard, while in 2002, President George Bush denounced Iran as part of an "axis of evil" along with Iraq and North Korea and accused Iran of operating a secret nuclear weapons program. This was significant as it occurred while the reformist president Mohammad Khatami was in office, shattered hopes of rapprochement, and reinforced the power of conservative hardliners (Dehghan, 2018a).

Following the election of the conservative president Mahmoud Ahmadinejad and in the climate of increasing tensions between Iran and the West, nuclear negotiations between major powers and Iran were stalled and new rounds of sanctions imposed on Iran over the nuclear issue which immensely impacted on the country's economy. These sanctions had tremendous negative impacts on the Iranian economy and people, in general, and the tourism industry, in particular (Khodadadi, 2016a; see also Chapters 1 and 3, this volume). After the election of President Rouhani, a moderate, in 2013, the long-running dispute over Iran's nuclear program was ended in July 2015 in the signing of the nuclear agreement and Iran took steps to restrict its nuclear activities required under the Joint Comprehensive Plan of Action (JCPOA) (see Chapter 3, this volume). Further positive steps occurred in 2016, when the United States and Iran announced a prisoner swap which was "Another Victory for Diplomacy and Human Rights" (Marashi, 2016).

However, the opposition to the agreement by President Trump has curtailed many of the potential economic benefits of the agreement to the Iranian people. Nearly three years on from the signing of the agreement, not a single tier-one European bank is prepared to do business with Iran with the April currency crisis, demonstrating the extent of Iran's economic vulnerability (Dehghan, 2018a, 2018c). Significantly, the collapse of the deal will affect tourism not just because of its enormous economic effects but because of its internal and external political impacts. Internally, the collapse of the deal would according to one commentator

destroy the moderates and reformists in Iran for the foreseeable future. This is particularly important since the supreme leader, Ayatollah Ali Khamenei, is 78 … The time may soon come when a successor takes his place—the biggest political change in decades.

(Dehghan, 2018a)

Such a situation would also likely lead to further human rights abuses, including detentions of dual-national members of the diaspora, with links to external institutions that are seen as threats by religious conservatives, when they visit the country (Dehghan, 2018b), and further domestic crackdowns by domestic hardliners. Externally, the collapse of the agreement would also only serve to further increase tensions with Israel and Saudi Arabia.

The changing environment of tourism and tourism research

Such issues are, of course, nothing new for the country's tourism industry. Since the 1970s, Iran's tourism industry has undergone a series of dramatic shifts in its business environment due to changes in the ruling elite (Khaksari, 2014). The Iranian tourism industry has experienced two distinct periods, a pro-tourism approach, up to April 1979, and a conservative religious-oriented perspective after 1988. The politico–religious perceptions of the ruling class particularly in the post-revolutionary period have had enormous impacts on policy-making and orientation of the country's tourism (Khaksari, 2014). The establishment of the theocratic Islamic republic with its unique Islamic ideology, translated into strict Islamic value-judgment tourism policies, affected the type and extent of Iranian tourism development and its position in the country's economy as well as how the country was promoted. The influential politico–religious elite have not yet seen a way to ease some of these constraints, which has occurred in other Muslim countries. For example, Saudi Arabia, Iran's main rival in the Middle East, which has long been viewed as an ultra-conservative country in the region for its stringent enforcement of Islamic law as well as its codes of behavior and dress, has recently relaxed its strict Sharia laws such as bans on drinking alcohol and launched new initiatives for the development of its tourism in an effort to move its tourism economy away from the annual pilgrimage of the Hajj (Ali khan, 2017). However, in Iran, the power of religious elites to influence policies of tourism promotion should not be underestimated. In such circumstances, no matter how hard tourism planners and professionals try to accomplish it, it is extremely hard to secure the potential benefits of the tourism industry because the politically sensitive and defensive religious leaders are unwilling to implement plans and policies that have, from their perspective, any potential perceived negative impact on society. The greatest challenge in tourism development in Muslim countries is undoubtedly how to ensure a reasonable balance between gaining the economic advantages of tourism development while avoiding possible negative socio-cultural outcomes. Contributing to a moderate and tolerant political and religious environment in which Islamic and other values are respected, is therefore a major challenge for the tourism sector.

One significant outcome of Iran's relative isolation in recent years has been that it suffers considerable difficulties in its national tourism marketing and research. Iran has long been neglectful in using modern methods of marketing tools. The lack of digital marketing is one of the country's biggest weaknesses that reduces its competitiveness in the global tourism market (World Economic Forum, 2017). Because of a marked shortfall in using digital techniques, Iran lags far behind other states in the field of tourism marketing (Khodadadi, 2017). Even in social networks that have a large audience, tourism authorities lack plans to promote Iran's attractions. The only efforts in this regard are restricted to those of the private sector, where hotels and travel agencies have slightly improved conditions (Financial Tribune, 2017). Moreover, the absence of a reliable statistical system for tourism hampers evaluations of the effectiveness of marketing campaigns as well as providing appropriate data for planning, strategy, and assessment of tourism's impacts. For example, Iran has not developed its own tourism satellite account, a now standard statistical framework for tourism and the main tool for the economic measurement of tourism. As a result, many of the statistics and statements regarding tourism in Iran are, in reality, based on projections and estimates (Financial Tribune, 2017).

Box 14.1: Tourism research in Iran: challenges and barriers

Tourism programs at higher education institutions in Iran have been offered over the past two decades. There are four levels of tourism education offered at Iranian universities and higher education institutions: two-year associate degrees, four-year bachelor's degrees, master's degrees and doctoral degrees. Although there are no precise published statistics about the total number of tourism students in Iranian higher education, according to the quotas announced by the National Organization of Educational Testing (known as *Sazman-e-Sanjesh*) for yearly nationwide entrance exams (*Konkur*), it is estimated that in 2016, more than 6,000 students were studying two-year associate degree programs and nearly 5,000 students were enrolled in four-year tourism degree programs. With regard to graduate programs, for the 2016–2017 academic year, according to the list provided by this organization, 63 universities offered master's programs in tourism-related areas.

Tourism disciplines are not very varied in Iran. Tourism marketing and tourism planning have been offered since the beginning and, recently, some universities offer graduate programs in ecotourism and religious tourism. There are approximately 1,150 master's students in the country. With respect to the doctoral programs, the first ones were offered at the Allameh Tabataba'i University (ATU) and the University of Science and Culture in Tehran in 2012. For the 2016–2017 academic year, these two universities offered doctoral programs in tourism management with an estimated 17 doctorate students. There has been a substantial increase in the number of universities and colleges offering tourism programs since the establishment of the first four-year bachelor's degrees by ATU in 1995 along with the first master's degree in 2004. Yet, this growth has been quite rapid since its modest beginning, which is arguably associated in significant ways with the phenomenal expansion of the country's tertiary-level educational opportunities in general (Seyfi, Nikjoo, & Alaedini, 2018a). It can be argued that increasing demand for higher education has been a result of reduced job prospects especially faced by the youth. With respect to Iran, it is contended that part of the country's possible failure to achieve a proper position in the field of tourism returns to the lack of efficient and trained human resources which have affected the product and market development, infrastructure and investment (Seyfi, Nikjoo, & Samimi, 2018b; Ziaee, Saeedi, & Torab Ahmadi, 2012; Heydari Chianeh, Nasrollahzadeh, & Abdollahi, 2012). Moreover, the number of enrolled students and universities' capacities is not consistent with the number of teaching staff, particularly at graduate levels in private universities. Tourism higher education therefore faces some major challenges in terms of quality and efficiency of training and has recently been a subject of debate.

Historical background

Following the Islamic revolution, higher education became the subject of substantial ideological and political evaluation and intervention (Farasatkhah, Ghazi, & Bazargan, 2008). The 'Cultural Revolution' in Iran (1980–1983) in the context of convulsive conflicts at the universities, led to full governmental intervention, closure of the universities, and the formation of a centralized system of evaluation for higher education which hugely impacted the direction and orientation of research in Iran, particularly in the social sciences.

With regard to tourism, researching tourism in Iran has been facing some major difficulties and challenges. The novelty of tourism as a discipline in Iranian higher education has been viewed as the main challenge in tourism research (Seyfi et al., 2018a). At the beginning, due to the novelty of tourism, in the absence of qualified teaching staff and academics in the field, some academics from other disciplines, particularly from geography, economics, management, and linguistics moved into the tourism field and occupied key positions with no or little experience in the industry. As a result, this has had a negative impact on the teaching of practical subjects (Seyfi et al., 2018b). The first publications by these academics were mainly in domestic journals and with a major focus on more theoretical studies on tourism which were primarily translations of articles published in English language literature. In light of the increasing number of universities offering tourism programs, most undergraduate and graduate level courses in a majority of higher education institutes in Iran are taught by students who graduated from pioneer universities in this field, mainly ATU. More importantly, the lack of teaching materials along with the language barriers among Iranian tourism lecturers and students led to the translation of English language tourism books to be used for teaching, assessment, and providing the main references for nationwide entrance examinations for graduate and post-graduate levels. However, these translated books are often outdated yet are still used at many institutions for teaching and research purposes. The novelty of tourism studies, the dearth of qualified staff, and educational system bottlenecks have therefore led to significant weaknesses in tourism research in the country.

Barriers to tourism research

Despite improvements in the quantity and quality of higher education and research in tourism over the years, tourism researchers still face many challenges. Iranian professors are not paid high salaries and are not often hired or promoted on the basis of knowledge and talent, with some faculty members being under-qualified with out-of-date knowledge and skills (Arani, Kakia, & Malek, 2018). The 'publish or perish' pressure on academicians in many colleges and universities has also led to greater attention to the quantity of publications produced than the quality (Seyfi, Hall, & Kuhzadi, 2018).

Accessible and reliable tourism statistics is another major challenge for tourism research. In the absence of systematic data collection and the development of a Tourism Satellite Account for Iran, industry performance figures are considered estimates, often contradictory and unreliable. The number of inbound tourist arrivals and expenditure figures is often sketchy or overestimated to show the success of administrations in attracting foreign tourists. Figures are often inconsistent with the data announced by international bodies such as UNWTO. The scarcity of accurate official statistics and access to data by individual tourism researchers is a challenge for tourism research in Iran. Many organizations involved with statistics and official data in Iran, including ICHTO, as a national tourism administration, have access to their data restricted on the pretext of security matters. In many cases, however, the security issue is merely an excuse and no information exists or is not reliable (Arab, 2016).

In addition, some organizations related directly or indirectly to tourism in Iran are not interested in tourism research as they appear to believe that research outcomes may pose challenges to their organizations and compromise their success in and chance of obtaining state funds. As a result of limited access to knowledge and financial credit, the tourism and hospitality industry on one side and the training and education system on the other have their own separate agendas (Seyfi et al., 2018 a). Some managers have restricted research projects or have a huge influence on the results and orientations of research mainly on customer satisfaction, service quality, and comparative studies. In addition, in order to do research in state-run organizations or in sensitive areas such as airports or train stations, the researcher requires certification or evaluation by the bureau of intelligence or relevant organizations and this process may take months. Moreover, sensitivity could impact on any stage of the research process from design to implementation, dissemination, and application. Some research findings may be sensitive to religious and political establishments. Social and political barriers usually do not permit researchers to deeply research societal problems, because many research findings suggest change and reform in culture and politics (Farasatkhah et al., 2008; Arani et al., 2018).

Since the tax declaration in Iran is not completely transparent, many private companies involved with tourism, such as hotels and travel agencies, refuse to release their financial information. The limited access to data can lead to false data creation. Sketchy data creation and 'shady' practices in scientific publishing has been identified as a growing trend in Iran especially among graduate students (Stone, 2016).

A huge part of Iran's economy is centrally planned and dominated by oil and gas production. Despite tourism's important role in the national economy, tourism research is often ignored by policy-makers and is viewed as a low priority sector leading to an ad hoc policy development approach in which tourism researchers barely find relevant research opportunities. In some provinces, there are some 'tourism master plan' projects, but due to lack of transparency, some private companies appear to get these projects regardless of their expertise. However, in the case of Iran, these kinds of master plans are superficial at best and highly general in nature (Alipour & Heidari, 2005). In fact, many tourism and hospitality research projects are repetitive, devoid of any practical benefit to the industry, and stored in the forgotten corners of organizations, universities, and research centers (Alipour & Heidari, 2005).

Future of tourism research in Iran

In light of the rapid growth of inbound tourism following the softening of sanctions on Iran, and in view of the support from the Rouhani's administration in developing the tourism industry as one of the major pillars of Iran's economy during the post-sanctions era (Mozaffari et al., 2017), tourism in Iran has the potential to grow at a rapid pace and the demand for professionally trained people will continue to increase over the next decade. With the lifting of sanctions on Iran and the changing image of Iran from a pariah destination into an emergent one (WTTC, 2017), more opportunities are available for Iranian people who are interested in developing a career in the field of hospitality and tourism. Therefore, the numbers of hospitality and tourism vocational programs are expected to grow. Moreover, the number of courses held jointly by Iranian universities with international universities is increasing, and consequently the quality of higher education in the country is expected to improve significantly. The government's expected focus on developing tourism and improving hotel management must be complemented by quality education at domestic universities and hotel schools. With respect to tourism research, tourism educational institutions and practitioners should work together closely in order to align tourism research with industry to meet the needs of the hospitality and tourism industry. Finally, self-censorship has been practiced by faculty members and tourism researchers as a response to the obstacles that affect their academic freedom (Arani et al., 2018), as social and political barriers usually do not permit deeper research on the problems of society and the industry.

Siamak Seyfi

Tourism marketing

In addition to transport and accommodation infrastructure (see Chapters 1 and 2, this volume), the lack of high-speed Internet is another issue facing the sector. Online and digital marketing is expected to dominate the sector in the near future and Iran will be sidelined from the global market if it does not utilize this useful means of growth. However, in light of the advent of online booking and price comparison agencies, Iranian authorities admit that their previous system is outdated and needs massive overhaul. In recent years several online booking sites have opened up, some backed by traditional travel agencies, including Alibaba.ir, Zoraq. com, Rahoja.com, Eligasht.ir, Rahbal.ir, as well as hotel booking site hotelro.ir. The growth of businesses offering ostensibly comparable and competitive services comes at a time when established travel agencies are seeing their profits decline as more people opt for price comparison features of such websites (Raad, 2016). Several systems plug into the international booking systems, something which was impossible with international sanctions placed on the Iranian economy. At the time of writing Iranians were able to use international room reservation websites such as booking.com. The website has added the Iranian currency which was long denied to their system, enabling Iranian travelers to book hotels all over the world. Moreover, to facilitate the reservation of accommodations, tours, and also transportation services, some domestic platforms for booking in the English language have also been created. Nevertheless, a long-term issue with respect to the viability of online booking will be the extent to which the Iranian government encourages international connectivity or seeks to copy China's initiatives in restricting international access for reasons of social and political control.

In terms of more traditional tourism marketing channels, there has been a change in attitude and will toward tourism development activities in Iran. In recent years, international conferences have been held in the country and Iran has hosted several national and international guest speakers/participants from both industry and academia. Iran's government and the Promotion and Marketing Office at the Iran Cultural Heritage, Handcraft and Tourism Organization (ICHTO) has also introduced two main programs to promote tourism: (1) familiarization tours for travel agents, reporters, and tour operators, and (2) private sector participation in tourism fairs such as ITB Berlin, Fitur Madrid, participation at which was previously prohibited by the government. Although the outcome of these activities remains to be seen, such activities are a positive step toward building a better future for the tourism industry in Iran, yet remain vulnerable to any reintroduction of sanctions (Khodadadi, 2017).

Outbound and domestic tourism

The total population of Iran reached over 81 million in 2018, with the vast majority being below 30 years of age. The new socio-economic profile of Iran has substantially impacted outbound travel which has dramatically increased over the last decades; from 1 million in 1995 to over 9 million travelers in 2017 (ICHTO, 2018). Compared to many other outbound travel markets in the region who prefer destinations where they can practice their Islam easily and peacefully and have access to halal food (Almuhrzi, Alriyami, & Scott, 2017), Iranians tend to travel to the countries where they can escape from strict Islamic dress and laws. In this regard, Turkey, followed by Dubai and Georgia, are the most popular non-religious destinations for Iranians. Iraq, which is home to a number of holy sites, is usually the top destination for Iranian pilgrims. The number of Iranian tourists to Istanbul has grown in recent years and could soon surpass the number of German visitors, partially as a result of economic recovery experienced after a nuclear deal lifting sanctions on Iran and the actions of the Erdogan regime in Turkey which has strained relations with many European countries. Similar to people in many Arab counties, Iranians tend to travel with their families, stay longer, and spend more money than average in the destinations they travel to. The relatively high expenditure of Iranians has attracted attention to the outbound market. However, due to the immense drop in value of the Iranian currency, unprecedented exchange rate fluctuations, and the threefold increase in the departure tax, the number of outbound travelers is expected to decrease, and domestic tourism is expected to grow to an estimated 65 million trips in 2018.

Domestic tourism has been the main focus of tourism development since 1979 and especially during the period of international sanctions. For much of the past two decades Iran has experienced the development of a resistive economy, in which the country's aim has been to lay out policies that help Iran become more self-reliant in order to shield it from the impacts of international economic and political developments, such as sanctions, that would otherwise hurt the country's economy (see Box 14.2). Encouraging people to undertake domestic travel and restricting opportunities for international travel has been an important part of this strategy (see Chapter 2, this volume).

Box 14.2: Sanctions, tourism and Iran's resistive economy

Sanctions have become an increasingly common and recurring feature of the political landscape. As Galtung (1967) suggests, sanctions are policies and actions initiated by one or more international actors against one or more others for a variety of foreign policy goals with an aim to respond swiftly to political challenges and developments that go against the objectives and values of countries and international bodies. Sanctions, while a form of intervention, are generally viewed as a lower-cost, lower-risk, middle course of action between diplomacy and war. Notwithstanding, the effectiveness of economic sanctions as a function of the foreign policy apparatus has been questioned by scholars and policy-makers (Bolks & Al-Sowayel, 2000; Dizaji & van Bergeijk, 2013). From 1990, following the collapse of the Soviet Union and the end of the Cold War, the imposition of economic sanctions increased sharply (Hufbauer, Schott, & Elliott, 2008), and sanctions and boycotts have frequently been used as a means of international public and private diplomacy (Hall, 2005). Since the establishment of the Islamic Republic in 1979 with the removal of the monarchy, Iran has been under comprehensive economic sanctions by international bodies as well as individual states. These sanctions were intensified in 2012 because of the international community's uncertainty about the peaceful purpose of Iran's nuclear program and the inadequacy of trust-building actions (Oechslin, 2014). Among the recipient countries of imposed economic sanctions, Iran is well-known for having one of the largest and longest sanctions (Pratt & Alizadeh, 2017; Farahani & Shabani, 2013). Some have called the sanctions the toughest sanctions in history (Sadeghi-Boroujerdi, 2012) with the United States having the objective of attempting to change Iran's political regime.

In the second presidential term of Mahmoud Ahmadinejad (2009–2013), in the climate of rising tensions with the West, and with the intensification of sanctions by US and Western countries against Iran due to its disputed nuclear program, the term 'resistive economy' was introduced to the country's economic and political literature and discourse. The term is interesting because much sanctions research, particularly in tourism, has failed to examine the coping responses of countries to sanctions or boycotts. Historically, the term resistive economy was introduced in 2005 following the blockade of Gaza by Israel, and this term was primarily raised

Figure 14.1 Conceptual model of the resistive economy.

in Iran by the leader of the country in 2010 as a response to toughened and unprecedented international sanctions imposed over Iran's economic lifeline oil exports along with restriction on the central bank. The resistive economy is intended to primarily nullify the negative effects of Western sanctions, and make Iran's economy more self-sufficient, wean the country of its heavy dependence on oil revenue through fiscal belt tightening, increase industrial output, and strengthen the role of science in boosting technological innovation (Esfandiari, 2012) (Figure 14.1). While this notion that in other forms has been around for a long time – given that sanctions have a reasonably long history – however, it is not well covered.

Despite the lifting of sanctions in the wake of the 2015 nuclear accord, Iran's economy could not fully profit given the negative ongoing results of the toughened embargo along with the plunge in oil prices since the middle of 2014. Moreover, foreign investors are cautious about trading with or investing in Iran, fearing penalties from remaining unilateral US sanctions along with Trump's tough stance toward Iran (Wintour, 2018). On the other hand, domestic conservatives in Iran believe that if the resistance economy had been implemented fully and widely, Iran could witness a tangible difference in people's lives. However, the scope of this is still in great doubt as the dependence of domestic players in the industry has always resulted in corruption (Shahidsaless, 2016). Sanctions have always been viewed by political leaders in Iran as the West's economic tactic in the broader 'soft war' aimed at spreading Western political and cultural values and undermining the Iranian regime (Toumaj, 2014). As a result, the Iranian ruling elite views the economy as having a direct relationship or parallel to national security policy, and supports the introduction of resistive economy as a means to strengthen national security. Moreover, the reintegration of Iran into the global economy and the necessity of having sanctions lifted in order to implement resistive economy programs has been a subject of debate. One view believes that the country should reintegrate to the global economy by boosting ties with the West as they look at China and Russia as unreliable partners, while the conservatives remain highly suspicious of such ties, fearing that they would leave Iran vulnerable to renewed economic pressure over time. However, in general, the 'Economy of Resistance' policies are aimed at reducing vulnerability to Western economic pressures and the global financial crisis along with supporting the state's political objective of establishing an Iranian-led hegemony in the Middle East.

As shown in Figure 14.1, the resistive economy doctrine aims to lower domestic energy consumption. This is to be achieved by using the capacity of implementing targeted subsidies. It also aspires to achieve self-sufficiency in strategic products, food, and medicine. Producing basic goods domestically can safeguard against sanctions by excluding the production chain from the international economic system and prevent social unrest induced by economic challenges. In this regard, Iran would also increase investment abroad and reduce taxes in an attempt to encourage domestic industry. However, a fundamental transition away from a state-dominated economy is sought in order to create the necessary space and platform for the private sector's growth.

As a part of the resistive economy strategy, the country has aimed to detach itself from international monetary bodies such as the World Trade Organization (WTO), IMF, and the World Bank, and tried to adhere to the SCO (Shanghai Cooperation Organization). In this regard, the government has announced plans to replace the US dollar with the euro in official financial reporting as an effort to circumvent restrictions on accessing the US dollar amid tensions with Washington, as well as prevent market instability generated due to fluctuations in the value of the Iranian rial against the dollar. Moreover, Iran and neighboring trade partners like Turkey and Russia intend to trade in their local currencies in an effort to increase bilateral trade in order to avoid any unilateral US sanctions. As a continuation of resistive economy policy, the government plans to support locally made products rather than importing foreign brands in an effort to reduce dependence on imports and foreign (dollar-based) currencies and build local capacity. Nevertheless, public anxiety over the economy was heightened by the plummeting value of the Iranian rial in April 2018 (Dehghan, 2018c) and the effectiveness of resistive economy along with its ambiguous framework has therefore increasingly become a question of debate.

The resistive economy and tourism

The resistive economy has some implications for the tourism industry in Iran. First and foremost, in the climate of rising tensions with the Trump administration coupled with regional powers, the country's tourism image is damaged in a number of markets and it may have quick impact on the country's tourism industry which has been revived following the nuclear deal. In this regard, as a resistive strategy the country may try to increasingly attract tourists from 'friendly countries' such Russia and China and neighboring countries which may ignore American sanctions. As a response to American antagonism to Iran, the country is seeking to teach Russian at schools, rather than English, as strategic ties grow with Russia in order to challenge the United States (Iran Daily, 2018). The development of new sets of financial relationships by Iran in Central Asia, China, and Russia will only serve to strengthen tourism relations with these countries as well.

Domestic tourism is also a major focus of the resistive economy. The plummeting value of the rial may reduce outbound tourism and increase domestic tourism, especially as the government tries to optimize tourism's contribution in the country's balance of payments. In addition, Iran may be able to attract the Iranian diaspora to invest in their home country as well as encouraging visitation. Diasporic investment may also challenge foreign investment in the country's hotel and aviation industry and potential future investment in the country's tourism industry. Regardless, the overall strategy is to increase financial self-reliance and reduce dependence on foreign capital that may be susceptible to changed political and economic conditions.

Siamak Seyfi and C. Michael Hall

Conclusion

The rapidly changing political and economic environment in Iran means that there are a number of possible futures for tourism. An escalation of political tensions between either the United States and Iran, or with Saudi Arabia and Israel, will lead to a major change in the positive outlook for the Iranian tourism industry that existed prior to President Trump coming to power. Uncertainty over the long-term support for the nuclear agreement by the United States has meant that many potential foreign investors have been waiting for a more stable political environment in which long-term investments can occur (Euromonitor International, 2017). Renewed hostility between Iran and the West could also undoubtedly seriously jeopardize the progress made and the future of the now-flourishing Iranian tourism industry, because of its effect on investment, marketing, and access, as well as the well-being of the wider country.

An additional major challenge is the need to improve perceptions of Iran's brand in international markets, particularly in the West. Branding is a powerful tool not only in positioning a destination in its desirable target markets, but also in re-positioning a destination which suffers from negative imagery. The latter is particularly important in the case of Iran which for decades has suffered from negative imagery in many of its tourist generating markets. Despite which, little effort has been invested in the development of a clear and unified branding strategy for the country (Khodadadi, 2017). Indeed, the lack of interest in better communicating Iran's positive attributes reflects not only the isolationist tendencies of the conservative ruling elite but also the lack of appreciation of the importance of tourism, and services in general, in an economy dominated by oil and gas production.

Finally, and perhaps most fundamentally, the foreseeable future for tourism in Iran is a focal point of two different desired futures for the country as a whole. One based on an ultra-conservative interpretation of Shia Islam that grossly represses many human rights and is closed to engagement with much of the contemporary world. The other is grounded in a moderate Shia Islam that is more tolerant and open to the world and that seeks engagement rather than putting up barriers. The hospitality of Iranians to strangers is legendary. History would suggest that when the rulers of the country cease being open to others then difficult times follow; it is therefore hoped that regardless of the closed minds of some people to engagement with Iran, that the country remains open to the world, with tourism being an essential part of such relationships.

References

Ali khan, G. (2017). Saudi Arabia launches new tourism initiatives within Vision 2030. Retrieved from http://www.arabnews.com/node/1130646/saudi-arabia

Alipour, H. & Heydari, R. (2005). Tourism revival and planning in Islamic Republic of Iran: Challenges and prospects. *Anatolia, 16*(1), 39–61.

Almuhrzi, H., Alriyami, H., & Scott, N. (Eds.). (2017). *Tourism in the Arab world: An industry perspective*. Bristol: Channel View Publications.

Arab, A. (2016). Iran's Lack of Transparency and Accountability and its Underdeveloped Data & Statistics Infrastructure. Iran Human Rights Review. Retrieved from http://www.ihrr.org/ihrr_article/economy-en_irans-lack-of-transparency-and-accountability-and-its-underdeveloped-data-statistics-infrastructure/

Arani, A. M., Kakia, L., & Malek, M. J. (2018). Higher education research in Iran: Quantitative development and qualitative challenges. In J. Jung, H. Horta & A. Yonezawa (Eds.), *Researching higher education in Asia* (pp. 315–326). Singapore: Springer.

Bolks, S. M. & Al-Sowayel, D. (2000). How long do economic sanctions last? Examining the sanctioning process through duration. *Political Research Quarterly, 53*(2), 241–265.

Dehghan, S. K. (2018a). If Trump destroys the nuclear deal, Iran will fall to its hardliners. *The Guardian*, May 3. Retrieved from https://www.theguardian.com/commentisfree/2018/may/03/trump-nuclear-deal-iran-reform-netanyahu-tehran

Dehghan, S. K. (2018b). Iran arrests British Council employee as she visits home country. *The Guardian*, May 2. Retrieved from https://www.theguardian.com/world/2018/may/02/iran-arrests-british-council-employee-as-she-visits-home-country

Dehghan, S. K. (2018c). Iranian rial hits all-time low as citizens scramble for US dollars. *The Guardian*, April 11. Retrieved from https://www.theguardian.com/world/2018/apr/11/iranian-rial-all-time-low-us-dollars-tehran

Dizaji, S. F. & van Bergeijk, P. A. (2013). Potential early phase success and ultimate failure of economic sanctions: A VAR approach with an application to Iran. *Journal of Peace Research, 50*(6), 721–736.

Esfandiari, G. (2012). Iran looks to 'resistive economy' to fight sanctions. Radio Free Europe, August 12. Retrieved from https://www.rferl.org/a/iran-looks-to-resistive-economy-to-fight-sanctions/24674314.html

Euromonitor International (2017). Travel in Iran. Retrieved from https://www.portal.euro-monitor.com

Farahani, B. M. & Shabani, M. (2013). The impact of sanctions on Iran's tourism. *The Open Access Journal of Resistive Economics (OAJRE), 33*, 1–13.

Farasatkhah, M., Ghazi, M., & Bazargan, A. (2008). Quality challenge in Iran's higher education: A historical review. *Iranian Studies, 41*(2), 115–138.

Financial Tribune. (2017). Iran's 2025 tourism target elusive. *Financial Tribune*. Retrieved from https://financialtribune.com/articles/travel/61770/irans-2025-tourism-target-elusive

Galtung, J. (1967). On the effects of international economic sanctions, with examples from the case of Rhodesia. *World Politics, 19*(3), 378–416.

Graham-Harrison, E. (2017). The guidebooks and selfie-sticks arrive as Rouhani's Iran declares itself open to all. *The Guardian*, May 28. Retrieved from https://www.theguard-ian.com/world/2017/may/27/rouhani-iran-tourists-culture-guidebooks-selfie-sticks

Hall, C. M. (2005). *Tourism: Rethinking the social science of mobility*. Harlow: Pearson.

Heydari Chianeh, R., Nasrollahzadeh, M., & Abdollahi, M. (2012). An evaluation of tourism higher education in Iran based on SWOT model. *Tourism Planning and Management, 1*(1), 129–152 [in Persian].

Hufbauer, G. C., Schott, J. J., Elliott, K. A., & Oeggm, B. (2008). *Economic sanctions reconsidered* (3rd ed.). Washington, DC: The Peterson Institute for International Economics.

Iran Cultural Heritage, Handcraft and Tourism Organization (ICHTO). (2018). *Tourism statistics of Iran*. Retrieved from http://bogendesign-vr.ir/gardeshgari2/19.php

Iran Daily (2018). Minister proposes Persian language be taught at Russian schools. Retrieved from http://iran-daily.com/News/213518.html

Khaksari, A., Lee, T. J., & Lee, C. K. (2014). Religious perceptions and hegemony on tourism development: The case of the Islamic Republic of Iran. *International Journal of Tourism Research, 16*(1), 97–103.

Khodadadi, M. (2016a). A new dawn? The Iran nuclear deal and the future of the Iranian tourism industry. *Tourism Management Perspectives, 18*, 6–9.

Khodadadi, M. (2016b). Return to glory? Prospects of Iran's hospitality sector post-nuclear deal. *Tourism Management Perspectives, 19*, 16–18.

Khodadadi, M. (2017). Challenges of branding Iran: Perspectives of Iranian tourism suppliers. *Tourism Planning & Development*. https://doi.org/10.1080/21568316.2017.1415957

Khodadadi, M. (2018). Donald Trump, US foreign policy and potential impacts on Iran's tourism industry: Post-nuclear deal. *Tourism Management Perspectives, 26*, 28–30.

Marashi, R. (2017). *The US–Iran prisoner swap is yet another victory for diplomacy and human rights* (online). Retrieved from https://www.huffingtonpost.com/reza-marashi/us-iran-prisoner-swap_b_8989970.html

Mozaffari, A., Karimian, R., & Mousavi, S. (2017). The return of the 'Idea of Iran' (2005–2015). In R. Butler & W. Suntikul (Eds.), *Tourism and political change* (pp. 186–199). Oxford: Goodfellow.

Oechslin, M. (2014). Targeting autocrats: Economic sanctions and regime change. *European Journal of Political Economy, 36*, 24–40.

Pratt, S. & Alizadeh, V. (2017). The economic impact of the lifting of sanctions on tourism in Iran: A computable general equilibrium analysis. *Current Issues in Tourism*. https://doi.org/10.1080/13683500.2017.1307329

Raad, M. (2016). Foreign travel sites enter Iran. Financial Tribune. Retrieved from https://financialtribune.com/articles/sci-tech/55792/foreign-travel-sites-enter-iran

Revesz, R. (2016). Colin Powell leaked emails: Israel has '200 nukes all pointed at Iran,' former US secretary of state says. *The Independent*, September 16. Retrieved from https://www.independent.co.uk/news/world/americas/colin-powell-leaked-emails-nuclear-weapons-israel-iran-obama-deal-a7311626.html

Sadeghi-Boroujerdi, E. (2012). *Sanctioning Iran: Implications and consequences*. London: Oxford Research Group. Retrieved from http://www.oxfordresearchgroup.org.uk/publications/briefing_papers_and_reports/sanctioning_iran_implications_and_consequences

Seyfi, S., Hall, C. M., & Kuhzadi, S. (2018). Tourism and hospitality research on Iran: Current state and perspectives. *Tourism Geographies*. https://doi.org/10.1080/146166 88.2018.1454506

Seyfi, S., Nikjoo, A., & Alaedini, P. (2018a). Teaching tourism service quality in Iran. In L. Cai & P. Alaedini (Eds.), *Quality services experiences in hospitality and tourism*. Cheltenham: Emerald.

Seyfi, S., Nikjoo, A., & Samimi, M. (2018b). Tourism higher education in Iran. Past, present, and future directions. In C. Liu & H. Schänzel (Eds.), *Tourism education in Asia*. Singapore: Springer.

Shahidsaless, S. (2016). Corruption a way of life in Iran. *Middle East Eye*. Retrieved from http://www.middleeasteye.net/columns/corruption-has-become-way-life-iran-1127296548

Stone, R. (2016). A shady market in scientific papers mars Iran's rise in science. *Science*, September 14. Retrieved from http://www.sciencemag.org/news/2016/09/shady-market-scientific-papers-mars-iran-s-rise-science

Toumaj, A. (2014). Iran's economy of resistance: Implications for future sanctions. *Critical Threats*. Retrieved from https://www.criticalthreats.org/wp-content/uploads/2016/07/imce-imagesToumajA_Irans-Resistance-Economy-Implications_november2014-1.pdf

Wintour, P. (2018). Fears grow for future of Iran nuclear deal in wake of Tillerson's removal. *The Guardian*, March 13. Retrieved from https://www.theguardian.com/us-news/2018/mar/13/rex-tillerson-iran-nuclear-deal-us-eu

World Economic Forum (WEF). (2017). *The travel & tourism competitiveness report 2017. Paving the way for a more sustainable and inclusive future*. Gland: WEF. Retrieved from http://www3.weforum.org/docs/WEF_TTCR_2017_web_0401.pdf

World Travel and Tourism Council. (2017). *Travel and tourism economic impact Iran*. Retrieved from https://www.wttc.org/-/media/files/reports/economic-impact-research/countries-2017/iran2017.pdf

Ziaee, M, Saeedi, A., & Torab Ahmadi, M. (2012). Exploring the state of tourism in Iran's higher education. *Tourism Studies, 7*(17), 61–86 [in Persian].

Index

Revolutionary Guards 16, 230
Rey 78
risk 28, 236; image 56; investment 60–1,
    63; socio-cultural 121
Rose and Rosewater Festival 145, 149–55
routes 6, 27, 39, 52, 74, 77
rural tourism 121, 196
Russia 10, 11, 29, 41, 56, 238–9

Sadeh 76, 117
sanctions 4–6, 11, 15, 17–19, 24, 25,
    28, 30, 55–65, 226–7, 229–30, 236–9;
    see also resistive economy
Saudi Arabia 3–4, 9, 10, 11, 59, 180, 209,
    226, 228, 239; political relations with
    Iran 79, 81, 228, 230
Sea of Oman 47
seaside resorts 25; *see also* coastal tourism
seasonality 47, 79, 187
second homes 46, 49–50
security 60, 81, 91, 154, 183, 226
services 14, 30, 43, 227, 234
Shanghai Cooperation Organization 238
Shia 10–11, 17, 57, 69–70, 80, 240; as
    official religion of Iran 7, 71; and
    political institutions 22; sacred sites 46,
    58, 72–5, 89, 100; sectarian rivalry 4,
    76; *see also* Islam; pilgrimage
Shiraz 100; Shah e Cheragh 9
shopping 46, 78, 90, 100, 168
Silk Road 39
Singapore 11
small business 199
social impacts 87, 99, 101, 115, 119,
    129–30; of faith tourism 102–7
Somalia 24
souvenirs 90
space 89–90; green 50; public 88, 91;
    socio-economic 85
spatial behaviour 48, 50, 59
spatial development 78, 106
special interest tourism 51, 117, 123
spiritual tourism *see* religious tourism
spirituality 86–7, 101, 106
state 134, 181, 228, 233, 238
Sufi 72, 76; *see also* Islam
Sunni 3–4, 17, 70, 71, 75–6, 80; Hanafi
    71; and Iranian policy 76; Khalid Nabi
    cemetery 75–6; Masjed Jama Sanandaj
    75; sectarian rivalry 4, 76; Sheikh
    Ahmad Jami tomb 75; *see also* Islam
sustainable development 51, 114, 115,
    123, 179; and community-based
    tourism 193

sustainable tourism 99, 106, 199, 200;
    see also sustainable development
Syria 11, 24, 28, 76, 79, 147, 228, 229
Syrian civil war 3, 10, 228
Syrian conflict *see* Syrian civil war

Tajikistan 11, 76, 209
taste 159
tax 62, 129, 233; departure 19, 43, 235;
    exemption for religious institutions 29;
    income 31, 62
Tehran 15, 30, 39, 47, 48–9, 50, 52, 62, 63,
    71, 72, 209
terrorism 57, 145, 147, 229
theocracy 13, 15, 28, 39, 51, 230; and
    cultural heritage management 114; and
    tourism policy 22, 23, 230
tourism communities 198
tourism development 13–25, 78–9, 101,
    116
tourism image 28, 239; role of events in
    rebuilding 144–5
tourism industry 11, 22, 38–9, 161,
    177, 199, 226, 230, 238; business
    environment 27–32, 230, 239;
    constraints 27–32; development 13–17;
    and food 169; and hospitality 162; and
    women 179–81, 183–91
tourism marketing 230–1, 235
tourism planning 19, 20, 101, 129, 196;
    before the 1979 revolution 26–30;
    see also Iran Cultural Heritage,
    Handcraft and Tourism Organization
    (ICHTO)
tourism policy 15, 18, 19–25, 28–9, 69,
    155, 179; before the 1979 revolution
    26–30
tourism research 231–4
tourism resources 6–13, 70
Tourism Satellite Account (TSA) 231, 233
tourism statistics 14; reliability of 233
tourist experience 115, 158, 165, 202
tourist flows 28
tourist motivation 46–8, 69, 84, 86, 88, 92,
    207; *see also* pilgrimage
tourist typologies 77
trade 56, 58, 60, 238; in Islam 87; *see also*
    sanctions
transport 6, 14, 30–1, 40, 44, 45, 51–2;
    public 44
trip characteristics 43, 44, 46
Turkey 10, 11, 12, 13, 42, 61, 116, 144,
    235, 238
Turkmenistan 10, 11, 76, 115

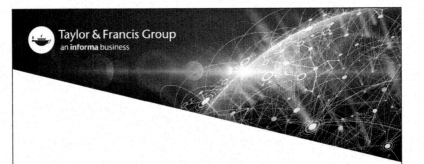